DONATA MAGGIPINTO

REAL-LIFE entertaining

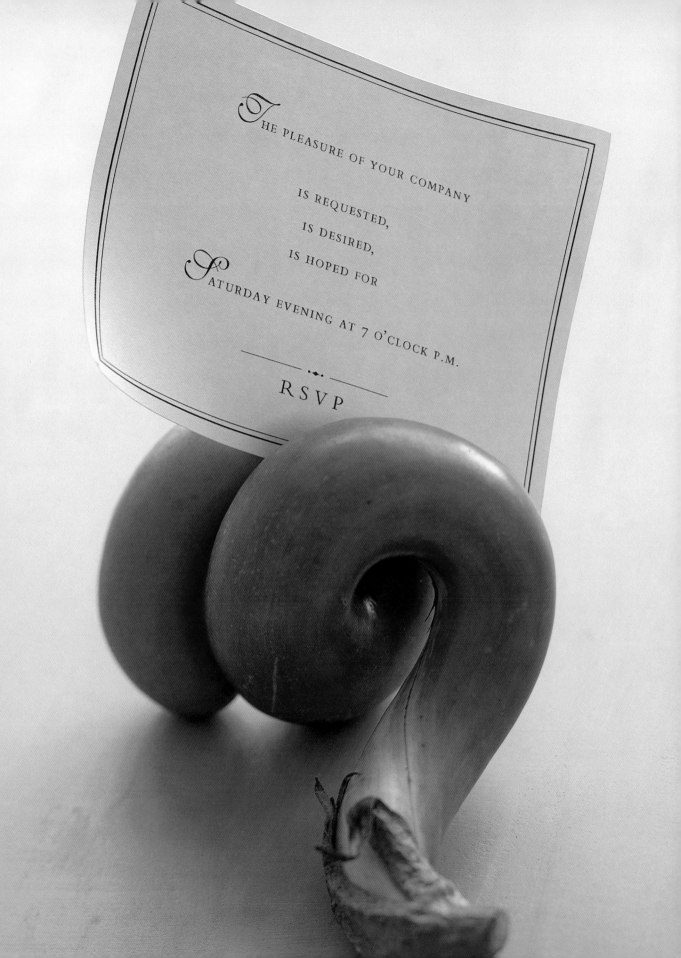

DONATA MAGGIPINTO

REAL-LIFE entertaining

great food and simple style for hectic lives

PHOTOGRAPHY BY RICHARD JUNG

DESIGN BY COURTNEY REESER & KRISTIN KONZ

 CLARKSON POTTER/PUBLISHERS NEW YORK

Published by Clarkson N. Potter/Publishers, 201 East 50th
Street, New York, New York 10022. Member of the Crown
Publishing Group.

Random House, Inc. New York, Toronto, London, Sydney,
Auckland
www.randomhouse.com

CLARKSON N. POTTER, POTTER, and colophon are
trademarks of Clarkson N. Potter, Inc.

Printed in China

Library of Congress Cataloging-in-Publication Data
Maggipinto, Donata.
   Real-life entertaining / Donata Maggipinto.
   1. Entertaining. 2. Cookery. 3. Menus. I. Title.
TX731.M32   1998
642'.4—dc21   97-46875
                   CIP

ISBN 0-609-60111-3

10 9 8 7 6 5 4 3

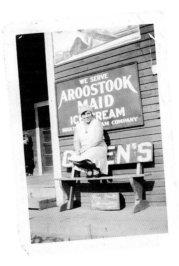

To Anna Borelli,

Katherine Graham

and

Anne Maggipinto

Great Cooks All

With Appreciation

to

MY HUSBAND (AND DESIGNER extraordinaire), Courtney Reeser, love and heartfelt gratitude for his many contributions to this book, including the inspiration and direction for its design, great styling ideas, and superb creative judgment. A big hug and kiss to my stepson, Chance, for his razor-sharp opinions and good humor.

I am very grateful to Richard Jung for his exceptional photography, his creative input, and his infinite patience. I am in awe of Pouké and her artistic finesse with food—brava!!! Many thanks, too, to Carol Hacker and Tableprop for listening so well and zeroing in on the beautiful things that turned our tables into canvasses of ideas and beauty. Hugs and thanks to Lissa Ivy, Michelle Syracuse, and Melissa Hacker. I was blessed with an extraordinarily creative team who spun magic every day. I love you guys.

Thanks to Williams-Sonoma, Pottery Barn, John Boyajian/Boyajian Caviar, Barbara Chambers, Draegers, Gardiner Hempel, Myles Henry/Maine Diner, June Taylor Baking Company, Ver Brugge Meats, and Zinc Details for props and specialty foods for use in photography.

A bear hug to Kristin Konz of Landor Associates who worked with Courtney on the design for this book and gave it a fresh look with exuberance that emanates from each page. Thanks for giving me this jewel.

I sincerely thank Kathleen Prisant and John Phillip Carroll for their recipe testing expertise and contribution. Many thanks and a warm embrace to Chuck Williams and Mary Risley who educated and inspired me and continue to do so every single day.

My heartfelt thanks to Amanda and Jeffrey Marcus for the use of their gorgeous home, and for giving me carte blanche to borrow items from their personal collections for photography. To Susan Turner, for the beautiful plants as well as for her horticultural advice.

To Angela Miller, my agent, for her insight and tenacity and wicked sense of humor. Thank you for guiding me on this maiden voyage. To Pam Krauss, my editor at Clarkson Potter who is my personal Max Perkins, thank you for giving me the room to spread my wings while ensuring that I did not stray too far into the wild. Thanks also to the rest of the A-team at Clarkson Potter—Robin Strashun, Margot Schupf, Chip Gibson, Andy Martin, Marysarah Quinn, Barbara Marks, Wendy Schuman, Amy Boorstein, Joy Sikorski, and Lauren Shakely, and everybody else who worked behind the scenes on behalf of my book.

Last but most definitely not least, love and thanks to my wonderful family and friends who continually endow me with inspiration and strength, and in doing so have contributed invaluably to my book, especially Mom and Dad, my sisters, Deidre, Diane, and Dina, Frank and Michael, Hal and Dionne, Stacy and Guy, Kevin and Ruth, Andrea Sandvig, Connie McDonald, Vicky Kalish, Richard Degnan, Katy Keck, Karen Kempf, Neal Ward and Jeff Gibson, Bill Thompson, Nancy and Ed Vick, Susan Bolle and Harold Sogard, Gates McKibbin (thanks for letting in the light), and Patti and Joe O'Neill, and everybody at the *Weekend Today* show, especially Beatrice Myers, Nicole Ciofalo, Carole Lee Carroll, Jack Ford, and Jodi Applegate.

contents

my

LIFE IS INCREDIBLY COMPLICATED

(which may be the understatement of the decade) and because you picked up this book, I am going to presume that yours is likewise.

Today, organizing a party—or even a casual dinner for friends—can seem too daunting to contemplate. In a time when we're all operating at full throttle seven days a week, juggling work, family, and the myriad responsibilities they entail, it's all we can do to get our friends to agree on a date! But being short on time doesn't necessarily mean we're short on style, taste, or the desire to entertain our friends and family in creative and memorable ways. We just need a simpler route to "wow." Enter **Real-Life Entertaining.**

For me, entertaining satisfies the most basic of human needs: to express ourselves, to give of ourselves, to receive acknowledgment for our efforts, and to create memorable moments with family and friends. But it's hard to approach these occasions as the festive events they should be if they invariably result in stress, anxiety, and angst for the host, discomfort for the guests, and anything but the convivial, comfortable evening you envisioned.

Although my job revolves around creating delicious food and stylish accoutrements, there are days when even I am too busy to make a Herculean effort. But I am not willing to scrimp on the details. The food must be delicious, the presentation must be beautiful, and the occasion, whether it's casual, a big deal, or a no-holds-barred party, must be memorable.

Real-Life Entertaining is a cookbook and style guide for the way we live today. Real-life entertaining does not require a lot of time, a battery of full-time help, or exceptional talent; all you need is an enthusiastic attitude and a desire to share your home and hospitality with others.

My recipes are simple, straightforward, and as time-efficient as I could make them. Because they're founded on using the freshest, best-quality ingredients you can find, the dishes really need very little embellishment. When you use seasonal ingredients and delicious, locally produced fruits and vegetables, the food speaks for itself.

My mind naturally groups entertaining occasions into three distinct categories. **Casual Suppers** feature simple yet stylish food and relaxed presentation that brings an unexpected touch of excitement or luxury to an otherwise humble-but-satisfying meal. **Big-Deal Meals** don't necessarily mean more work but they often include more impressive presentations of costly ingredients such as a crown roast of pork, duck breasts, or caviar than I normally choose for casual suppers. **Parties!** mean more people, more food, and a bit more orchestration than is usually the norm. But they're so worth it!

Acknowledging the immense time constraints on us and the time-saving, sanity-preserving aspects of purchasing prepared foods, I've also included a chapter called **"Ways with Take-Away,"** in which I give you ideas for enhancing prepared foods for entertaining and every day.

You'll also find ideas for table settings and the other visual details that elevate ordinary meals into extraordinary ones, along with tips on making your entertaining less stressful and more memorable.

I truly believe that the rewards of entertaining justify the effort required to fit it into your real life. Consider this book your guide and your inspiration for entertaining with style—your own, personal distinctive style—and having fun doing it!

Cheers!

Donata

we

all have role models whose taste we admire and strive to emulate. At age five, my ideal was my best friend Laura Williamson's mom, Janet, who was the be-all and end-all when it came to elegance and élan. Everything about her entertaining style was simple, smooth, and seemingly effortless. She cut the crusts off her luncheon sandwiches and cut the sandwiches into shapes. She served mixed drinks in heavy crystal glasses. And she offered vegetables along with the usual bread at her fondue parties.

Imagine my surprise when, years later, my friend told me how much she admired *my* mother and her casual, "the more, the merrier" approach to entertaining. She liked the way children were always included. She thought it was "cool" that my mother served chicken broth dusted with freshly grated Parmesan cheese.

As an adult, I have come to appreciate the distinctive entertaining styles of the Europeans I met when I lived in Vienna and Madrid and the people I came to know via my visits to Italy.

Their influences have contributed immeasurably to my own approach to cooking and entertaining. Yet I could not articulate this philosophy adequately until a recent

business trip to Venice afforded me the pleasure of meeting Arrigo (Harry) Cipriani, scion of the Harry's Bar restaurant and hotel empire. We enjoyed a lunch of perfectly cooked tagliarini pasta with unsalted butter and fresh Parmesan cheese followed by a salad of tender lettuces dressed with lemon juice and fruity green olive oil. Dessert was fragoline, wild strawberries that were in season at the time and so ripe that each one tasted how rubies must taste if they had a flavor. The table was set with a pale blue linen tablecloth and pale yellow linen napkins. They were soft from repeated launderings.

When I asked Arrigo to reveal the secret of his success, he repeated to me what his father had taught him and what I then realized had been my own touchstone all these years: "There is luxury in simplicity."

EMPLOYING THE PLEASURE PRINCIPLE

Have you ever walked from point A to point B, so intent on reaching your destination that you barely noticed—let alone enjoyed—the journey? All too often such is the case with entertaining. While the ultimate goal of entertaining is to please our guests, why bother if we can't enjoy the process as much as the result?

Give yourself enough time to immerse yourself in the pleasures of the entertaining process. Cooking can be calming, restorative, and very rewarding. Shelling peas, husking corn, stirring a risotto, and rolling out pastry dough are all simple tasks that require us to use our hands and participate in a time-honored tradition that, by its very nature, causes us to slow our normally harried pace of living and focus on the present.

■ *When it's time to cook, don't answer the phone (this is where technology, i.e., the answering machine, comes in handy).* Sometimes I listen to National Public Radio, sometimes to music, and often I simply revel in the sounds of onions sautéing or tomato sauce bubbling.

Occasionally I enjoy having a friend visit while I cook, but most times I prefer the comforting (and silent) presence of my two Labrador retrievers, who incidentally also double as spill picker-uppers and enthusiastic taste testers.

■ *Make the kitchen yours.* Bring in a comfortable chair and footstool so you can sit and peruse recipes. Let a French armoire or Amish pie cabinet hold your favorite linens or glasses. Hang old plates or prints with food motifs that you find in secondhand stores or while you're traveling. I have a map of Italy on my wall that never fails to prompt a daydream or fuel an inspiration. Collect antique tea towels from flea markets and use them to dry your hands between tasks, or display them when they're not in use. Hang a bulletin board and fill it with magazine photographs that spark ideas. Throw a colorful (washable) rug on the floor. Cultivate a collection of fresh herb plants on the windowsill—a practical and pretty kitchen accessory. Surround yourself with the colors, textures, and flavors that make you smile.

■ U*se cooking equipment that makes you happy.* Good-quality equipment really does produce better results, but just as important, you should like the look and feel of the equipment. I love my heavy restaurant cookware with its black anodized aluminum exterior, sturdy stainless steel handles, and what looks to me like fire-branded seals that affix the handles to the pots. Cooking with them just makes me *feel* good.

■ *Keep your treasures in plain sight.* An antique earthenware bowl from my mother sits on the sideboard filled with oranges and lemons and reminds me of the special aromas in her kitchen. A green-rimmed enamel colander from my great-grandmother holds red tomatoes ready to be rinsed. Wooden spoons, collected from everywhere, share space with other cooking utensils in a crock on the counter. And a cream-colored, animal-patterned Emma Bridgewater jar that I found in London holds the kosher salt next to the stovetop.

EXPRESSING YOUR PERSONAL STYLE

So often, we bend toward the "more is better" credo when it comes to entertaining, when in most cases, less is truly more. Above all, however, the golden rule is: "Be yourself."

If you are yourself, you will be less stressed and your guests will be more comfortable. Cook dishes that are delicious to you. Set the table with dinnerware and glassware that make you happy. Decorate the table with colors and objects that appeal to you. Listening to these preferences will help you develop a personal style that is uniquely your own. Banish the invisible demons who sit on your shoulder and whisper "shoulds" or "shouldn'ts" in your ear. Please yourself and others will be pleased, too.

You can derive inspiration from many places. What you experience in restaurants, gardens, museums, friends' homes, florists, and your travels will pique each of your senses. How you interpret in your own home what you encounter "out there" is an expression of your personal style. For example, a walk through a farmers' market may give you the idea to use herbs in bouquets instead of flowers. You may come home with deep purple eggplants and decide to display them on a cut-glass cakestand. You may purchase just-picked corn on the cob and mix the sweet, raw kernels with tiny heirloom cherry tomatoes and minced basil for a fresh, seasonal salad.

Often, I look to magazines and books for ideas. It's relaxing for me to page through magazines and clip articles that I'll read on a rainy weekend, and cut out pictures that will stir my creative juices when I'm planning a party. I don't limit myself to food magazines; I pore over home, lifestyle, and fashion magazines from the United States and abroad, pasting the photos, along with my own notes, in notebooks or binders. When it's time to host a party, I tap my "inspiration arsenal" and interpret the ideas in a way that pleases me.

COMPOSING A MENU

In my opinion, food is the keystone of entertaining. The ingredients you choose, the dishes you prepare with them, and the menu you compose set the tone for the evening and should excite each of the senses.

Every menu creates a distinct mood. Dishes with caviar or white truffles have a definite big-deal attitude, the degree of which increases proportionally with the quantity served. Elegant does not always mean expensive, though. A small bowl of perfectly ripe golden raspberries with a splash of framboise would be a fitting end to a fancier dinner. Purple figs with lavender honey or Cornish game hens spell romance. Saturday night ribs with 'slaw most definitely spell fun. Throughout this book you will find menu suggestions for some of my favorite food combinations. But because it is meant as a workbook, you should feel comfortable mixing and matching dishes based on your own preferences.

There are only a few guidelines that you may want to consider when composing a menu. They are:

Color Strive for a variety of colors on the plate. An all-white menu of poached fillet of sole, cauliflower, and mashed potatoes is as boring to look at as it is to eat. On the other hand, poached fillet of sole, steamed asparagus, and sautéed cherry tomatoes are fresh and vibrant.

Texture Again, variety is key. A menu composed of cream of broccoli soup, chicken with a mushroom cream sauce and spinach puree, and a dessert of vanilla ice cream with chocolate sauce would define the word *creamy* in a definitely unappetizing way. The mouth wants to be entertained, too. Opt for a combination of chewy, creamy, and crunchy foods.

Flavor This is probably the most tricky. The rule of thumb is: Don't go overboard on any one flavor. A chicken breast marinated in soy sauce, which is quite salty, should not be served with asparagus with black olives and bread crumbs because the olives are salty, too. Likewise, the sweet richness of lobster or scallops would not do very well with a puree of sweet potatoes,

which might be too cloying. If you stick with fresh, seasonal ingredients and vary them, you'll be fine.

Another note on flavor: It really is essential that you taste the food as you are preparing it. Seasoning can make the difference between a bland, flat-tasting meal and a stellar one. Seasoning as you cook, with salt and other ingredients such as herbs and spices, helps build the layers of flavor that exemplify great cooking. Relying on your guests to use salt and pepper at the table just doesn't cut it.

The flavors of ingredients vary with the season and by brand. For this reason, my recipes all direct you to "season with salt and pepper to taste" and to "adjust seasoning according to taste." Don't be afraid of salt! It truly is a flavor enhancer. A little bit can go a long way. Taste at each step and add a pinch when you think it's needed.

The number of dishes you choose to serve at a meal is entirely up to you, but I am never compelled to serve a separate first course when I am entertaining casually. For big-deal meals, I will generally serve a first course, a main course with one or two side dishes, sometimes a salad, and then the dessert. Again, remember that less can be more, especially if preparing fewer dishes means you can afford to be more generous with the shellfish in the bouillabaisse or spend more time making the table pretty—or enjoying a glass of wine with your guests!

CREATING A BEAUTIFUL PRESENTATION

The first thing your guests will experience when you set their plates in front of them is the aesthetics of the food. We feast with our eyes as well as our palates. Consider the colors and shapes that will be on the plate and strive for variation. A grilled salmon fillet would look wonderful served beside whole new potatoes and whole baby zucchini. Chicken potpie, chock-full of generous chunks of chicken, large mushrooms, and bright green peas, makes a less composed and more casual

statement, yet still retains distinct texture and color variety.

The more natural you stay with the food, the better. It's not necessary or even desirable to produce plates that look whisked out of a restaurant kitchen. Think about each element that you will be arranging on the plate and give each room to breathe. Cutting vegetables into fancy shapes is not only time-consuming but also can come off a bit fussy. Food used to build architectural towers on the plate may be pretty to look at but it will generally be a hazard to eat. The purpose of food presentation is to delight your guests, not intimidate them.

THE TABLE IS A CANVAS

Just as food contributes to the mood of the occasion, dinnerware, glassware, flatware, and linens go beyond their practical functions to help create ambience even for casual gatherings. The mantra here is *simplicity* with another watchword, *harmony*.

First the practical elements: The table should be set correctly, not for stodginess's sake but because a correctly set table is a comfortable one. It would be quite off-putting, not to mention confusing, for your guests to be reaching from one side of the table to the other for their wineglasses and utensils (though it might be slightly amusing). In this case, the rules of etiquette exist for a good reason.

Share the things that bring you joy with your guests. Different patterns of dinnerware, flatware, and glassware can be mixed. Establish aesthetic harmony by setting the table with complementary colors, patterns, textures, and materials. Or, simply stay with white. It can do no wrong.

Natural elements lend themselves nicely to table decoration and they need little embellishment. A branch with pinecones attached or beach rocks scattered on the table create a serene and comfortable aura.

Flowers and found objects and treasures that you have collected add personality and warmth to the table. Unscented candles are always correct for an evening table setting.

Consider the details. Your guests will be grateful for comfortable chairs, cotton or linen napkins, water glasses along with their wineglasses (and the water to go in them), and salt and pepper shakers that are within reach.

In short, think about what makes you happy and secure, then provide the same for your guests.

MEETING AND GREETING

Speaking of happiness, who hasn't attended a party and felt horribly self-conscious and insecure upon arrival? This is perhaps the most important time to make your guests feel comfortable. Even if you are behind schedule and a tad harried, take the time to greet your guests as they enter your home.

Asking early-arriving guests to join you in the kitchen for a drink or to lend a hand will immediately put them at ease. You can ask guests to help themselves to drinks or you may put someone in charge of making drinks for other guests (inevitably, you'll have a volunteer). Direct them to the garden or invite them to wander through the house.

Think about your guest list. Choose guests with complementary and divergent interests and introduce them to each other based on one or the other. This is a fine line to tread. Too many similar interests can transform the party into a convention while a plethora of strangers can leave everyone feeling tongue-tied.

Tricks abound for matching guests and promoting conversation. When guests arrive, have them select a card with a play or movie character's name from a basket. Each guest must find his or her companion character (Romeo and Juliet, for example) and reveal the play or

movie plot at the table. Or, as guests arrive, tell them that they have something in common with one, two, or three other guests at the party. In order to be seated at the table, they must divine what the commonality is and with whom they share it. This may be their birth dates, colleges they attended, number of children they have, or any number of amusing things. Alternatively, do as I usually do and designate one of your more gregarious friends to ensure that no one is standing alone for too long.

What if *you're* the nervous one? Entertaining is a bit like being onstage, having to remember your lines and wanting to please your audience. Channel that nervousness into energy and direct it into action, then take three deep breaths before answering the door, smile, and you'll be fine. Never forget, this party is for you, too!

HAVING IT ON HAND:
THE ESSENTIAL PARTY PANTRY

So much of the time we devote to planning entertaining occasions is spent in the market. Keeping these staples on hand will not only free up that time, but will also ensure that you're well supplied for last-minute "get-over-here-at-eight" get-togethers. Come to think of it, these pantry items are great to have on hand whether you're entertaining or not. Knowing they're in your kitchen will make you happy.

dry storage

Arborio rice

couscous

pasta (one long variety and one shaped variety)

polenta

chicken and beef broths (low sodium)

Dijon mustard

canned tomatoes and sun-dried tomatoes

artichoke hearts

roasted red peppers in oil

curry paste

soy sauce

vinegars: balsamic, sherry, red wine

olive oil

sesame oil

canned tuna in olive oil

tapenade or black olive paste

an assortment of crackers and cookies

canned black, cannellini, and garbanzo beans

dried mushrooms

pesto

chocolate sauce

dried basil and oregano

saffron

herbes de Provence

kosher salt and black peppercorns

clam juice

red wine

garlic

onion

lemons and limes

sugar

flour

pure vanilla extract

the fridge

eggs

unsalted butter

Parmesan cheese

ricotta cheese

any interesting cheese that you like

salad greens

a selection of olives

white wine

champagne

beer

sparkling and still waters

seasonal vegetables

heavy cream

the freezer

ice cream and sorbet

coffee beans

frozen peas

frozen berries

phyllo dough or puff pastry or both

good bread (wrap well to prevent freezer burn)

foccacia

pancetta or bacon

pound cake

cookies (homemade, if possible)

On the following pages you'll find some examples of meals I've thrown together without leaving the house, or with just a quick stop at the market for something fresh such as tomatoes or ripe fruit to round out what I've stocked in the pantry.

risotto

Risotto *with* Artichoke Hearts *and* Porcini Mushrooms

Salad *of* Slivered Fennel, Radicchio, *and* Orange Slices

A selection *of* sorbets

pasta

Pasta *with* Peas, Sun-dried Tomatoes, *and*
   Chicken Broth

Green Salad *with* Balsamic Vinaigrette

Angel Food Cake *with* Cocoa Whipped Cream

frittata

Frittata *with* Parmesan *and* Herbs

Roasted Red Peppers *with* Garlic *and* Lemon

Pound Cake *with* Pureed Blueberries

spaghetti

Spaghetti *with* Clam Sauce

Broiled Radicchio Halves *with* Parmesan Cheese

Red Wine Poached Pears *with* Star Anise

niçoise

Niçoise Salad *with* Tuna, Black Olives, *and* Canned
   White Beans

An assortment *of* crackers

Lemon Sherbet *with* Gingersnaps

pizza

Individual Pizzas topped *with* black olives, sun-dried
   tomatoes, capers, *and* goat cheese

Simple Green Salad *with* Olive Oil *and* Lemon Juice

Fresh fruit *and* cookies

TAKING STOCK—AND KEEPING IT: THE ESSENTIAL EQUIPMENT CLOSET

Though I have subscribed with success to my version of real-life entertaining for many years, I can count more times than I'd like to admit when party planning became paranoia and I wasted as much energy as a chicken with her head cut off trying to mine my house for supplies.

To prevent a recurrence and simplify my entertaining life, I created "entertaining central." Mine is in an antique Irish linen press; you can create a home for your entertaining essentials in a trunk, a box, a large picnic basket, or an empty cupboard or closet. Inside the press, wicker baskets hold entertaining essentials like candles, candleholders, matches, and napkin rings. A deep bowl holds place cards and invitations. Assorted

tchotchkes that may make interesting table accessories and other items that can't be stacked reside on a low pull-out shelf. Pitchers, tureens, a gravy boat, and over-sized platters sit on a top shelf. Tablecloths and napkins reside on padded retractable wardrobe hangers in a nearby closet.

Take stock of your supplies and categorize them by use, size, and storage need, then establish one or more places that are devoted exclusively to their keep. I store all my tabletop and serving supplies in the linen press and closet, my flower arranging supplies in a garage cupboard adjacent to my kitchen, and outdoor party supplies in a weatherproof box alongside my gardening equipment.

19

CASUAL SUPPERS

after

a long day at the office or ferrying kids from point A to point Z, or a Saturday full of errands and household chores, what I want most is to fall into a cushy chair and read a magazine. When real life presses in it's tempting to surrender to its hulking demands, but the rejuvenating effect of a good meal with family or friends is worth a bit of effort (especially if you can press someone else into service for the cleanup).

When I was a kid, I remember having people in our house and around our table very often. Neighbors and friends of my parents would drop in. Pals from my sister's soccer team would converge upon the kitchen. We'd arrive home from a semester at college with friends who would stay and stay and stay.

My mother may have been an organized woman but there is no way that she could have orchestrated every one of those dinners in advance. Since I so often find myself in a time-pressed situation, as I'm sure you do, I wanted to duplicate the ease with which my mother was able to prepare a quick meal that prompted conviviality and contentment. Wouldn't it be fun to bring a friend home from work, or invite your daughter's best friend's parents to drop by after dance class, or arrange a barbecue with the neighbors on the fly—and not be stressed out about it?

In this chapter, I've assembled a collection of recipes that answer the question, "What's for dinner?" with "relaxed" as my byword. The recipes are based on fresh ingredients and robust flavors with vibrant presentation. Many of the dishes can be prepared entirely ahead of time, or you can prepare the ingredients for the dishes and assemble them later on.

Don't discount carry-out foods as a way of easing the effort. Specialty take-out shops and supermarket delis offer a range of prepared foods that you can use to augment the meal—or compose an entire dinner. In *Ways with Take-Away* (page 220) I share ideas on using take-out foods to enhance entertaining.

When I'm entertaining in a casual mode, I often opt for dishes that can be cooked communally. Invite your guests into the kitchen to lend a hand—with a glass of wine or lemonade to fortify them. Everybody likes to get in on the act, whether they're chopping or mixing or "supervising," and the end result is that much better!

These recipes can be plated individually or served family style in big bowls and on large platters that are passed around the table. They can even be grouped as a buffet, too, which has the advantage of being beautiful for your guests to see and so easy for you to serve.

SETTING THE CASUAL TABLE

A welcoming, comfortable table enriches any occasion, regardless of the dinner's degree of formality. Casual tables can be set anywhere—in the dining room, in the kitchen, outdoors under a shady tree, or around the coffee table by the fireplace. The ease of casual meals overflows to the aesthetics of the table and gives you free rein to decorate and adorn as much or as little as you like.

First and foremost, however, a table ought to be set properly. This has nothing to do with snobbishness or stuffiness and everything to do with practicality. A properly set table simply makes the meal easy for your guests to enjoy.

The dinnerware is always set directly in front of the diner and the flatware is always set to either side of the dinner plate in order of use, arranged from the outside in toward the plate. The forks are set on the left, the knife and spoon on the right. The knife blade always faces in toward the plate. Dessert utensils are brought out with the dessert. Bread-and-butter plates are generally not used for casual settings.

The napkin is placed either on top of the plate or to the left of the fork. No utensils should be placed on the napkin. Glasses are always placed to the upper right of the plate, directly over the knife and/or soup-spoon. The water goblet is the largest glass and is placed first, followed by the wineglass at a slight distance to the right.

CASUAL COVERAGE

My pine farmhouse table has as many surface imperfections as I do, each of which is a loving reminder of the many happy times spent around this table. For that reason, I tend to keep the surface uncovered when I entertain casually and rely on chargers (oversized plates on which dinner and salad plates can be placed) or place mats to create atmosphere and protect the wood from hot plates.

During the holidays, I use colored leaves or evergreen cuttings as place mats. I drape the table in translucent gauze or organza and arrange leaves or flowers underneath it so both the patina of the table and the decorations are visible. Sometimes in the autumn and winter, I will place a runner of brocade or velvet from end to end, or put larger swatches of the fabric under plates.

I have tied bamboo branches with twine to create exotic resting places for plates. I've cut place mats out of chicken wire and decorated them with flowers and leaves. Big white handkerchiefs (remember when our dads carried those?) look crisp against wood surfaces. Ceramic tiles add both color and texture to the table; I have used them singly as coasters, placed end to end as a runner, assembled into rectangular place mats, and I've covered the entire table with them, too.

For a summer supper after a day at the beach, I once lined the table with small boat flags. Their graphic and bold designs herald "summer" and "shore." I've used mirrors and old books and flats of real grass (line the bottoms with plastic) as place mats and chargers, each of which lent its singular characteristics and helped define the occasion. Look around your house and garden with a new eye and you will no doubt recruit everyday items for an entertaining role.

Candles always have a place on the table if it's dark outside. They lend warmth and an aura that creates a sense of occasion. For casual suppers, I opt for votives and pillar candles that I wrap with twine or ivy, or set in terra-cotta flowerpots or muffin tins, or on fanciful plates that I've found at secondhand stores.

I am particularly fond of flowers, and I use them liberally. I think flowers have distinct personalities. Some are more casual than others and therefore great for informal occasions; daisies, black-eyed Susans, daffodils, asters, dahlias, and sunflowers come to mind. Of course, the container that holds the flowers plays a role in the overall effect. I like to employ everyday items as impromptu vases. A cookie jar, a gravy boat, or a row of perfume bottles imbues the table with character. Put it all together and you'll come up with engaging compositions like garden roses in a florist's bucket, pansies in teacups, and hydrangeas in a steamed pudding mold!

CASUAL MENUS

Casual is as casual does. From a simple summer dinner of pasta with fresh-from-the-garden zucchini and basil, tossed with creamy ricotta and served on the porch, to a cozy autumn supper of pumpkin chowder and crusty bread by the fireside, the watchwords for casual entertaining are simplicity and ease.

The menu composition guidelines I share with you in the introduction apply to casual menus, too. Along with the basic considerations of color, texture, and flavor, I always think about seasonality—are the dishes I want to make and the ingredients I want to use in season and therefore appropriate? I consider the weather, too. If it's cold and blustery, I err on the side of warm and robust, and if it's hot and muggy, I veer toward the cool and refreshing.

I'm usually pretty selfish when it comes to the foods I serve. I figure if I'm doing the cooking, I deserve to cook what I like to eat. This works very well unless you are particularly fond of nonpopulist foods like anchovies and tripe. It's thoughtful, too, to cook foods that you know are particular favorites of one of your guests.

Those considerations aside, when it comes to casual entertaining, anything goes. As a rule, I don't serve a first course and I serve the side dishes (and often a salad) on the same plate as the main course. Sometimes I serve nothing more than a soup with a selection of crackers followed by cookies and ice cream. Often, I offer pasta and a salad, with fresh fruit for dessert.

Time is an important part of menu planning. If you know that you're going to be running in the door from your son's tennis match, to be followed soon by a gaggle of guests, you'll want to serve something that requires little labor or can be made largely ahead. In this case, when the weather's nice, the grill is a great tool. Rib-Eye Steaks with Chive Butter or Grilled Swordfish with Lemon-Rosemary Aioli, accompanied by Tomato, Red Onion, and Skinny Lemon Salad, fit the bill. Oven-friendly foods (those whose preparation time is spent largely in the oven) are a good bet, too. You can't go wrong with Perfectly Simple Roast Chicken or Roast Loin of Pork with Cider Glaze. When you have the luxury of more time, dishes that require a bit more assembly, like Lamb, Swiss Chard, and Sweet Potato Curry or a special dessert such as Jumbleberry Potpies, are appealing choices.

Here's the 3-point formula for figuring out a casual menu:

1. Consider the amount of time (or the inclination) you have to cook.

2. Determine what you'd like to cook—taking into account the season and how the foods you select get along together in terms of color, texture, and flavor.

3. Gauge how hungry you and your guests will be. This will help you decide whether to cook robustly or lightly and how many courses to serve.

FINAL WORDS

In the pages that follow you'll find four casual menus, one for each season, plus dozens more recipes that work well when the occasion is loose and the company familiar. Prepare the menus in their entirety or use them as a template for creating your own menus.

And remember, the struggle for perfection can be a noose. This is about having a good time. Cook and they will come!

PRIMER

D-I-Y Bar

Let your guests make their own drinks as you put the finishing touches on dinner. Stock the do-it-yourself bar with standards like wine and beer, then add an unexpected selection such as a pitcher of frosty margaritas in the summer or hot mulled wine in the winter, as well as a nonalcoholic offering like fresh-squeezed pink grapefruit juice or sparkling cider. I always have a bottle of Champagne on ice, for as my friend Roberta Klugman, director emeritus of the American Institute of Wine and Food so eloquently states, "A day without Champagne is stupid."

A basic yet interesting D-I-Y cocktail bar might include:

iced vodka

scotch

gin

dry sherry (chilled)

an aperitif such as campari

beer (a lager or an ale and a stout or porter)

red wine

white wine (chilled)

Champagne (chilled)

sparkling water

diet sodas and/or fruit juices

mixers: tonic, club soda

lemons, limes, oranges

green olives, cocktail onions

ice (in an ice bucket or bowl)

equipment: corkscrew, lemon zester, knife, small pitcher, cocktail shaker, swizzlers, cocktail napkins

casual menu

Spinach Salad *with* Pancetta *and* Pine Nuts

Green Pea, Mushroom, *and* Goat Cheese Risotto

Fresh Berries *with* Balsamic Cream

spinach salad with pancetta and pine nuts

This salad takes the Italian route with the addition of pancetta, pine nuts, and balsamic vinegar.

SERVES 6

- 3 tablespoons pine nuts
- 1/4 pound pancetta or slab bacon, cut into bite-size pieces
- 3 tablespoons balsamic vinegar
- 1 teaspoon red wine vinegar
  Kosher salt and freshly ground pepper
- 1/3 cup extra-virgin olive oil
- 8 cups spinach leaves

METHOD

Preheat the oven to 350°F.

Spread the pine nuts on a baking sheet. Place in the oven and toast until lightly browned, 3 to 5 minutes. Watch them carefully, as they will burn in an instant!

In a medium skillet, cook the pancetta over medium heat until crisp; drain on paper towels.

In a large salad bowl, whisk together the vinegars and salt and pepper. Whisk in the oil in a steady stream. Add the spinach and toss to coat with the dressing. Divide among 6 plates, sprinkle with the pancetta and pine nuts, and serve immediately.

green pea, mushroom, and goat cheese risotto

If you like goat cheese, this dish is for you.

SERVES 6

- 6 cups chicken stock or low-sodium canned broth
- 2 tablespoons extra-virgin olive oil
- 2 tablespoons (1/4 stick) unsalted butter
- 1/2 medium onion, chopped
- 1 shallot, chopped
- 2 cups Arborio rice
- 1/2 cup white wine
- 1 cup fresh or frozen peas
- 1 cup sliced button mushrooms
- 2 teaspoons fresh thyme leaves
- 1 tablespoon chopped fresh parsley
- 1/2 cup crumbled mild goat cheese, such as chèvre
  Kosher salt and freshly ground pepper
  Thyme sprigs, for garnish

METHOD

Bring the stock to a boil in a medium saucepan; cover and keep at a simmer.

Heat the olive oil and butter in a large saucepan over medium heat. Add the onion and shallot and cook until soft, about 3 minutes. Add the rice and cook, stirring to coat it with the oil, for 3 minutes. Add the wine and stir until absorbed, about 1 minute.

Slowly add 1 cup of the hot stock. Stir and let simmer, reducing the heat if necessary, until the rice absorbs the stock. Continue in this way, adding 1/2 cup stock at a time and stirring continuously, until the rice is beginning to soften, 10 to 15 minutes. Stir in the fresh peas, if using, the mushrooms, and herbs and continue cooking, stirring, and adding stock 1/2 cup at a time until the rice is creamy and al dente, about 10 minutes more. Add the goat cheese and frozen peas, if using, and stir until the cheese melts and the peas are heated through. Season to taste with salt and pepper. Serve immediately, garnished with thyme sprigs and more crumbled goat cheese if you wish.

fresh berries with balsamic cream

It may seem odd, but balsamic vinegar is a perfect complement to strawberries. Use a good-quality balsamic vinegar and serve this when berries are at their most flavorful. You can whip the cream about an hour beforehand without losing its fluffiness.

SERVES 6

- 4 cups strawberries, at room temperature
- 2 cups berries of your choice, such as blackberries or raspberries, at room temperature
  Grated zest of 1 lemon
- 1 cup heavy cream
- 1/4 cup confectioners' sugar
- 2 tablespoons balsamic vinegar

METHOD

Gently mix the berries with the lemon zest.

Whip the cream with the sugar and balsamic vinegar. Spoon over the berries and serve.

style note

**GREAT-AUNT MILLIE'S CRYSTAL
(OR SILVER OR CHINA)**

Don't save your "good" things just for
formal occasions. Beautiful dinnerware
and glassware is meant to be enjoyed
and unless you have somone in your life
who suffers from terminal butterfingers,
why not? If it gives you pleasure use
your "good" things as often as possible.

I like to put crystal candlesticks on my
wood farmhouse table and serve wine in
antique Waterford glasses. My mother-
in-law gave me silver nut cups (tiny
dishes to be placed at each place setting which were popular in the fifties)
one Christmas, and I use them to serve
after-dinner mints with coffee. I use an
old set of lusterware demitasse cups for
custard desserts or rich cream soups.

Why not use silver flatware for a casual
dinner for friends? With plain white
plates, silverware would be a contemporary yet elegant statement. Fine china,
whether mixed with everyday plates or
with other patterns, always makes a
table more beautiful. You could use
your everyday plates for the main
course and serve a star dessert (think
Almond Red Pavlova with Berries) on
your Royal Doulton.

We're subjected to so much blight in
the world today, a bit of beauty is much
appreciated. So if Aunt Millie wanted
you to have some of her lovely things,
go ahead and enjoy them.

SUMMER

casual menu

Tomato, Red Onion, *and* Skinny Lemon Salad

Tequila-Grilled Shrimp *on* Smashed Avocado

Flour *and* Corn Tortillas

A Selection *of* Summer Melon *and* "Go With" Cookies

tomato, red onion, and skinny lemon salad

Lemons marry very well with tomatoes as long as they are sliced very, very thinly. Make this salad when tomatoes are ripe and sweet. If you can find small, sweet Meyer lemons, definitely use them!

SERVES 6

4 medium tomatoes, cut into thick slices
1 large red onion, thinly sliced
2 lemons, sliced paper thin, seeds removed
3 tablespoons honey or white wine vinegar
1 teaspoon kosher salt
 Freshly ground pepper
½ teaspoon sugar
½ cup extra-virgin olive oil
1½ tablespoons finely chopped fresh tarragon

METHOD

On a platter, arrange the tomatoes in rows alternating with slices of red onion and lemon.

In a small bowl, combine the vinegar, salt, pepper, and sugar. Whisk in the olive oil in a steady stream. Stir in the tarragon. Pour over the salad and serve immediately.

tequila-grilled shrimp on smashed avocado

A virtual fiesta of color and flavor, this dish is as much fun to make as it is to eat. Serve it with tortillas and margaritas. Perfecto!

SERVES 6

Shrimp

2 tablespoons tequila
 Juice of 4 limes
4 garlic cloves, peeled and crushed
1 jalapeño pepper, seeded and finely chopped
1 tablespoon finely chopped cilantro
 Kosher salt and freshly ground pepper
24 jumbo shrimp, peeled and deveined
6 wooden skewers, soaked in water for 30 minutes

Smashed Avocado

2 small ripe avocados, peeled and pitted
2 small plum tomatoes, seeded and diced
3 tablespoons minced red onion
 Juice of ½ small lime
3 tablespoons finely chopped cilantro
 Hot pepper sauce
 Kosher salt

6 limes, quartered, for garnish
 Cilantro sprigs, for garnish
 Small flour tortillas

METHOD

Prepare a fire in the grill.

In a large bowl, combine the tequila, lime juice, garlic, jalapeño, cilantro, and salt and pepper to taste. Add the shrimp and toss to coat with the marinade. Cover and refrigerate 30 minutes.

Cut the avocados into 1-inch cubes. Place in a medium bowl with the tomatoes, onion, lime juice, cilantro, and hot pepper sauce and salt to taste.

Gently toss to mix. Using the back of a spoon, gently press on the mixture to "smash" the avocado. Cover and refrigerate.

Remove the shrimp from the marinade and thread 4 onto each of 6 skewers. Grill just until pink, about 2 minutes per side; don't overcook.

To serve, remove the shrimp from the skewers. Divide the smashed avocado among 6 plates. Top with the shrimp and squeeze a bit of lime juice over each. Garnish with the lime quarters and cilantro sprigs. Serve with warm flour tortillas. Alternately, you can prepare "wraps" by rolling the tortillas into cone shapes and filling them with the smashed avocado and shrimp.

"go with" cookies for fruit and ice cream

There is something about fruit and ice cream that demands a partner, preferably a crunchy one. "Go With" cookies are neither overly sweet nor overly rich, plus they contain an interesting ingredient—a kick of fragrant herbs—that makes them a perfect topic for conversation—and for eating with fruit or ice cream. I have suggested three herbs that would be ideal for these cookies because they have a sweeter flavor and are most often associated with desserts. A more esoteric choice would be basil, which complements berries very well. Edible, fragrant flower petals such as rose geranium and rose would be a pretty choice, too.

**MAKES ABOUT TWENTY-FOUR
2$^{1}/_{2}$-INCH COOKIES**

- 1 cup (2 sticks) unsalted butter, at room temperature
- $^{1}/_{4}$ cup granulated sugar
- 5 tablespoons confectioners' sugar
- 2 cups unbleached all-purpose flour
- 2 tablespoons minced fresh lemon verbena, lavender, or mint
  Pinch of kosher salt

METHOD

Preheat the oven to 350°F. Line 2 baking sheets with parchment.

In a large bowl, use an electric mixer to beat the butter until pale yellow and fluffy. Gradually add the sugars and beat well.

In a small bowl, stir together the flour, herb, and salt. Add to the butter mixture and beat until thoroughly combined. Turn the dough out onto a lightly floured surface and pat into a disk. Wrap with plastic wrap and chill for 1 hour.

When the dough is firm, transfer to a well-floured surface. Roll out the dough to about $^{1}/_{4}$ inch thick and cut into desired shapes. Transfer the cookies to the prepared baking sheets, arranging them about $^{1}/_{2}$ inch apart. Prick each cookie with the tines of a fork, sprinkle with additional granulated sugar, and bake until golden around the edges, 10 to 12 minutes. Transfer the cookies to a wire rack to cool. Store for up to 7 days in an airtight container. These cookies (as well as the dough) freeze very well.

PRIMER

The Art of Cleaning Up

Just as meal preparation benefits from advanced planning, so too does cleanup. With a bit of organization, this dreaded part of entertaining won't seem as daunting and will progress much more quickly.

- This is tip number one: Clean as you go. If you've cleaned as you've cooked throughout the day, you will be a giant step ahead of the game.

- Begin the evening with an empty dishwasher.

- Consider using a rolling cart for transporting dirty dishes from the table to the kitchen so you only need to make one trip. A laundry basket lined with plastic works well, too.

- Establish an area in the kitchen for dirty dishes: one part for dishwasher-safe things and another part for handwashables.

- Have a trash container handy so you can scrape the dishes as you bring them into the kitchen, then stack them in their appropriate areas. If you wish, you can put the dirty dishes in buckets of soapy water. I use a baby's plastic bathtub for this.

- Put dirty flatware in a bucket or pot filled with soapy water so it's not strewn about.

- Allot glassware its own area so glasses are not tipped over and broken during the course of cleaning up.

- At the end of the evening (not during the dessert course!), put the dishwasher-safe items in the dishwasher and start it. Since you've scraped all the plates, put the flatware in soapy water, and emptied the glasses, you can leave them until the morning to wash.

- Listen to music or chat with your significant other as you clean. It helps pass the time.

- If someone offers to help, accept.

AUTUMN

Pumpkin Chowder

Westphalian Ham, *a* Wedge *of* Gruyère, *and* Cornichons

Triple Ginger Cake *with* Lemon Glaze

style note

FASHION PLATES

It used to be that "fine china" made its appearance only on special occasions. Nowadays, anything goes, in any combination. The only limit is your imagination. Go for it!

• Establish a theme either with color or pattern and use it to link various pieces of dinnerware patterns. The elegance of an all-white or all-ivory table, in various values or shades, the crispness of a blue and white motif, a rose theme, brought to life with hand-painted earthenware, etched glassware, and rose-shaped porcelain dessert plates are all examples of how to make this work.

• Use large service plates or chargers beneath the dinner plates to create a mood. Gold underplates lend glamour. Frosted glass chargers add depth to clear glass plates or bowls. Bamboo chargers anchor fire-glazed green rice bowls.

• Stack china for drama and dimension. A stack of creamware dinnerware may include a scalloped underplate, a plain plate, and a soup bowl or salad plate with a pierced rim.

• Mix the contemporary with the antique. Pink depression glass matched with white porcelain makes a fresh yet refined statement. Traditional blue and white Spode (in the Blue Italian pattern) earthenware looks terrific with contemporary blown glass in the style of Kosta Boda.

pumpkin chowder

The earthy flavors of this hearty chowder make it an ideal choice for an autumn or winter supper. If you can't find fresh pumpkin, substitute butternut or hubbard squash. For a dramatic presentation hollow out small pumpkins and serve the soup in these natural bowls.

SERVES 6

- ½ pound thick-sliced bacon, diced
- 2 cups chopped onions
- 2 teaspoons curry powder, preferably Madras
- 2 tablespoons flour
- 1 pound eating or sugar pumpkin, peeled, seeded, and cut into 1-inch chunks
- 2 large potatoes, peeled and cut into 1-inch chunks
- 4 cups chicken stock or low-sodium canned broth
- 1 cup half-and-half
  Kosher salt and freshly ground pepper
  Toasted pumpkin seeds, for garnish
  Chopped green onions, for garnish

METHOD

Put the bacon in a large soup pot over low heat and cook gently until it releases its fat, about 5 minutes.

Add the onions and cook, stirring occasionally, for 10 minutes. Stir in the curry powder and flour and cook, stirring, for 5 minutes. Add the pumpkin, potatoes, and stock. Increase the heat to medium-low and cook until the pumpkin and potatoes are tender, 10 to 15 minutes.

Add the half-and-half and season with salt and pepper to taste. Simmer for 5 minutes, or until heated through. Do not allow to boil.

Serve the soup in warm bowls, garnished with pumpkin seeds and a sprinkle of green onions.

Sides for Soups

Casual meals based on hearty soups are so wonderfully simple for the cook because they require nothing more than punctuation when it comes to side dishes. I like to serve a selection of the best-quality delicatessen meats and a wedge of ripe, full-flavored cheese. Tart cornichons balance the richness of the cheese and meat.

triple ginger cake with lemon glaze

If you like ginger, this cake has your name all over it. It tastes even better if made the day before you serve it.

MAKES ONE 8-INCH CAKE

- 1½ cups unbleached flour
- 1 teaspoon ground ginger
- ¾ teaspoon baking powder
- ¾ teaspoon baking soda
- ¾ teaspoon kosher salt
- ½ cup (1 stick) unsalted butter, at room temperature
- ½ cup packed dark brown sugar
- 1 large egg
- ½ cup light (unsulphured) molasses
- 1 tablespoon grated fresh ginger
- ½ cup milk
- 3 tablespoons finely chopped crystallized ginger

Glaze

- 2 tablespoons ginger liqueur or dark rum
- ¼ cup fresh lemon juice
- ½ cup confectioners' sugar

METHOD

Preheat the oven to 350°F. Butter and flour an 8-inch square or round cake pan.

In a medium bowl, sift together the flour, ground ginger, baking powder, baking soda, and salt. In a large bowl, using an electric mixer on medium-high speed, beat the butter until light and fluffy. Add the brown sugar and beat until fluffy, 2 minutes. Add the egg, molasses, and fresh ginger and beat until well blended. Reduce the speed to low and in 3 batches, beat in the flour mixture alternately with the milk, beginning and ending with the flour. Fold in the crystallized ginger. Pour the batter into the prepared pan.

Bake until the center springs back when touched lightly with a fingertip, about 35 minutes. Transfer to a rack and let the cake cool in the pan for 5 minutes. Invert onto a rack and turn right side up. Cool 15 minutes.

In a small bowl, combine the glaze ingredients. Stir until well blended, then brush onto the top and sides of the cake. Let cool before serving.

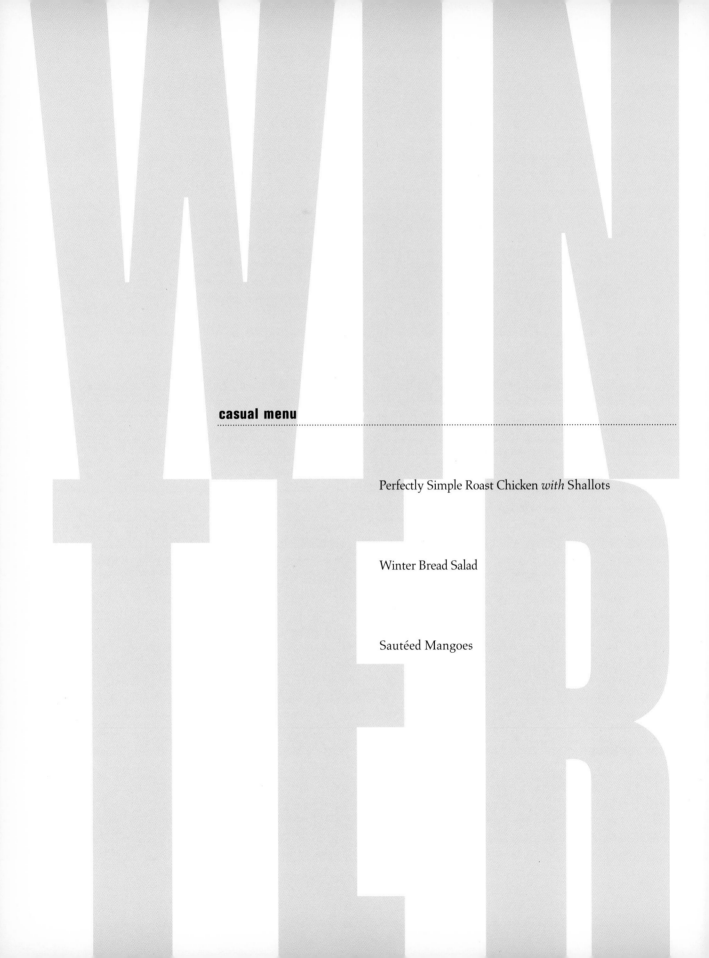

WINTER

casual menu

Perfectly Simple Roast Chicken *with* Shallots

Winter Bread Salad

Sautéed Mangoes

perfectly simple roast chicken with shallots

It's said that the mark of a good cook is a perfectly roasted chicken. This recipe will win you kudos every time. The shallots are a nice addition but not essential.

SERVES 6

- 1 chicken, about 3½ pounds
- 1 lemon, cut in half
  Kosher salt and freshly ground pepper
- 2 sprigs of any herb you like (rosemary, bay, or sage is nice)
- 2 tablespoons extra-virgin olive oil

Roasted Shallots

- 2 tablespoons extra-virgin olive oil
- 1 tablespoon unsalted butter
- 24 shallots, peeled
- 2 teaspoons balsamic vinegar

METHOD

Preheat the oven to 450°F. Pat the chicken dry and rub inside and out with a lemon half. Discard the lemon half. Squeeze the juice of the remaining lemon half into the cavity, then place the lemon half in the cavity. Season the cavity with salt and pepper.

Use your fingers to gently separate the skin from the breast meat and slip 1 herb sprig between the skin and meat of each breast. Truss the chicken. Rub the chicken with the olive oil, season it with salt and pepper, and place it breast side up, on a rack if you desire, in a roasting pan. Place in the center of the oven, legs toward the back of the oven, and roast until the thickest part of the thigh registers 175°F. to 180°F. on an instant-read thermometer, about 1 hour.

While the chicken roasts, prepare the shallots. Heat the remaining oil and the butter over medium heat in an ovenproof skillet. Add the shallots, salt, pepper, and vinegar and toss to coat. Cook, stirring, until the shallots begin to brown, about 5 minutes. Set aside.

When the chicken is done, remove it from the oven, reducing the oven temperature to 350°F. Tent it with aluminum foil, and let rest at least 15 minutes before carving. Place the skillet with the shallots in the oven and bake until tender, about 15 minutes.

Carve the chicken and serve with pan juices and the shallots.

winter bread salad

Zuni Cafe in San Francisco serves a creative rendition of stuffing in the form of a bread salad. From the moment I tasted it, I knew I had to try to re-create it. Bursting with the savory flavors of sage, parsley, arugula, and red onion and a whisper of sweetness from currants, this is a wonderful salad to serve with roasts and is especially good with roast chicken. Arrange the salad on individual plates and place slices of the roasted meat on top of the salad. The juices will seep into the salad—it's delish!

SERVES 6

- ½ pound day-old country bread, crust removed, cut into thick slices
- 2 tablespoons extra-virgin olive oil
- ½ medium red onion, thinly sliced
- 1 bunch arugula, trimmed and washed
- 2 celery stalks, thinly sliced crosswise
- ⅓ cup currants

Dressing

- 3 tablespoons balsamic vinegar
- 1 teaspoon Dijon mustard
  Kosher salt and freshly ground pepper
- ⅓ cup extra-virgin olive oil
- 2 tablespoons chopped fresh parsley
- 1 tablespoon chopped fresh sage

METHOD

Preheat the oven to 450°F. Brush the bread slices on both sides with the olive oil. Cut into 1-inch cubes (you should have about 3 cups of cubes). Arrange in a single layer on a baking sheet and bake until crisp and golden, about 10 minutes. Check frequently to be sure the bread doesn't burn.

As the bread is toasting, make the dressing. Combine the vinegar and mustard in a small bowl with salt and pepper to taste. Whisk in the olive oil, then stir in parsley and sage.

To serve, combine the onion, arugula, celery, and currants in a bowl. Drizzle half the dressing over the salad and mix well. Add the warm bread, drizzle with the remaining dressing, and mix again. Serve immediately.

style note

I can't resist the juxtaposition of a bright blooming bulb at a window against the backdrop of white snow. I like to breathe in the warm aroma of paperwhites as I look at the crystal-cold air outside the window. And I adore the surprise flash of red I get from an amaryllis when I turn on the lights in the living room before my guests arrive.

Whether you force bulbs for yourself or to give as gifts (they make wonderful party favors for a holiday dinner), follow a few simple steps.

Place pebbles or marbles in a water-proof container (anything from a mixing bowl to a sugar bowl will do). Place bulbs an inch apart, leaving the top third exposed to light. Pour in water to reach the bottom of the bulbs. Keep in a cool spot (some types of bulbs require darkness—check with your nursery) until green shoots appear, then move to a sunny windowsill. You can enjoy your blooms in four to six weeks.

sautéed mangoes

Serve this tropical dish as a topping for vanilla ice cream or with a splash of cream. Coconut macaroons would be a delightful partner for this easy but unusual fruit dessert.

SERVES 6

- ½ cup (1 stick) unsalted butter
- 2 tablespoons minced fresh ginger
- ½ cup dark rum
- 2 tablespoons fresh lime juice
- 4 ripe but firm mangoes, peeled and cut into ½-inch slices
- ⅓ cup packed dark brown sugar

METHOD

Melt the butter in a large sauté pan over medium heat. Add the ginger, rum, and lime juice and stir to combine. Add the mangoes, sprinkle with the brown sugar, and cook, stirring, until the sugar is dissolved and the mangoes heated through.

PRIMER

How to Peel and Slice a Mango

Anchor the mango on a cutting board with its stem end up. With a sharp knife, cut away the flesh on either side of the pit. Hold a mango half in the palm of your hand (place it on a dish towel for safety) and cut around the perimeter to free the fruit from the peel. Cut into slices.

more

casual supper recipes

Beet Salad with Roquefort provides a vibrant counterpoint to Scallop and Corn Chowder with big chunks of cut-from-the-cob corn. Small starfish do double duty as decorative touches and nautical fork rests.

scallop and corn chowder

Scallops and corn have a natural affinity and in this chunky chowder, they get along splendidly! It's a nice change from traditional clam chowder.

SERVES 6

3 ounces salt pork, diced
1 medium onion, finely chopped
3 medium waxy potatoes, peeled and cut into ¾-inch cubes
1½ cups bottled clam juice
½ cup dry white wine
1 cup half-and-half
1 cup milk
1½ pounds bay scallops
1 tablespoon fresh thyme leaves
1½ cups cooked corn kernels
Kosher salt
Cayenne
2 tablespoons chopped fresh parsley

METHOD

In a medium saucepan over medium-low heat, cook the salt pork until it softens and releases its fat, 8 to 10 minutes. Add the onion and potatoes and sauté for 3 minutes. Add the clam juice and wine, cover, and simmer until the potatoes are tender, 8 to 10 minutes. Add the half-and-half and milk and bring to a boil, then immediately reduce the heat to low. Add the scallops with their juice, cover, and simmer for 1 minute. Stir in the thyme and corn and cook gently just until the corn is heated through. Season to taste with salt and a dash of cayenne. Ladle into hot soup bowls and sprinkle with parsley.

your favorite vegetable soup

Master this recipe and you can make as many different soups as you can find vegetables to use. If you wish, enrich the soup before serving by swirling in a bit of heavy cream. Definitely garnish it with herbs and/or herb flowers and serve it with Parmesan toasts.

SERVES 6

2 tablespoons (¼ stick) unsalted butter
1 tablespoon extra-virgin olive oil
1 medium onion, finely chopped
1 large potato, peeled and diced
2 pounds vegetable of your choice, such as broccoli, asparagus, or zucchini, peeled if necessary and coarsely chopped
6 cups chicken stock or low-sodium canned broth
2 parsley sprigs
1 thyme sprig
1 bay leaf
Kosher salt and freshly ground pepper
⅓ cup heavy cream (optional)
Chopped fresh herbs, such as chives and chive flowers or thyme and thyme flowers
Parmesan Toasts (recipe follows)

METHOD

In a medium saucepan, heat the butter and oil over medium-low heat. Add the onion and cook until it softens, 4 to 5 minutes.

Add the potato, vegetable, and chicken stock. With kitchen string, tie together the parsley, thyme, and bay leaf into a bouquet garni and add to the saucepan. Bring to a boil, then reduce the heat, cover, and simmer until the vegetables are very tender, about 15 minutes.

Discard the bouquet garni. In batches, puree the soup in a food processor or blender. Return to the saucepan and reheat over low heat if necessary. Season with salt and pepper to taste and swirl in a bit of heavy cream, if desired. Ladle into warm soup bowls, garnish with chopped fresh herbs, and serve with Parmesan Toasts.

parmesan toasts

The perfect "go with" for soups and salads, these toasts can be made beforehand and stored in an airtight container. You can also vary the cheese by using Gruyère or Cheddar if you wish. If you like, use small cookie or canape cutters to cut the toasts into shapes before broiling.

MAKES 12

12 $\frac{1}{4}$-inch-thick baguette slices, cut on the diagonal
$\frac{1}{2}$ cup extra-virgin olive oil
1 cup coarsely grated Parmesan cheese

METHOD

Preheat the broiler.

Brush both sides of each bread slice with olive oil and arrange on a baking sheet. Toast the bread under the broiler until crisp but not too brown, about 1 minute per side. Remove and sprinkle the bread slices evenly with the Parmesan and place under the broiler until the cheese melts and begins to brown, about 2 minutes. Watch carefully to prevent burning!

cool as a cucumber salad

On a muggy summer day or as an accompaniment to a spicy meal, cucumbers beat the heat. Tart and refreshing with a hint of mint, this salad also happens to be low-fat.

SERVES 6

1 cup plain yogurt
2 tablespoons rice wine vinegar
$\frac{1}{2}$ teaspoon celery seed
2 long seedless (English) cucumbers, peeled and cut into $\frac{1}{4}$-inch slices
$\frac{3}{4}$ cup finely chopped fresh mint (approximately 1 large bunch)
Kosher salt and freshly ground pepper

METHOD

In a small bowl, combine the yogurt, vinegar, and celery seed. Put the cucumbers in a medium bowl and pour the yogurt mixture over them. Stir in the mint and add salt and pepper to taste. Refrigerate at least 1 hour to allow the flavors to blend.

Your Favorite Vegetable Soup makes a refreshing chilled soup, too. For summer lunches, I pair zucchini, spinach, and parsley and float Parmesan "stars" and "moons" and "suns" on top.

THE OUTDOOR TABLE

Bring your pine farmhouse table out-doors, place it under a big, shady tree, and think Italian country. Cover it with a piece of fabric patterned with lemons or cherries, a blue and white patchwork quilt, or Nantucket red sailcloth. If your table won't travel, find a grassy spot and spread out a quilted movers' blanket.

Just because you're outside doesn't mean you're obligated to use paper. Cloth napkins, whether coolly elegant white linen or bright bandannas and tea towels, add a special touch—plus they're so much more pleasant to they are far more effective with messy summer fare like barbecued ribs or chicken. White and ivory antique table linens offer a refined but warm welcome. You can often find them for a song in sec-ondhand stores and at yard sales. If you're so inclined, embroider them with brightly colored floss or with a mono-gram in a complementary value of the same color (ivory on white, for exam-ple).

Sew small stones into the corners of tablecloths or clip the edges with fish-ing weights to keep them from taking flight in the wind. Put napkins under a fly screen so they don't blow away. Use beach rocks to "collar" the bases of vases so they don't tip over in the breeze.

Using real glassware—not to mention crystal—does lend an air of devil-may-care refinement (think Scott and Zelda).

Wrapping tumblers in raffia or cloth will help save them from breaking should they be dropped. Bring the wine to the table in a big ice-filled planter or flow-erpot. Cover open pitchers with lace doilies threaded with fishing weights or narrow ribbons. Serve drinks with col-ored straws.

For serving food, enameled tinware adds color, plus it's inexpensive and practi-cal. Baskets of various shapes and sizes can hold chips, breads, and raw vegeta-bles. Line Chinese steamer baskets with large kale leaves for portable buffet-to-table servers.

For a daytime party, wrap sunglasses and suntan lotion in bandannas and place a bundle at each setting, or offer spray bottles filled with water and lemon essence or rosewater. At night, set sparklers at each place and light them when you give the welcome toast.

roasted beet and roquefort salad

Okay, I know it takes time to roast beets but it's all baking time, freeing you to do other things. If you don't have the time to wait out the roasting but you simply must have this salad, use canned beets or check out the take-out section for roasted beets.

SERVES 6

- 8 medium beets
- 3 to 4 tablespoons balsamic vinegar
     Grated zest from 1 orange
     Kosher salt and freshly ground pepper
- ½ cup walnut oil
- 1 medium red onion, thinly sliced
- 6 large curly endive leaves
- 3 tablespoons coarsely chopped toasted walnuts
- ¾ cup (3 ounces) crumbled Roquefort or other blue cheese

METHOD

Preheat the oven to 400° F.

Trim off the beet tops leaving just a bit of green stem and wrap the beets well in aluminum foil. Bake until tender, about 45 to 60 minutes. When the beets are cool enough to handle, slip off the skins and slice.

In a large bowl, combine the balsamic vinegar, orange zest, and salt and pepper to taste. Stir to dissolve the salt. Whisk in the walnut oil.

Toss the beets and the onion with the vinaigrette and marinate for 30 minutes.

To serve, arrange 1 curly endive leaf on each of 6 individual plates. Spoon the beet salad onto the leaves and garnish with the toasted walnuts and cheese.

'slaw

American to the core and so familiar to all of us, coleslaw need not be relegated to summer picnics. Serve it with roasted and grilled foods throughout the year.

SERVES 6

- ¼ cup apple cider vinegar
- 1 tablespoon Dijon mustard
- 2 teaspoons honey
     Kosher salt and freshly ground pepper
- ¾ cup safflower oil
- ½ medium head green cabbage, shredded
- ½ medium head red cabbage, shredded
- 2 Granny Smith apples, unpeeled, cored and chopped
- 1½ teaspoons celery seed

METHOD

Combine the vinegar, mustard, honey, salt, and pepper in a large bowl. Stir to dissolve the salt. Whisk in the oil. Add the cabbages, apples, and celery seed and toss to coat with the dressing.

red lettuces with citrus vinaigrette

Mixing the vinaigrette in the bottom of the bowl in which I toss the lettuce not only saves time but also coats the lettuce with the dressing more thoroughly.

SERVES 6

- ½ teaspoon grated orange zest
- 3 tablespoons orange juice
- 1 tablespoon lemon juice
     Kosher salt and freshly ground pepper
- ¼ cup extra-virgin olive oil
- 6 large handfuls of red leaf greens, such as red oak leaf lettuce, radicchio, lola rosa, or red-tipped endive
     Garnish: Edible flowers such as red and orange nasturtiums, marigolds, and scented geranium

METHOD

In the bottom of a large salad bowl, combine the orange zest, orange juice, lemon juice, salt, and pepper. Whisk in the olive oil in a steady stream.

Add the lettuces and toss gently with the vinaigrette. Garnish with the edible flowers.

soy-glazed salmon

Though this recipe calls for marinating the fish for 30 minutes, it doesn't require any additional effort on your part and in fact gives you the opportunity to make a salad and set the table or help with homework while the fish marinates.

SERVES 6

Marinade

- ¼ cup soy sauce
- 2 teaspoons sesame oil
- 3 tablespoons rice wine vinegar
- 2 garlic cloves, minced
- 2 tablespoons light brown sugar
- 1 tablespoon peanut oil
  Kosher salt and freshly ground pepper to taste

- 6 salmon steaks, about ¾ inch thick

METHOD

Combine the marinade ingredients in a small bowl. Place the salmon fillets in a baking dish. Pour the marinade over the fish, turning the salmon to coat. Cover with plastic wrap and marinate in the refrigerator for 30 minutes, turning once.

Preheat the broiler. Oil a broiler pan or baking sheet.

Remove the salmon steaks from the marinade and arrange on the broiler pan. Broil for 4 minutes, turn, and broil for another 4 minutes, or until the fish is opaque when tested with a knife.

I applied the salmon's Asian theme to the table setting by tying together green bamboo shoots into a rectangular "plate frame." An arrangement of ornamental grasses or a bowl of goldfish would make a whimsically elegant centerpiece.

grilled swordfish with lemon-rosemary aioli

Swordfish stands up well to high heat so I prefer to grill it. You can do so in the traditional way, on an outdoor grill, or you can use a ridged grill pan on your stovetop. Broiling works well, too. If you have the time, prepare the aioli in advance so the flavors have time to marry.

SERVES 6

- ¾ cup mayonnaise (store-bought is fine)
- 2½ tablespoons extra-virgin olive oil
- 2 cloves very finely chopped garlic
- 3 teaspoons finely grated lemon zest
- 2 teaspoons finely chopped fresh rosemary
  Fresh lemon juice
  Kosher salt and freshly ground pepper
- 6 8-ounce swordfish steaks, ½ inch thick

METHOD

If grilling outdoors, prepare a fire in the grill.

In a small bowl, combine the mayonnaise with 1½ tablespoons of the olive oil, garlic, the lemon zest, rosemary, lemon juice, and salt and pepper to taste.

If using a ridged grill pan, place it over medium-high heat to preheat it. When the fire is hot or when the grill pan is hot, brush the swordfish on both sides with the remaining 1 tablespoon olive oil. Grill for 2 minutes, then turn and grill the other side until done, 2 to 3 minutes more. If using a stove-top grill pan, the fish may require a bit more cooking.

Transfer the swordfish to a platter or individual plates. Serve with a dollop of the lemon-rosemary aioli and pass the remainder.

steamed clams with lemongrass-ginger broth

Steamed clams are one of my all-time favorite foods and I like to eat them straight out of the black enamel pot I cook them in. In this version, the clams have gone uptown for a dish with Asian influences. Serve it as a main course for a casual supper or as a first course for a more uppity do.

SERVES 6

- 2   tablespoons extra-virgin olive oil
- 1   2-inch piece fresh ginger, thinly sliced
- 2   shallots, thinly sliced
- 1   lemongrass stalk, cut into 2-inch pieces and crushed with the back of a knife
- 3   green onions, white and green parts, chopped
- ½   cup chopped fresh cilantro
- 1   carrot, peeled and finely chopped
- 3   plum tomatoes, diced
- 2   cups bottled clam juice
- 2   cups dry white wine
- 4   dozen medium clams (cherrystone or littleneck) or 6 dozen small clams, such as Manila
- ⅓   cup chopped fresh cilantro, for garnish

METHOD

In the bottom of a steamer pot, warm the oil over medium-high heat. Add the ginger, shallots, lemongrass, green onions, ½ cup of cilantro, carrot, and tomatoes and sauté 3 minutes, stirring and tossing frequently. Add the clam juice and wine and bring to a boil, then reduce the heat to low and simmer for 15 minutes.

Place the steamer basket in the pot. Add the clams, cover, and steam until the clams open, 5 to 10 minutes. (Manila clams may need only 4 to 6 minutes.)

To serve, divide the clams among 6 shallow soup bowls. Strain the broth through a sieve and pour some over each serving. Sprinkle with the remaining chopped cilantro.

chatham lobster rolls

Every summer when we're on Cape Cod, we visit the Kream-n-Kone on Route 28 near Chatham. Along with the world's best clam rolls (but that's another story), we feast on lobster rolls jam-packed with chunks of lobster meat on buttery toasted buns. If you're near the shore when you eat these, heed your mother's advice and wait an hour before swimming—they're rich!

SERVES 6

- 3   cups cooked lobster meat, in chunks (about 1½ pounds lobster meat) (see Note)
- 6   tablespoons finely chopped celery
- 2   tablespoons finely chopped green onions
- ¾   cup Hellmann's or Best Foods mayonnaise
- 2   tablespoons lemon juice
      Dash of hot pepper sauce
      Kosher salt
- 6   hot dog rolls
- 3   tablespoons butter, melted

METHOD

In a medium bowl, toss together the lobster, celery, green onions, mayonnaise, and lemon juice. Season to taste with hot pepper sauce and salt.

Brush the rolls with the melted butter and toast them on a grill or in a heavy skillet. Mound the lobster mixture into the toasted buns and serve immediately.

Note: Two 1½-pound lobsters will yield enough meat for 6 lobster rolls.

crunchy herb chicken breasts

I love these chicken breasts. The cornflake crumbs add a pleasing crunch and impart a subtle corn flavor that complements the delicately flavored chicken.

SERVES 6

- 1 cup chopped fresh mixed herbs, such as parlsey, thyme, and rosemary
- 2 tablespoons minced shallots
- 2 tablespoons lemon zest
- 4 tablespoons Dijon mustard
- 3 tablespoons extra-virgin olive oil
  Kosher salt and freshly ground pepper
- 3 cups cornflakes, crushed into coarse crumbs (see Note)
- 6 skinless, boneless chicken breasts

METHOD

Preheat the oven to 350°F. Line a baking sheet with parchment paper.

Combine the herbs, shallots, lemon zest, mustard, and olive oil in a small bowl and add salt and pepper to taste. Put the cornflake crumbs on a large plate.

Brush the chicken breasts with the mustard mixture and roll them in the bread crumbs until well coated. Drizzle with olive oil or, even easier, spray with a bit of vegetable cooking spray.

Arrange on the baking sheet and bake, turning once after 15 minutes, until golden brown and the juices run clear when pierced with a fork, 30 minutes.

Note: To make cornflake crumbs, put them in a sealable plastic bag and crush with a rolling pin.

turkey burgers with goat cheese

Fire up the grill, give your guests a glass of Champagne (it's a nice juxtaposition to the casual nature of a barbecue), and enjoy life!

SERVES 6

- 6 ounces mild goat cheese, such as chèvre
- 2 pounds ground turkey (preferably a combination of light and dark meats)
- 2 tablespoons chopped fresh parsley
- 2 teaspoons chopped fresh rosemary
  Kosher salt and freshly ground pepper
- 6 hamburger buns
  Roasted red peppers
  Thinly sliced red onion
  Dijon mustard

METHOD

Prepare a fire in the grill.

Cut the cheese into 6 pieces and shape each into a 2-inch disk. Reserve.

In a medium bowl, quickly combine the turkey, herbs, and salt and pepper to taste. Do not overmix. Divide the turkey into twelve 4-inch patties. Place a cheese round on 6 of the patties and top with the remaining patties, pressing the edges together to seal.

Grill the burgers on one side for 5 minutes without turning. Turn and cook 4 minutes more, or until cooked through, as poultry should never be served rare.

While the burgers cook, split the buns and toast them on the outer edges of the grill.

Serve the burgers on toasted buns topped with the roasted red peppers, onion, and mustard.

I give presentation punch to the one-dish Ratatouille Chicken Breasts by serving the ratatouille in a pedestal bowl on the same plate as the chicken.

ratatouille chicken breasts

The famous Provençal vegetable dish makes a flavorful bed for baked chicken breasts—an easy main course and side dish in one.

SERVES 6

4	tablespoons extra-virgin olive oil
1	large red onion, thinly sliced
3	garlic cloves, thinly sliced
1	red bell pepper, seeded and thinly sliced
2	medium zucchini, cut into $\frac{1}{4}$-inch slices
3	large plum (Roma) tomatoes, cut into $\frac{1}{4}$-inch slices
2	Japanese eggplants or 1 small globe eggplant, coarsely chopped
$\frac{1}{4}$	cup chicken broth
1	tablespoon fresh thyme leaves
2	tablespoons chopped fresh basil
	Kosher salt and freshly ground pepper
6	skinless, boneless chicken breasts
3	tablespoons capers, rinsed and drained

METHOD

Preheat the oven to 350°F.

Lightly brush a baking dish that is large enough to hold the chicken breasts in one layer with 1 tablespoon of the olive oil.

Heat the remaining 3 tablespoons of olive oil in a large skillet over medium heat. Add the onion and garlic and sauté until soft. Add the pepper, zucchini, tomatoes, eggplants, and chicken broth. Cover and simmer over low heat, stirring occasionally, until the vegetables begin to soften, about 10 minutes. Stir in the thyme and basil. Season with salt and pepper.

Transfer the vegetables to the baking dish. Place the chicken breasts on the vegetables, season with salt and pepper, and spoon a bit of the vegetables on top of the chicken breasts. Bake until the chicken is golden brown and the juices run clear when pierced with a fork, 30 minutes.

To serve, spoon some of the vegetables onto each plate, top with a chicken breast, and add a sprinkling of capers.

rib-eye steaks with chive butter

Rib-eye steaks are particularly flavorful so they need very little embellishment. Don't sweat the fat content; the protein will make you strong and the great taste will make you happy. Don't crowd the steaks in the pan or they will steam rather than brown. I like to use 2 large skillets so I can cook all the steaks at once.

SERVES 6

- 1 tablespoon dry mustard
- 1 tablespoon dry white wine
- 8 tablespoons (1 stick) unsalted butter, at room temperature
- ¼ cup snipped fresh chives
  Kosher salt and freshly ground pepper
- 6 boneless rib eye steaks, ½ pound each and 1 inch thick
- ¼ cup extra-virgin olive oil

METHOD

In a small bowl, stir together the mustard and wine. Add the butter and chives and mix well. Season with salt and pepper. Transfer the mixture to a piece of plastic wrap and form it into a log shape about 1 inch in diameter. Wrap tightly and refrigerate until ready to serve.

Heat 2 large skillets over medium heat until very hot. Season the steaks with salt and pepper. Add 2 tablespoons olive oil to each pan. When hot, fry the steaks, 3 in each skillet, without turning for 5 minutes. Turn the steaks and cook another 3 minutes for rare or 4 minutes for medium-rare or to your liking. If you're using only one skillet, transfer the cooked steaks to a warm platter, cover, and keep warm while you fry the second batch.

To serve, slice the butter into ½-inch rounds and top the steak with it.

beef stroganoff with chanterelle mushrooms

When beef tenderloin took the place of ground beef in my mother's stroganoff, it became company food. Here, I've taken the tactic one step further by adding chanterelle mushrooms. They imbue this stroganoff with a sweet richness that plays off the tart sour cream. It's comfort food with a grown-up attitude.

SERVES 6

- 6 tablespoons (¾ stick) unsalted butter
- 1 shallot, finely chopped
- 2 pounds beef tenderloin, cut into 1-inch strips
- ¾ pound chanterelle mushrooms, well cleaned and sliced
- ¼ cup dry red wine
  Kosher salt and freshly ground pepper
- 1 cup sour cream (don't use low-fat), at room temperature
- ¾ pound egg noodles, cooked
- ¼ cup chopped fresh parsley

METHOD

Melt the butter in a large sauté pan over medium heat. Add the shallot and cook until soft, about 3 minutes. Add the mushrooms and cook for 5 minutes. With a slotted spoon, transfer the mushrooms to a plate; reserve.

Increase the heat to high, add the beef strips in a single layer, and sear, turning once, until brown, about 1 minute per side. Transfer the beef to a plate and keep warm. Add the wine to the skillet and cook, scraping the bottom of the pan to release the meat and mushroom bits, until the wine reduces by half, a minute or so. Season with salt and pepper and reduce the heat to low. Whisk in the sour cream and heat through but do not allow it to boil. Return the beef and mushrooms to the pan and cook for about a minute more. Serve over the egg noodles, sprinkled with parsley.

PRIMER

Isn't It Wild?

Wild mushrooms are truly one of nature's finest gifts. They add luxe to the simplest meals and impart elegance to anything they touch. And while they're expensive, since they're so rich and flavorful, just a few go a long way.

Chanterelles, morels, oysters, porcini, portobellos, and shiitakes are now widely available. Look for mushrooms that are tight, firm, and definitely *not* slimy to the touch. When you buy them, put them in a paper bag and store them in the crisper section of your refrigerator with the bag open so the mushrooms can breathe. Most are extremely perishable, so use them within 2 to 3 days.

When you're ready to use wild mushrooms, don't wash them. Mushrooms are quite porous and will absorb moisture, which will dilute their flavor. Instead, trim the stems and use a mushroom brush or a soft tea towel to brush any dirt away.

If you can't get fresh wild mushrooms, consider dried mushrooms as an acceptable alternative. Look for whole dried mushrooms rather than pieces. Soak in hot water or broth to cover for 20 to 30 minutes to reconstitute them. Use them as you would fresh wild mushrooms. Don't discard the steeping broth—strained, it's a delicious addition to soups, risottos, and sauces.

sunday night pot roast

It's wholesome. It's authentic. Paired with a good friend and a tall story, Sunday night pot roast makes the weekend.

SERVES 6

 1 (3-pound) boneless beef chuck or rump roast, with
    fat on one side
    Kosher salt and freshly ground pepper
 3 tablespoons extra-virgin olive oil
 1 tablespoon flour
 1 cup dry red wine
 ¼ cup balsamic vinegar
 ¼ cup water
 1 medium carrot, chopped
 1 medium onion, chopped
 3 garlic cloves, chopped
 1 bouquet garni: 1 large bay leaf, 2 thyme sprigs, 2
    parsley sprigs tied together with kitchen string
 4 small turnips, peeled and quartered
 4 medium red potatoes, peeled and quartered
 12 pearl onions, peeled
 2 large carrots, peeled and cut into 2-inch pieces

METHOD

Season the roast with salt and pepper. In a large ovenproof casserole or heavy pot, heat the oil over medium-high heat. Add the beef, fat side down, and brown well on all sides. Remove the roast to a platter and stir the flour into the pot. Cook, stirring, for 2 minutes, then add the wine, vinegar, and water and cook for 5 minutes longer. Add the chopped carrot, chopped onion, and garlic; return the roast to the pot, add the bouquet garni, and bring to a boil. Cover the pot tightly, reduce the heat, and simmer for 2 hours. Add the turnips, potatoes, onions, and carrot chunks, cover, and continue to simmer until the vegetables are tender, 40 to 45 minutes. You may need to add about ½ cup of water along with the vegetables so they are just covered with liquid.

Transfer the pot roast to a cutting board and let it rest 10 to 15 minutes before carving. Slice the pot roast across the grain and serve with the vegetables and a gravy boat of the pan juices.

saturday night spareribs

Cover the table with newspaper, add 'Slaw (page 49) and pitchers of beer, and you're all set for a down-home meal! Because of the messy (but fun!) nature of this dish, you might consider offering tea towels moistened with lemon-infused water to your guests at the end of this meal.

SERVES 6

 6 pounds pork spareribs, in whole racks
 2 cups flat dark beer
 ¼ cup soy sauce
 2 teaspoons dry mustard
 2 tablespoons brown sugar
 2 garlic cloves, minced
 ½ teaspoon kosher salt
    Dash of hot pepper sauce

METHOD

Bring a large pot of water to a boil. Add the spareribs and parboil for 3 minutes. Drain and pat dry with paper towels.

Combine the remaining ingredients in a measuring cup or pitcher. Place the spareribs in a shallow baking pan and pour the beer mixture over them. Cover with aluminum foil and marinate at room temperature for at least 1 hour, turning occasionally.

Preheat the oven to 350° F. Cover the pan tightly with aluminum foil and bake for 45 minutes. Uncover and bake until tender, about 40 minutes more.

A spareribs dinner presents the perfect opportunity for a micro-brew beer tasting. Offer a sampling of light and dark beers from across the USA.

black and white sesame pork chops

Sesame seeds are simple ingredients, yet the combination of black and white seeds in this dish gives it an air of sophistication. They also help keep the pork moist. I like to serve this with roasted Yukon gold mashed potatoes, a nice foil for the subtle spiciness of the pork. A salad of Red Lettuces with Citrus Vinaigrette (page 49) served right on the same plate would finish the course nicely.

SERVES 6

- $\frac{1}{4}$ cup black sesame seeds (available at Asian groceries and in gourmet food markets)
- $\frac{1}{4}$ cup white sesame seeds
- 3 tablespoons flour
- 2 tablespoons toasted sesame oil
- 1 tablespoon fresh lemon juice
- $\frac{1}{2}$ cup soy sauce
- 2 tablespoons dry mustard
- 3 garlic cloves, minced
  Dash of hot pepper sauce
- 3 tablespoons peanut oil
- 6 center cut pork loin chops, each about 6 ounces and 1 inch thick

METHOD

Preheat the oven to 375°F.

In a small bowl, combine all ingredients except the peanut oil and pork chops to form a paste. Brush the chops on both sides with the sesame paste.

Heat the oil in a large ovenproof sauté pan or skillet over medium-high heat. When hot, add the pork chops and sauté, turning once with a spatula, until lightly browned on each side, about 3 minutes per side. Transfer the skillet to the oven and bake until the chops are barely pink in the center, about 10 minutes.

roast loin of pork with cider glaze

This recipe pairs pork with all of its favorite partners: apple cider, citrus, and pungent spices. This would make a wonderful autumn dinner, accompanied by Classic Potato Gratin (page 73).

SERVES 6

- 1$\frac{1}{3}$ cups apple cider
- 1 bay leaf
- 1 boneless pork loin, about 3 pounds, trimmed of excess fat

Marinade

- 4 large garlic cloves, finely chopped
- 1 teaspoon grated orange zest
- 2 teaspoons powdered ginger
- 2 teaspoons crumbled dried rosemary
- $\frac{1}{2}$ teaspoon kosher salt
- 2 tablespoons fresh lemon juice
- 4 tablespoons canola oil

- 1 cup dry white wine

METHOD

In a small saucepan, boil the cider with the bay leaf over medium-high heat until it has reduced by half. You should have $\frac{2}{3}$ cup cider remaining. Discard the bay leaf.

Place the pork on a rack in a small roasting pan. In a small bowl, combine the marinade ingredients. Rub the mixture over the pork, cover with plastic wrap, and marinate for 30 minutes at room temperature.

Preheat the oven to 500°F. Pour the white wine into the roasting pan, place the pork in the oven, and roast for 15 minutes. Remove the pork from the oven and brush it generously with the cider. Return the pork to the oven and reduce the heat to 350°F. Roast the pork, basting frequently with the cider mixture, until an instant-read thermometer inserted into the center of the roast registers 145°F. to 150°F., about 30 minutes longer. The meat should be pale pink in the center.

Remove the pork from the oven and transfer it to a cutting board. Cover loosely with aluminum foil and let it rest 10 minutes before carving.

To serve, slice the pork into $\frac{1}{2}$-inch-thick slices and drizzle with the pan juices.

oven-braised lamb shanks with flageolet beans

This is comfort food at its finest. Serve it with crusty
French bread, a wedge of Cantal cheese (or Cheddar if
you can't find the Cantal), and a hearty red wine. This
dish ought to be started a day or two ahead of time.
Often, I will soak the beans 3 or 4 days ahead of time,
toss them in olive oil to keep them moist, and store
them in the refrigerator until I am ready to finish the
recipe later in the week.

SERVES 6

  2   cups dried flageolet beans
  ¼   cup extra-virgin olive oil
  6   large, meaty lamb shanks (5 to 6 pounds total)
       Kosher salt and freshly ground pepper
  1   medium onion, chopped
  2   medium carrots, peeled and chopped
  3   garlic cloves, finely chopped
  1½   cups chopped tomatoes
  2   teaspoons herbes de Provence
  1   bay leaf
  1   cup dry sherry
  4   cups chicken broth

METHOD

One day in advance, put the beans in a pot with water
to cover by 2 inches and soak overnight. The next day,
drain the beans well and set aside.

In a deep, heavy ovenproof casserole, heat the oil over
medium heat. Season the shanks with salt and pepper.
Add the shanks to the casserole and sear until brown on
all sides. Transfer to a platter.

Reduce the heat to medium. Add the onion, carrots,
and garlic to the casserole and cook, stirring, until the
onion softens, about 3 minutes. Add the soaked and
drained beans, tomatoes, herbes de Provence, and bay
leaf to the pot along with the sherry and chicken broth.
Bring to a boil, then reduce the heat to low and simmer
for 1 hour.

Preheat the oven to 350°F. Add the lamb shanks to
the casserole, spooning some of the beans and liquid
over the shanks. Cover, bring to a boil, then transfer to
the oven. Cook until the meat and the beans are tender,
about 1½ hours.

Edible accompaniments to the
main course can double as decorative elements. The pyramid of
Cantal cheese set on a pewter
plate and the deep red of the
wine in a handblown glass
carafe imbue this humble dish
and simple setting with country
elegance.

PRIMER

Dried Beans

- Sort through dried beans before
cooking and discard any pebbles.
Cover with water and discard any
beans that rise to the surface.
Drain, then cover with fresh water
if soaking.

- To reduce overall cooking time,
dried beans should be soaked
before cooking. Soak them
overnight or, if you're time-
pressed, quick-soak them by boiling for 1 minute, covering the pot,
and letting the beans stand for
1 hour. Drain the beans and continue with the recipe.

- When cooking beans, rely on this
ratio: 3 parts liquid to 1 part
beans.

- Cooking times depend upon the
size of the bean. Always cook
beans at a simmer so they don't
burst forth from their jackets.

- Never salt beans until the end of
cooking or they will toughen.

lamb, swiss chard, and sweet potato curry

Lamb takes exceptionally well to the rich pungency of curry and in this dish it simmers to tender perfection. Use the best curry powder you can find, preferably a Madras blend; it does make a difference.

SERVES 6

- ½ cup all-purpose flour
- 3 pounds boneless lamb shoulder, cut into 1-inch cubes
  Kosher salt and freshly ground pepper
- ¼ cup peanut oil
- 2 large onions, finely chopped
- 4 garlic cloves, minced
- 1 tablespoon grated fresh ginger
- 3 to 4 tablespoons curry powder, preferably Madras
- ½ teaspoon ground coriander
- ¼ teaspoon crushed red pepper flakes, or more to taste
- 4 large ripe, firm tomatoes, peeled, seeded, and chopped
- 2 cups chicken broth
- 3 cups water
- 2 sweet potatoes, peeled and cut into 1-inch cubes
- 1¼ pounds Swiss chard, including stems, coarsely chopped
- 6 to 8 cups cooked basmati rice

METHOD

Place the flour on a large plate. Season the lamb with salt and pepper and dredge in the flour. Heat the oil in a large casserole or Dutch oven. Working in batches, add the lamb to the casserole in a single layer and sear over medium-high heat until brown on all sides. Transfer each batch of lamb to a plate as it is cooked.

Return the lamb to the pot. Add the onions and garlic and cook over medium heat until the onions are translucent, 3 to 4 minutes. Add the ginger, curry powder, coriander, and red pepper and cook, stirring, for 2 minutes. Stir in the tomatoes, then the chicken broth and water, scraping the bottom of the pan to dislodge any caramelized bits. Reduce the heat to low, cover, and simmer for 1 hour.

Add the sweet potatoes to the pot. Cook until the potatoes are just tender and the sauce has thickened a bit, about 20 minutes. Add the Swiss chard and cook for 5 minutes more. Season with salt and pepper. Serve with basmati rice

loin lamb chops with lemon-thyme butter

Lamb chops are quick and easy to prepare, as is the lemon-thyme butter that transforms the chops into a special dinner. You can make the butter a few days ahead of time and refrigerate it until you're ready to prepare the chops. Make extra lemon-thyme butter and freeze it and you will be able to put this dish together even more quickly the next time. If you can find lemon thyme, use it and decrease the lemon zest to 1 teaspoon.

SERVES 6

- 6 tablespoons (¾ stick) unsalted butter, at room temperature
- 3 tablespoons chopped fresh thyme
- ½ tablespoon grated lemon zest
- 4 teaspoons chopped shallots
  Kosher salt and freshly ground pepper

- 12 loin lamb chops, 1 inch thick
- 2 tablespoons extra-virgin olive oil

METHOD

In a small bowl, combine the butter, thyme, lemon zest, and shallots and blend well. Season with salt and pepper to taste. Spoon the butter onto a sheet of plastic wrap and roll into a log about 1 inch in diameter. Wrap it tightly and refrigerate until ready to use.

Preheat a broiler or prepare a fire in the grill. Brush the chops with olive oil and season with salt and pepper to taste. Broil or grill the chops without turning for 5 minutes. Turn the chops and broil another 5 minutes for medium-rare, or to your taste.

To serve, cut the butter into ¼-inch slices. Place 2 lamb chops on each plate and top each with a lemon-thyme butter slice.

METHOD

Preheat the oven to 375°F. Butter a 1½-quart baking dish; set aside.

Melt 3 tablespoons of the butter in a medium saucepan over moderate heat. Stir in the flour and cook, stirring, until the flour bubbles and cooks a bit, about 2 minutes; do not brown the flour. Gradually add the milk and cook, stirring, until the sauce thickens. Stir in the Gorgonzola and the Tabasco. Season to taste with salt and pepper.

Combine the macaroni with the sauce, stirring gently to combine. Pour into the baking dish. Mix together the bread crumbs and the Parmesan; sprinkle over the macaroni. Dot with the remaining butter. Bake until the sauce is bubbling and the top is golden, 20 to 30 minutes.

PRIMER

baked macaroni and gorgonzola

Served as a main course, this is definitely an indulgence, but what the heck! Served in more restrained proportions, it's an ideal accompaniment to grilled steak or roasted tenderloin. So the macaroni retains its texture and does not turn to mush, boil it just until it's al dente, as it will continue to cook in the oven.

SERVES 3 AS AN ENTRÉE, 6 AS A SIDE DISH

- 5 tablespoons unsalted butter
- 3 tablespoons all-purpose flour
- 2 cups whole milk, heated
- ⅓ pound Gorgonzola cheese, crumbled
  Dash of Tabasco sauce
  Kosher salt and freshly ground pepper
- ½ pound elbow macaroni, cooked al dente
- ½ cup unseasoned bread crumbs
- 2 tablespoons freshly grated Parmesan cheese

Dinner in Front of the TV

Though it may seem an abomination to suggest such a thing, there are a few occasions that may warrant communion with the black beast: the final round of the U.S. Open, the Academy Awards, a Barbara Walters special, monitoring the progress of a really big tropical depression on the weather channel. If you do indulge, do it in style:

- Set up small folding tables or cover a large coffee table with a cloth. Set each place with flatware, glasses, napkins, and individual salt and pepper shakers.

- Plate each serving of food in the kitchen. Stock a tiered trolley cart with dinnerware and the prepared dinner plates, plus wine and water (top tier), and a bread basket, condiments, dessert, and dessert plates (bottom tier). Roll the trolley out to the den or living room and serve.

- When the main course is finished, move bottom tier items up to the top tier and stow away dirty dishes on the bottom tier. When dessert is finished, put dirty dishes on the bottom tier, wheel the trolley away to the kitchen, and return with the coffee.

- Serve casual food that does not require much effort on the part of your guests, as they won't have much room to maneuver (and they're sitting on your nice furniture). A Caesar salad and pasta or sliced roast chicken and mashed potatoes would be nice.

- A dinner in front of the TV is a great opportunity for serving take-away food.

pasta with broccoli rabe and spicy sausage

Broccoli rabe is the pungent, often bitter green that comes tied in bundles. The headiness of garlic and the spiciness of the sausage give broccoli rabe a run for its money. All told, the many vibrant flavors in this dish will have a resonant and pleasing effect on the palate.

SERVES 6

Kosher salt
1½ pounds tube-shaped pasta, such as rigatoni
1½ pounds broccoli rabe
⅓ cup extra-virgin olive oil
1½ pounds spicy Italian sausage, cut into 1-inch pieces
6 garlic cloves, finely chopped
1 cup water
Freshly ground pepper
Freshly grated Parmesan cheese

METHOD

Bring a large pot of water to a boil. Add 2 large pinches of salt and when the water has returned to a boil, add the rigatoni and cook until al dente. Drain.

While the pasta is cooking, cut the broccoli rabe stems into ½-inch pieces and coarsely chop the leaves and florets.

Warm 2 tablespoons of the olive oil in a large skillet over medium heat and sauté the sausage pieces until well browned on all sides. Transfer to a plate lined with paper towels.

Pour off all but 2 tablespoons of the fat from the skillet. Add the garlic and cook over medium-low heat until golden. Add the broccoli rabe and sauté until wilted, about 1 minute. Add the water, heat to a simmer, and cook for 5 minutes. Drain.

In a large bowl, toss the pasta with the remaining olive oil. Add the broccoli rabe, sausage, and salt and pepper to taste. Serve with Parmesan cheese.

I like to grate the Parmesan over the large holes of the grater so its flavor is "bigger" and it can hold its own with the bitter Broccoli Rabe and Spicy Sausage.

pasta with zucchini, basil, and ricotta

I like the fresh taste and color of this pasta dish as well as the texture of the sauce, which is creamy but not cloying. The effect is one of richness and indulgence, yet your guests won't swear at you when they look in the mirror the next morning.

SERVES 6

Kosher salt
1½ pounds ziti or rotelle
6 tablespoons extra-virgin olive oil
3 small zucchini, quartered lengthwise and cut into thin slices
Freshly ground pepper
¾ cup ricotta cheese
2 large plum tomatoes, seeded and chopped
¾ cup chopped fresh basil leaves
Freshly grated Parmesan cheese

METHOD

Bring a large pot of water to a boil. Add 2 large pinches of salt and when the water has returned to a boil, add the ziti and cook until al dente. Drain, reserving about ¾ cup of the cooking water.

While the pasta is cooking, heat the olive oil in a large sauté pan over medium heat. Add the zucchini and sauté until just beginning to brown. Season with salt and pepper. Add the ziti and cook, stirring, for 3 minutes.

Remove from the heat and stir in the ricotta and as much cooking water as needed to create a sauce. Stir in the tomatoes, basil, and salt and pepper to taste. Serve with Parmesan.

style note

HAVE A SEAT

To enhance the comfort of your guests, place small pillows at the backs of unupholstered chairs. If you have the time and inclination, you can stencil the guest's name on the pillow with fabric paint or, if you're really handy, you can embroider it.

Mismatched chairs give the dining table a certain whimsy. If you want a more unified look, place slipcovers over the chairs or simply pull fabric "slippers" over the chair backs.

The back of the chair is the first thing guests see when they enter the dining room. Hang little herb bouquets or tassels on chair backs or make place cards and adhere them to the backs of the chairs.

For a lucky number party, I hung blue and white enamel house numbers on the chair backs. Guests took them home as party favors.

pappardelle with mussels and sage

This is a rich pasta dish that, served as a first course, would complement a simple roast chicken or beef tenderloin. If served as a main course, consider accompanying it with a green salad with a citrus vinaigrette or Tomato, Red Onion, and Skinny Lemon Salad (page 34), which would balance the pasta's richness.

SERVES 6

1½	cups dry white wine
3	pounds mussels in the shell, scrubbed and debearded
3	tablespoons unsalted butter
1	tablespoon extra-virgin olive oil
18	fresh sage leaves
1	shallot, finely chopped
2	tablespoons minced fresh sage
2	cups heavy cream
2	teaspoons grated lemon zest
	Kosher salt
1¼	pounds pappardelle or other wide pasta noodles
	White pepper

METHOD

In a large saucepan or skillet, bring the white wine to a boil over medium-high heat. Add the mussels, decrease the heat to low, cover, and steam the mussels until they open, 3 to 5 minutes. Remove to a bowl with a slotted spoon, discarding any mussels that did not open. Strain the steaming liquid through a fine-mesh sieve; reserve. When the mussels are cool enough to handle, remove them from their shells and discard the shells.

In a small saucepan over medium-low heat, melt the butter with the olive oil. When the foam subsides, add the whole sage leaves, decrease the heat to low, and cook until the leaves are crisp, 3 to 5 minutes. Remove with a slotted spoon and drain on paper towels. Increase the heat to medium, add the shallot and minced sage, and sauté until translucent, 4 to 5 minutes. Add the cream and lemon zest and simmer until reduced by half, 12 to 15 minutes.

Meanwhile, bring a large pot of water to a boil. Add 2 generous pinches of salt and when it returns to a boil, add the pasta and cook until al dente, 10 to 12 minutes.

Stir a few tablespoons of the reserved steaming liquid into the cream sauce. Stir in the mussels and cook over low heat just until heated through.

Drain the pasta and transfer to a large warm bowl. Pour on the sauce and toss well. Season to taste with salt and white pepper. Serve in individual bowls, garnished with the whole sage leaves.

spaghetti with fresh tomatoes, basil, and smoked mozzarella

This dish depends on the flavor and juice of ripe tomatoes so it's best made when tomatoes are in season. I think that the skins and seeds of the tomatoes deepen the flavor of this dish but if they bug you, go ahead and remove them before chopping the tomatoes.

SERVES 6

6	large, ripe tomatoes, coarsely chopped
2	cups chopped fresh basil
	Kosher salt
1½	pounds spaghetti
⅓	cup extra-virgin olive oil
¾	pound smoked mozzarella, cut into 1-inch cubes
	Freshly ground pepper

METHOD

Bring a large pot of water to a boil over high heat.

Meanwhile, in a large bowl (this can be the bowl you will use to serve the pasta), toss the tomatoes with 1½ cups of the basil. Set aside.

Add 2 large pinches of salt to the boiling water. When it returns to a boil, add the spaghetti and cook, stirring occasionally, until al dente. Drain.

Add the hot pasta to the tomatoes, drizzle with the olive oil, and toss. Add the mozzarella and toss again. Season with salt and pepper, sprinkle with the remaining basil, and serve.

risotto with black olives, lemon, and vodka

Lemon vodka has a spirited kick that balances the saltiness of the olives and deepens the risotto's overall flavor.

SERVES 6

- 6 to 7 cups chicken stock or low-sodium canned broth
- 2 tablespoons extra-virgin olive oil
- 2 tablespoons (¼ stick) unsalted butter
- 1 large onion, chopped
- 1 large shallot, peeled and finely chopped
- 2 cups Arborio rice
- ¾ cup lemon vodka (such as Absolut Citron)
- 1 cup pitted slivered black olives, such as kalamata
  Grated zest of 1½ lemons
- ¼ cup freshly grated Parmesan cheese
  Kosher salt and freshly ground pepper
- 3 tablespoons finely chopped chives, for garnish

METHOD

Bring the stock to a boil in a medium saucepan; cover and keep at a simmer.

Heat the olive oil and butter in a large saucepan over medium heat. Add the onion and shallot and cook until soft, about 3 minutes. Add the rice and cook, stirring to coat it with the oil, for 3 minutes. Add the vodka and stir until absorbed, about 1 minute.

Slowly add 1 cup of the hot stock. Stir and let simmer, reducing the heat if necessary, until the rice absorbs the stock. Continue in this way, adding stock ½ cup at a time and stirring frequently, until the rice is creamy and al dente, about 20 to 25 minutes. Add the olives and cook to heat through, about 1 minute. Stir in the lemon zest and Parmesan cheese. Season to taste with salt and pepper, sprinkle with chives, and serve immediately.

For this minimal but warm table motif, I composed an "orbit" for each setting by anchoring an olive branch in a small aperitif glass with olives. If you can't find olive branches, any decorative stem would work fine.

risotto milanese with shrimp

Risotto Milanese is a traditional Italian rice dish that glows with the pungent flavor and deep yellow hue of saffron. In this rendition, the sweet flavor of shrimp plays off saffron's slight bitterness and their pink color contrasts smartly with the bright yellow rice.

SERVES 6

- 2½ to 3 cups chicken stock or low-sodium canned broth
- 2½ to 3 cups bottled clam juice
- ¼ teaspoon crushed saffron threads
- ¼ cup extra-virgin olive oil
- 1 large onion, chopped
- 2 garlic cloves, finely chopped
- 2 cups Arborio rice
- ½ cup dry white wine
- 1½ pounds large shrimp, peeled and deveined
  Kosher salt and freshly ground pepper
- 2 tablespoons chopped fresh parsley

METHOD

Combine the chicken stock and clam juice in a medium saucepan. Bring to a boil, cover, and keep warm. Ladle ¼ cup of the broth into a small bowl and dissolve the saffron in it, pressing it against the sides of the bowl with the back of a spoon; reserve.

In a flameproof casserole or Dutch oven, heat the olive oil over medium heat. Add the onion and garlic and sauté until the onion is soft, about 2 minutes. Add the rice and cook, stirring to coat it with the oil, for another 5 minutes. Add the wine and cook, stirring, for 1 minute.

Increase the heat to medium-high. Slowly add 1 cup of the warm broth to the rice. Cook, stirring, until the rice has absorbed almost all the broth. Add ½ cup more broth and continue in this way, stirring frequently, until half the broth has been added. At this point, stir in the saffron mixture and continue cooking, adding the broth ½ cup at a time, until all but ¼ cup has been added, 18 to 22 minutes total cooking time.

Stir in the shrimp and another ¼ cup broth and cook until the shrimp are pink, about 3 minutes, adding the remaining broth if needed. The risotto should be creamy and the rice should be cooked but firm to the bite. Season to taste with salt and pepper. Serve immediately, sprinkled with chopped parsley.

baked zucchini with parmesan

Baking is a rather untraditional way to prepare zucchini but it ensures that the squash retains its crunchiness and endows it with a golden crust.

SERVES 6

3 medium zucchini, sliced crosswise ¼ inch thick
3 tablespoons chicken broth or water
3 tablespoons extra-virgin olive oil
  Kosher salt and freshly ground pepper
5 tablespoons freshly grated Parmesan cheese

METHOD

Preheat the oven to 375°F.

Place the zucchini in a 9×13-inch baking dish. Add the chicken broth or water. Drizzle the olive oil over the zucchini and season with salt and pepper. Sprinkle the top evenly with the cheese. Bake until the zucchini is tender and the tops are golden, about 30 minutes.

roasted asparagus

Roasting asparagus brings out its earthy flavor. Choose medium asparagus spears rather than the thin, tender shoots; they will hold up better in the oven's heat.

SERVES 6

  Kosher salt
2 pounds medium asparagus, trimmed
2 tablespoons extra-virgin olive oil
2 tablespoons balsamic vinegar
  Freshly ground pepper

METHOD

Preheat the broiler.

Fill a large sauté pan with water and bring to a boil. Add a generous pinch of salt and the asparagus. Cook 2 minutes. Remove from the pan with tongs and drain on paper towels.

Transfer the asparagus to a baking sheet. Drizzle with the olive oil and turn the spears to coat with the oil. Place under the broiler and roast 3 to 5 minutes, depending upon the size of the asparagus, turning the asparagus frequently.

Remove from the oven, transfer to a platter, and drizzle with balsamic vinegar. Season with salt and pepper to taste.

grilled corn with chive-chili butter

Many cookbooks recommend soaking corn in the husks before grilling but I find this step unnecessary and the flavor result is smokier and "roastier" without it. Be sure to turn the corn frequently as it cooks, however.

SERVES 6

6 tablespoons (¾ stick) unsalted butter, melted
2 tablespoons snipped chives
1 tablespoon chili powder, or more to taste
  Kosher salt and freshly ground pepper
6 ears of corn, in their husks
3 limes, cut into wedges

METHOD

Prepare a fire in a grill.

In a small bowl, mix together the butter, chives, chili powder, and salt and pepper to taste.

Trim the stems of each ear of corn and peel back the husks, but do not remove them entirely. Remove the corn silk.

Brush each ear of corn with chive-chili butter and pull the husks back up over the corn. Tie the husks at the top with kitchen string.

Grill the corn, turning frequently, for 10 to 20 minutes, depending upon the size of the ears. To serve, pull back the corn husks and tie them with a piece of husk or kitchen string. Serve with more melted butter and the lime wedges.

Serving grilled corn in a wire clam basket gives it the down-home feel it deserves.

scented rice

Rice is like an artist's canvas in the way it absorbs flavors and colors. Here, I've combined aromatic spices with jasmine rice, a fragrant rice from Thailand.

SERVES 6

- 2 tablespoons (¼ stick) unsalted butter
- 1 tablespoon safflower oil
- 1 2-inch piece cinnamon stick
- ¼ teaspoon whole cardamom seeds
- 1½ tablespoons minced fresh ginger
- 3 cups jasmine rice
- 6 cups warm chicken broth
  Kosher salt and freshly ground pepper
- ¾ cup golden raisins (optional)

METHOD

In a large saucepan, melt the butter with the oil over medium-high heat. When hot, add the cinnamon and cardamom and cook, stirring, for 1 minute. Add the ginger and cook 1 minute more. Add the rice and cook, stirring, for 2 to 3 minutes, coating the grains with the spice mixture. Add the chicken broth and bring to a boil, then reduce the heat to low, cover, and cook until all the liquid is absorbed, 15 to 20 minutes. Do not remove the cover until close to the end of the cooking time. Remove from the heat and let stand, covered, for 10 minutes. Season to taste with salt and pepper. Fluff with a fork and serve garnished with raisins, if desired.

roasted yukon gold mashed potatoes

Yukon Gold potatoes are so sweet and rich that, if you're counting calories, you can forgo the butter and barely notice. If you're really calorie adverse, substitute chicken broth for the olive oil and half-and-half. I leave the skins on for the flavor as well as for the presentation—it's so honest.

SERVES 6

- 3 pounds Yukon Gold potatoes, halved
- 3 tablespoons extra-virgin olive oil
- ¾ cup half-and-half
- 6 tablespoons (¾ stick) unsalted butter
  Kosher salt and freshly ground pepper

METHOD

Preheat the oven to 400° F.

Toss the potatoes in the olive oil, coating them well. Put in a roasting pan cut side down and roast, shaking the pan occasionally, until tender and golden brown, about 40 minutes.

Combine the half-and-half and butter in a small saucepan over medium heat. Cook until the half-and-half begins to bubble around the edges and the butter melts. Remove from the heat; keep warm.

Transfer the roasted potatoes to a large bowl. Using a potato masher or fork, mash the potatoes, adding the half-and-half as you do so, until the potatoes reach the desired consistency. Season to taste with salt and pepper.

PRIMER

Potatoes Plus

Sometimes even the perfect potato needs a lift. For a spin on plain mashed potatoes, try one of the following:

- Mash with cooked celery root or parsnips, corn and scallions, pureed chipotle chile peppers, or caramelized shallots.

- Sprinkle in Parmesan cheese.

- Drizzle in a flavored oil.

- Fold in sour cream or crème fraîche.

- Use chicken broth instead of cream.

- Add chopped smoked ham or smoked salmon.

- For a bit of presentation flair, pipe mashed potatoes into a shallow baking dish, brush with melted butter, and place under a broiler to brown the peaks.

classic potato gratin

A few dishes earn the designation "classic" because they are so appealing and appropriate for any occasion. This is one of them. Cooking the potatoes with the half-and-half and seasonings infuses them with flavor and ensures that they are well cooked. The result is a gratin that is crispy and golden on the outside and sumptuously creamy on the inside. If that doesn't say "classic," I don't know what does.

SERVES 6

- ½ tablespoon olive oil
- 2 cups half-and-half
- 1 garlic clove, peeled and smashed
- 1 bay leaf
- 1½ teaspoon salt
- ½ teaspoon freshly ground black pepper
- 2 pounds russet potatoes, peeled and sliced ⅛-inch thick
- 1 tablespoon unsalted butter, cut in small pieces

METHOD

Preheat the oven to 375° F. Lightly brush a shallow 1½-quart baking dish with the olive oil.

Combine the half-and-half, garlic, bay leaf, salt, pepper, and potatoes in a large, heavy sauté pan or saucepan over medium-high heat (the half-and-half should barely cover the potatoes). Bring to a boil, stirring occasionally, then reduce the heat to low and simmer until the liquid thickens a bit, about 8 to 10 minutes, stirring frequently.

Bake, uncovered, until the top is golden brown, about 45 minutes, or until the potatoes are very tender.

baked cheese grits

This is rich, rich, rich—and worth it!

SERVES 6

- 4 cups whole milk
- ½ cup (1 stick) unsalted butter, cut into 4 pieces
- 1 cup quick-cooking or regular grits
- 1½ cups shredded sharp Cheddar cheese
  Kosher salt and freshly ground pepper

METHOD

Preheat the oven to 350° F. Butter a 1½-quart baking dish.

Combine the milk and butter in a medium saucepan. Cook over medium-high heat until the butter melts and bubbles appear on the edges of the milk. Gradually whisk in the grits and cook, stirring constantly, until the mixture is soft and thick, about 10 minutes. Stir in 1 cup of the Cheddar cheese, season to taste with salt and pepper, and pour into the baking dish. Sprinkle with the remaining cheese, and bake until crusty on top, 40 to 45 minutes. Let cool 5 minutes, then serve.

baked bananas tropicale

When liberated from their customary role as breakfast cereal topper, bananas take on an entirely new—and zippy!—personality. Here, I have paired them with tropical flavors in a wonderful dessert for a cold winter night or after a spicy dinner anytime.

SERVES 6

  6 medium ripe bananas
 ¼ cup dark rum
  2 tablespoons pineapple juice
  2 tablespoons fresh lime juice
  6 tablespoons (¾ stick) unsalted butter, melted
  2 tablespoons minced fresh ginger
 ⅓ cup packed dark brown sugar
 ¼ cup sweetened flaked coconut
     Sweetened heavy cream or vanilla ice cream

METHOD

Preheat the oven to 350°F. Peel the bananas and cut in half lengthwise.

  In a small bowl, stir the rum, pineapple juice, and lime juice into the melted butter. Place 1 banana in each of 6 individual shallow baking dishes large enough to accommodate them or arrange the bananas in a baking dish large enough to accommodate them in a single layer. Pour the butter-rum mixture over the bananas. Sprinkle with the ginger, brown sugar, and coconut and bake for 15 minutes. Serve warm with sweetened cream or vanilla ice cream.

jumbleberry potpies

My grandmother made pies like nobody's business and in the heat of New England summers when berries were fat and sweet, she would mix them in a beautiful and tasty jumble in potpies that demanded a big spoon for catching all the juices. Using prepared puff pastry makes this one of the quickest baked desserts to throw together.

SERVES 6

  4 tablespoons (½ stick) unsalted butter
  2 tablespoons quick-cooking tapioca
  1 cup sugar
 ¼ teaspoon salt
  6 cups mixed berries, such as raspberries, blueberries, and blackberries
  1 tablespoon fresh lemon juice
 1½ sheets prepared puff pastry, thawed
     Vanilla ice cream

METHOD

Preheat the oven to 400°F.

  Using 1 tablespoon of the butter, lightly grease six 1-cup ramekins or individual baking dishes. Set aside.

  In a large bowl, combine the tapioca, sugar, and salt. Add the berries and lemon juice and toss to mix. Divide the berry mixture evenly among the ramekins. Dot with the remaining butter.

  Using one of the baking dishes as a guide, cut the puff pastry to fit on top of the berry mixture and place over filling.

  Place the pies on a baking sheet and bake until the pastry is golden and the filling is bubbling, about 25 minutes. Serve with vanilla ice cream.

strawberry-rhubarb crumble

This is a great all-purpose crumble recipe that's extremely versatile. It can be baked family style and served at the table or in individual ramekins, which looks a bit more refined. Vary the fruit according to your liking and what the season has to offer and cover with the crumble topping. Strawberry and rhubarb are a classic spring combination, but some other combinations I like are blueberry-peach, apple–pear–dried cherry, apple-raspberry, and blackberry-nectarine.

SERVES 6

- 1 pound fresh or frozen rhubarb, cut into 1-inch pieces
- 1 pint strawberries, stemmed and halved
- ¾ cup granulated sugar
- 1¼ cups all-purpose flour
- ¾ cup packed light brown sugar
- ¾ cup regular or quick-cooking oatmeal
- 1 teaspoon ground cardamom
- ½ teaspoon salt
- ¾ cup (1½ sticks) chilled unsalted butter, cut into ½-inch pieces
- 1 cup heavy cream, whipped with 2 teaspoons vanilla or orange extract

METHOD

Preheat the oven to 375°F.

Generously butter an 8- or 9-inch baking dish or 6 individual 1-cup ramekins or custard cups.

In a medium bowl, combine the rhubarb, strawberries, and granulated sugar; toss gently to combine. Transfer to the baking dish or dishes.

In another medium bowl, stir together the flour, brown sugar, oatmeal, cardamom, and salt. Using a pastry blender or 2 knives, cut the butter into the flour mixture until it resembles coarse crumbs. Spread the topping over the fruit, covering it completely, and bake until the fruit is bubbling and the topping is golden, about 30 minutes. Serve with the flavored whipped cream.

pink grapefruit sherbet

I don't know what's more delicious, the pale pink color or the flavor of this sherbet. It's the perfect ending to a rich or spicy meal.

MAKES 1 GENEROUS PINT; SERVES 4 TO 6

- 2 cups freshly squeezed pink grapefruit juice (about 3 medium grapefruits)
- 2 teaspoons grated grapefruit zest
- ½ cup whole milk
- ½ cup light corn syrup
- ¼ cup sugar

METHOD

In a medium bowl, combine all the ingredients, stirring until the sugar dissolves. Transfer to an ice cream maker and freeze according to the manufacturer's directions. When firm, transfer to a sealable container and freeze until ready to serve. For best flavor, the sherbet should be served within 2 days.

style note

HOW TO ASSEMBLE A SIMPLE BOUQUET

This technique works best with thinner and shorter-stemmed garden blooms, such as sweet peas, poppies, daffodils, ranunculus, and tulips. Thicker and longer-stemmed varieties, such as calla lilies and ginger blossoms, are better off displayed as single stems or spaced apart in a larger vase.

• Fill a water glass three-quarters full with cool water.

• Grasp a bunch of flowers and trim the stems to the same length. Arrange stems, one by one, to form a circle around the perimeter of the glass. Repeat the circle arrangement, filling in the gaps and spaces (inserting the stems vertically). Continue this pattern until the glass is full.

• Grasp the bouquet with both hands and lift out of the glass. Transfer to one hand and trim the stems to an even length again.

• Place a rubber band around the stems. Tie with raffia or a ribbon, if desired, and insert into a vase.

BIG
DEAL MEALS

certain

occasions seem to demand a more formal observance, both in terms of menu and ambience. For such special occasions, a big-deal meal is in order. These are the dishes that, by their nature, taste extravagant and look gorgeous. Match these with a creatively set table and people you love and you will have achieved entertaining nirvana.

A big-deal event doesn't necessarily mean a big amount of work. It's the nature of the recipes and their ingredients, and particularly their presentation, that make them a bit more luxurious. But before you get too intimidated, rest assured: They're not overly fancy or formal and they don't require you to attend culinary school to cook them nor to master origami to assemble them. Think softly scrambled eggs with caviar served in an eggshell, sliced duck breast fanned on a plate with cherry-cabernet sauce, or milk chocolate pôts de crème in small pudding dishes. The techniques required to prepare these dishes are not much different from those you'd use to make a casual family dinner, yet somehow they add up to an *important* dinner.

Many of the recipes in this section can be prepared completely ahead of time or in stages. They make a big impression but they fit into your real life.

Presentation plays a big role in creating the aura that you want. I recommend plating big-deal meals individually in the kitchen and serving your guests at the table. This suspense results in delight (not to mention kudos to the cook) when the plates are set in front of your guests. Don't forget, there is an element of theater in the most successful events.

SETTING THE (MORE) FORMAL TABLE

Formal settings have assigned rules of placement that create a certain symmetry and avert confusion for your guests. They also send a signal that this is not just your ordinary occasion and, in fact, it's a big deal. Formally set tables look like a million bucks and make us sit a little taller and act a bit more grown-up (maybe . . .).

The dinner plate is always set directly in front of the diner. Often a charger or service plate that is one inch wider than the dinner plate anchors the dinner plate and assures that the place setting is never empty—which it never should be at a formal table.

The flatware is always set to either side of the dinner plate in order of use, from the outside in toward the plate. The forks are set on the left; the knives and soupspoon on the right. The soupspoon is placed to the right of the knives. The knife blade always faces in toward the plate. All handle bottoms should align.

The dessert utensils are centered above the dinner plate. The spoon is placed over the fork, facing toward the diner's left, with the fork facing in the opposite direction.

Following restaurants' lead, bread-and-butter plates and knives are now standard on American formal tables.

The bread-and-butter plate is placed directly above the forks, with the butter knife placed on the top of the butter plate, its blade pointing to the left, its cutting edge turned inward.

The napkin is placed either on top of the plate or to the left of the fork. No utensils should be placed on the napkin.

Glasses are always placed to the upper right of the plate, directly over the knife and/or soupspoon. The water goblet is the largest glass and is placed first, followed at a slight distance to the right by the wineglass. If Champagne is to be served with the first course, it is placed next to the water goblet, followed by the wineglass.

Salt and pepper shakers or cellars are placed above the settings, one pair for every two to four persons.

SERVING AND CLEARING

Your mother may have taught you the mnemonic "Lower (serve) from the left, raise (clear) from the right." It's an excellent rule of thumb, with these two exceptions:

If guests are engaged in conversation, don't reach through their talk. Serve or clear from the other side. Wine is always served from the right since this is the side on which wineglasses are placed.

At the conclusion of the main course, all tableware, including salt and pepper, relishes, and other enhancements, are removed from the table. All glasses, including water goblets and wineglasses, remain on the table.

EMBELLISHING THE (MORE) FORMAL TABLE

There are no hard-and-fast rules for decorating the more formal table. Once you fulfill the rules of dinnerware and glassware placement, the table should be a canvas for expressing your personal style. And a bit of luxe is definitely appropriate.

Decorating big-deal tables reminds me a bit of playing dress-up as a girl. I regard each element as an accessory that will enhance the overall look. Here are some considerations:

Candelight. Tapers, pillars, or votives? A mix of all? Candlesticks in silver, brass, or ceramic? A line of votives on a silver tray, or interspersed among a "runner" of lemons, oranges, and greens? A large pillar wrapped in ivy?

Flowers. A centerpiece or small bouquets, called orbits, strewn about the table? One type of flower or a profusion of many varieties? A simple statement of greens?

Linen. Antique or new? White or color? Pattern or solid? Tablecloth or place mats?

Dinnerware and Glassware. A mix of patterns and colors or a single statement? Red wine and white glasses? Chargers underneath dinner plates?

Silverware. Silver or stainless? Vintage or new? Mixed or matched? Butter knives, fish knives, soupspoons, dessert spoons?

Place Cards. Yes? No? Where?

The Effect. Minimal or profuse? An overall theme (Bastille Day or Moroccan)? Sophisticated and refined or no-holds-barred statement?

There are no correct answers to these rhetorical considerations; there are unlimited ways to express yourself without going horribly wrong. The fact is, you won't.

Here are a few examples: Consider a starched white antique damask tablecloth that showcases bird's egg blue linen napkins, a mix of hotel silverware found at flea markets, and blue-tinted pressed-glass goblets. To me this says antebellum. On the other hand, envision a deep crimson velvet runner that spans the length of a polished bird's-eye maple table and sets off gold-rimmed ivory china, stemmed crystal, and paisley-patterned napkins in a declaration of English refinement.

Taken singly, each element stands on its own but set on the table, each element plays off the next, linked by color or pattern or style, to create a complete picture.

PLACE CARDS AND SEATING ARRANGEMENTS

Though the table may be inordinately beautiful with everything set in its place, how many times have you stood around awkwardly, wondering where you should sit? The function of place cards is to balance table seating and enable guests to take their seats with ease and grace. They can also be decorative elements on the table.

But the true beauty of place cards is they allow you, as the host, to seat your guests exactly where you want them. (What power the host wields!) Place cards enable you to seat your best friend next to you and your best friend's boring husband at the opposite end of the table (but you wouldn't do that, would you?).

While I am more inclined to seat guests according to respective personalities and interests, traditional etiquette rules that a formal seating arrangement is thus: If there is an equal number of men and women, seat them alternately. If not, seat the guests so men and women are mixed. If there is a guest of honor, he or she may be seated to the host's or hostess's right or in the center of the table. The host and hostess generally sit at the heads of the table. The specific seating arrangement is decided by the host or hostess based on what he or she thinks will prompt the best conversation.

style note

Party favors, the little gifts that you offer your guests, make a party special and definitely elevate it into the realm of big deal. The thoughtfulness and generosity in the gesture will make your guests happy and the party memorable. Place favors at each place setting, in a basket by the front door, or rest them on the dining chairs as a lovely surprise. Favors need not be expensive or fancy—in fact, the more whimsical the better, I say. Let your imagination be your guide. Consider these possibilities:

• Jars and bottles of condiments, attractively packaged. Match the condiment to the guest's personality: vanilla sugar for your friend who likes to bake, Louisiana hot sauce for someone who adores spicy food.

• Bars of scented soap, wrapped in tissue paper and topped with a gold seal with the guest's name on it.

• Small pots of herbs or fraises de bois.

• Hand-packed boxes of gourmet chocolates.

• Picture frames (insert a photograph of each guest and they'll double as place cards).

• Pralines wrapped in cellophane.

• Mini-bouquets of flowers (violets or lily of the valley) in miniature colored glass vases.

• Seed packets and zip-lock bags of potting soil nestled in flowerpots.

• Small boxes made of paper, wood, or glass.

• If you garden or preserve, individual baskets of vegetables or jars of homemade jam.

"SIT A LITTLE
TALLER & ACT
A BIT MORE
GROWN-UP
(MAYBE...)"

There is no rule governing card placement. They can be situated to the top right, top left, or center of the plate; they can be placed on the plate, in a goblet, or hung on the back of a chair.

Once everybody sits down to a beautiful table and a spectacular meal, everyday cares will ebb, the conversation will flow, and your guests will remember an evening full of friendship and warmth.

BIG-DEAL MENUS

When I am hosting a big-deal occasion, it's a bit less "wash and wear," if you will, than an everyday affair. This is the time for wineglasses instead of jelly jars for before-dinner drinks. The overall flow of the occasion is more formulated and the menus are carefully thought out.

The defining differences between casual and big-deal menus is the number of courses and especially the mode of presentation. However, the basic considerations of flavor, color, and texture, along with seasonal appropriateness, remain the same.

It's especially nice to highlight a luxurious food or an uncommon ingredient in one course. Gravlax, duck, and saffron are not everyday foods and therefore make a meal distinctive. Likewise, a significant dish such as Spinach Herb Soufflé, which everybody knows requires a certain finesse (not really, but don't tell your guests), will be greeted with oohs and ahs.

With more dressy menus, it's easy to err on the side of richness, which, once the first course has been enjoyed, can begin to wear heavily on the palate and the constitution. I try not to serve too much of a rich thing. If I begin with Caviar Eggs, I'll follow it up with a straightforward beef entrée and end with creamy Milk Chocolate Pôts de Crème, which is light rather than densely chocolatey.

Generally, I will serve a separate first course, followed by a main course, sometimes a salad, and finally dessert. For a change of pace, I may include a cheese course in place of dessert (though you will inevitably be subjected to cries of distress from the sweet tooths among your guests) or offer cheese only to those who may prefer it instead of dessert. (See page 102 for more on serving cheese.)

Often, I serve dessert and/or coffee in another room to change the venue and give my guests an opportunity to trade conversation partners.

For big-deal menus, I try to allot myself more time to cook, not only because I'm preparing more dishes, but also because I like to take special care with the presentation. As with the table decoration, the details of the food and how it looks enhance the occasion, too.

I have created four big-deal menus—one for each season. Use them as is or choose from the recipes that follow to create your own big-deal menus that will make your guests know they have been part of a very special evening.

SPRING

big-deal menu

Asparagus *with* Toasted Bread Crumbs *and* Olives

Rack of Lamb *with* Moroccan Gremolata

Lemony Pea Puree

Spicy Couscous *with* Orange Zest and Scallions

Almond Pavlovas *with* Red Berries

asparagus with toasted bread crumbs and olives

In southern Spain, spring heralds the asparagus crop and a wealth of culinary variations on the asparagus theme. Here, I have paired asparagus with other Spanish flavors, such as sherry vinegar and black olives, in a robust first course that would also be appropriate as a side dish.

SERVES 6

Vinaigrette

   3 tablespoons sherry vinegar
   1 tablespoon fresh lemon juice
      Kosher salt and freshly ground pepper
   6 tablespoons extra-virgin olive oil

   3 tablespoons unsalted butter
1½ cups fresh bread crumbs (see Note)
   ½ cup slivered black olives
1¼ pounds asparagus, trimmed

METHOD

In a small bowl, stir together the sherry vinegar, lemon juice, and salt and pepper to taste. Slowly add the olive oil in a steady stream, whisking constantly. Set aside.

In a medium skillet, melt the butter over medium heat. When the foam subsides, add the bread crumbs and sauté, stirring and tossing, until crisp and golden, 2 to 3 minutes. Transfer to paper towels. When cool, toss with the olives in a small bowl.

Bring a large sauté pan of water to a boil. Add a pinch of salt and when the water returns to a boil, add the asparagus. Lower the heat and cook at a gentle simmer until crisp-tender, 3 to 8 minutes, depending upon the size of the asparagus. Remove from the water with tongs and drain on paper towels.

To serve, arrange the asparagus on plates, sprinkle the olives and bread crumbs over the top, and drizzle with the vinaigrette. Serve warm.

Note: To make fresh bread crumbs, put 2 to 3 slices of firm-textured white bread in a food processor. Pulse until coarse crumbs form.

rack of lamb with moroccan gremolata

Rack of lamb is proof that there is elegance in simplicity. Because it's so easy to prepare and lends itself readily to an impressive presentation, I serve rack of lamb frequently, varying the flavors of its crust with the seasons. Here, I've created a fragrant Moroccan rendition of the traditional Italian gremolata, which is a mixture of lemon zest, garlic, and parsley. I've substituted mint for the parsley and added orange zest and cumin to the mixture. Have your butcher trim off, or french, the thin strip of meat and fat between each chop.

SERVES 6

   ¾ cup chopped fresh mint
   8 garlic cloves, finely chopped
   ¼ cup grated orange zest
   1 tablespoon grated lemon zest
   2 tablespoons ground cumin
      Kosher salt and freshly ground pepper
   6 tablespoons extra-virgin olive oil
   3 racks of lamb (8 chops each), cut in half

METHOD

Preheat the oven to 400°F.

In a small bowl, combine the mint, garlic, citrus zests, cumin, salt and pepper to taste, and olive oil. Pat the mint mixture over the fat sides of the racks to form a crust.

Place the racks on a baking sheet, crust side up, and roast until an instant-read thermometer registers 130°F. to 135°F. for medium-rare, 25 to 30 minutes. Let rest 10 minutes before carving.

To serve, slice the lamb between the ribs and serve 3 to 4 chops per person.

Bring a medium saucepan of water to a boil. Add a generous pinch of salt and the peas. Cook at a gentle boil for 1 minute, then drain, reserving a few tablespoons of the cooking water. Place the peas in the bowl of a food processor, along with the lemon zest, thyme, and 2 to 3 tablespoons of the cooking water. Puree the peas, then pass through a sieve into a bowl, using the back of a wooden spoon to help press the peas through. Season with salt and pepper, then stir in the heavy cream, a bit at a time, until smooth.

spicy couscous with orange zest and scallions

Couscous is made from the same grain as pasta, but it has its own special characteristics that make it particularly appealing as a side dish. It's light, fluffy, and versatile. As an added benefit, couscous is easy to make beforehand and reheat when it's time to serve the meal.

SERVES 6

- 6 cups chicken stock or low-sodium canned broth
- 3 cups couscous
- 1 tablespoon grated orange zest
- ¾ cup finely chopped green onions
- ¼ cup currants
- 1 teaspoon chili oil (available in Asian groceries and many supermarkets), or more to taste
  Kosher salt and freshly ground pepper

METHOD

Place the broth in a medium saucepan and bring to a boil. Stir in the couscous, remove from the heat, cover, and let stand for 15 minutes. Mix in the remaining ingredients. Season to taste with salt and pepper.

lemony pea puree

Believe it or not, frozen peas actually work better than fresh peas in this recipe as they tend to be more uniformly sweet and soft. Don't cover the peas while they're cooking or they'll turn gray, which would be a very sad turn of events.

SERVES 6

  Kosher salt
- 2 cups frozen petite peas
  Grated zest of ½ lemon
- ½ teaspoon fresh thyme leaves
  Freshly ground pepper
- ¼ cup heavy cream

almond pavlovas with red berries

Featherlight meringues become sweet nests for a mix of red, ripe berries to provide an elegant ending for a special dinner. Pavlovas also transform store-bought ice creams and sorbets into luxurious statements.

SERVES 6

6 egg whites, at room temperature
Pinch of kosher salt
1¾ cups superfine sugar
2 teaspoons fresh lemon juice
1 teaspoon almond extract

1 pint raspberries
1 pint strawberries
¾ pound fresh pitted cherries
¼ cup granulated sugar
¼ cup kirsch
1 cup heavy cream
2 tablespoons confectioners' sugar
1 teaspoon pure vanilla extract
1 cup prepared lemon curd (see Note)

METHOD

Preheat the oven to 275°F. Line 2 baking sheets with parchment.

Place the egg whites and salt in a large nonreactive bowl, preferably stainless steel. Using an electric mixer, beat on low speed until bubbles form. Increase the mixer's speed and beat until the egg whites form very soft peaks, about 1½ minutes.

With the mixer running, gradually beat the sugar into the egg whites, then add the lemon juice and almond extract and beat until the whites form very stiff, shiny peaks, about 3 minutes.

Scoop about 1 cup of the meringue onto one of the baking sheets. Using the back of a spoon, form a shallow well in the center of the meringue. Repeat with the remaining egg whites, placing 3 meringues on each baking sheet.

Bake without opening the oven door until the meringues are crisp on the outside and very lightly colored, about 1½ hours. Turn off the oven, open the door slightly, and allow the meringues to cool in the oven. If you need the oven for another use, remove the meringues from the oven and cool completely on a rack.

While the pavlovas cool, combine the fruits, granulated sugar, and kirsch in a medium bowl. Macerate at room temperature for 1 hour, stirring occasionally.

To serve, whip the cream with the confectioners' sugar and vanilla until soft peaks form. Place a meringue on each plate. Spoon a bit of lemon curd into the well of each meringue and top with some of the berries. Spoon whipped cream over the berries. Top with the remaining berries.

Note: Lemon curd is available at gourmet groceries and specialty retailers.

PRIMER

The Secret to Perfect Meringues

The sweet cloud called meringue is nothing more than egg whites and sugar. The secret to achieving the cloud effect is to trap air inside the egg whites. Here's how:

Be sure the bowl in which you whip the egg whites is perfectly free of any fats or grease that will prevent the egg whites from whipping to cloud level. Many soaps contain fat, so if you have recently washed the bowl, you need to get rid of the residue. To do so, rub half a lemon inside the bowl and dry it thoroughly.

Begin whipping egg whites at a very low speed. When they begin to foam, increase the speed to medium and beat until the egg whites resemble the head on a draught beer. Increase the speed to high and whip until stiff peaks form.

Some additional pointers:

- A pinch of salt or cream of tartar will help egg whites achieve volume.

- Room-temperature egg whites are easier to beat than cold egg whites.

- If you overbeat the whites and they begin to resemble Styrofoam, add an unbeaten white and whip until they're at the level they should be.

- Never attempt to make meringue on a muggy day. They really need a dry atmosphere to puff in a way that will make you proud.

SUMMER

Heirloom Tomato Salad *with* Chive-Parsley Dressing

Tuna au Poivre

Spicy Green *and* Yellow Beans

Gingered Sweet Potatoes

Bellini Peaches

heirloom tomato salad with chive-parsley dressing

Heirloom tomatoes are the descendants of seeds that have passed down through generations of farmers. Often irregularly shaped, or interestingly mottled or striped, they offer vibrant color and flavor. Because they are not commercially grown, farmers' markets (or your own garden!) are the likeliest source for heirloom tomatoes, but if you cannot find them, substitute the best vine-ripened red tomatoes.

SERVES 6

- 3 tablespoons extra-virgin olive oil
- 3 tablespoons chopped chives
- 1 tablespoon chopped parsley

- 8 medium ripe heirloom tomatoes in assorted colors

Dressing

- 2 teaspoons sherry vinegar
- 2 tablespoons finely chopped shallot
- $\frac{1}{4}$ teaspoon kosher salt
- $\frac{1}{4}$ teaspoon sugar
- 1 teaspoon fresh thyme

- 1 log (6 ounces) fresh goat cheese, such as chèvre, cut into rounds
  Fresh or dried lavender, for garnish

METHOD

Combine the olive oil, chives, and parsley in a blender or food processor and puree. Set aside.

Slice the tomatoes and put them in a large, shallow bowl.

In a small bowl, whisk the vinegar, shallot, salt, sugar, and thyme until blended. Pour the vinegar mixture over the tomatoes and gently toss to coat them thoroughly.

To serve, divide the chive-parsley puree evenly among 6 plates, using the back of a spoon to spread evenly. Arrange some of the tomatoes and goat cheese on top of the puree. Garnish with the lavender.

Alternatively, you can build tomato towers (as seen on page 93) by arranging two tomato slices on the plate, placing the goat cheese on top of the tomato, and topping the cheese with two more tomato slices.

tuna au poivre

A seashore-inspired rendition of the classic French dish, my version substitutes meaty-textured tuna for the usual beefsteak. You can make this into a one-dish meal by serving the tuna on top of dressed salad greens such as the Red Lettuces with Citrus Vinaigrette (page 49). I do this a lot.

SERVES 6

- $\frac{1}{2}$ cup crème fraîche
- 3 teaspoons grated lemon zest
- $\frac{1}{4}$ cup extra-virgin olive oil
- 3 tablespoons cracked multicolored or black peppercorns
- 6 tuna steaks, about $1\frac{1}{2}$ inches thick
  Kosher salt

METHOD

Preheat the broiler.

In a small bowl, combine the crème fraîche and lemon zest; set aside.

Pour the olive oil on a plate large enough to accommodate a tuna steak. Place the cracked peppercorns on another plate. Pat the tuna steaks dry with a paper towel. Dip each steak in the oil, then press the cracked peppercorns evenly onto both sides of the steak. Season with salt.

Place the tuna steaks on a broiler pan and broil 4 inches from the heat for 3 minutes. Turn the steaks, return to the oven, and continue to cook until medium-rare, about 3 minutes more.

Transfer the tuna to serving plates and pass the lemon crème fraîche at the table.

I like to use multicolored peppercorns for a summer presentation of tuna au poivre because they lighten the visual palette.

I wrapped an Asian long bean around the shorter beans to create a "bouquet" effect. The beans are offset by bean sprouts sprinkled with black sesame seeds and rice wine vinegar.

spicy green and yellow beans

Green and yellow beans benefit from being tossed with Asian ingredients—the delicious result proves it. If you can find Asian long beans, available in Asian groceries and some supermarkets, use them as they round out the recipe nicely. Be sure to dry the beans before stir-frying so the oil won't spatter.

SERVES 6

1½ pounds green beans and yellow beans, trimmed
2 to 3 tablespoons peanut oil
2 garlic cloves, minced
1½ teaspoons grated fresh ginger
¼ teaspoon red pepper flakes
2 tablespoons soy sauce
1 tablespoon sesame oil
½ cup coarsely toasted chopped almonds (optional)

METHOD

In a large pot of boiling salted water, cook the green beans for 2 minutes. Drain and immediately plunge into cold water to chill. Drain again and pat dry.

In a wok or a large skillet, heat the peanut oil over medium-high heat. When hot, add the garlic and cook, stirring, for 30 seconds. Add the ginger and red pepper flakes and cook, stirring, for 10 seconds.

Increase the heat to high, add the beans and soy sauce, and cook until tender, about 3 minutes, stirring and tossing constantly. Drizzle with sesame oil. Taste for seasoning, adding more soy sauce or red pepper flakes as desired. Sprinkle with almonds, if using, and serve.

PRIMER

Herbal Excellence

It's easy to plant herbs in containers and pluck them for cooking, and they'll do double-duty as scented centerpieces, too. Cultivate them in red-lacquered window boxes, pastel-hued pots, or old concrete planters. Fill the containers with rich potting soil and tuck in herb plants to your heart's content. Combinations to consider include purple basil and lavender; lemon verbena and musky sage; rosemary and thyme. If you're really dedicated, you can include summery edible blooms such as pansies and nasturtiums. Let the herbs live in a sunny spot, and when it's time to set the outdoor table, give them center stage. (P.S. They're natural pest repellents, too.)

gingered sweet potatoes

An unexpected and appropriate addition to a summer menu, sweet potatoes balance the spiciness of the tuna.

SERVES 6

- 2 pounds sweet potatoes, peeled and quartered
  Kosher salt
- 4 tablespoons (½ stick) unsalted butter
- 1 tablespoon finely chopped fresh ginger
- 1 tablespoon freshly grated orange zest
- ½ cup sour cream
  Freshly ground pepper

METHOD

Place the sweet potatoes in a medium saucepan with cold water to cover. Bring to a boil over medium-high heat, add a large pinch of salt, and cook until tender, about 30 minutes.

Drain the potatoes and put them through a ricer or mash them with a potato masher or fork. Add the butter, stirring to melt it, to the potatoes. Add the ginger, orange zest, and sour cream and mix well. Season to taste with salt and pepper

bellini peaches

The lovely Bellini, a cocktail made with white peach puree and Prosecco, the Italian sparkling wine, was made famous at Harry's Bar in Venice (what wouldn't taste lovely at Harry's Bar in Venice?). I've reinterpreted the ingredients of the famous Bellini in this fetching dessert. *Salute!*

SERVES 6

- 6 large ripe peaches (use white peaches if you can find them)
- 1 cup plus 2 teaspoons sugar
- 3 cups Prosecco (Italian sparkling wine)
- 1 vanilla bean, split lengthwise
  Peel from ½ lemon
- ⅔ cup crème fraîche
- 1 tablespoon crème de cassis

METHOD

Bring a large pot of water to a boil. Drop a few peaches at a time into the boiling water and blanch for 15 seconds, then remove them with a slotted spoon to a bowl of ice water. Carefully slip off the peels.

In a large saucepan, combine 1 cup of sugar, the Prosecco, vanilla bean, and lemon peel and bring to a boil over medium heat. Decrease the heat to a simmer and carefully add the peaches. Poach until tender, 8 to 10 minutes, depending upon their degree of ripeness. Remove the saucepan from the heat and let the peaches cool in the liquid.

In a medium bowl, combine the crème fraîche, remaining 2 teaspoons of sugar, cassis, and 1 tablespoon of the poaching liquid. Whip just until soft peaks form.

Remove the peaches from the liquid with a slotted spoon. Put in individual bowls or goblets and spoon the crème fraîche over them.

early AUTUMN

big-deal menu

Celery Root Remoulade

Tuscan Bread Salad

Veal Chops *with* Sage Butter

Hearts *of* Romaine *with* Blue Cheese Vinaigrette

Caramelized Figs *with* Lavender Honey

celery root remoulade

Celery root is proof positive that beauty is only skin deep and that good taste lies within. Sometimes called celeriac, celery root is the knobby globe-shaped vegetable that resides with the other root vegetables in the produce section. It is not the root of stalk celery, but a distant cousin. It possesses a subtly sweet flavor and appealing crunchiness. A classic French bistro offering, this creamy, crunchy celery root slaw is a refreshing first course and a fine accompaniment to roast meats and fish.

SERVES 6

1 egg
1 tablespoon Dijon mustard
  Generous pinch of kosher salt
  Dash of Tabasco Sauce
$\frac{1}{2}$ cup safflower oil
$\frac{1}{4}$ cup extra-virgin olive oil
$1\frac{1}{2}$ tablespoons fresh lemon juice
$1\frac{1}{2}$ tablespoons heavy cream
1 large celery root

METHOD

Put the egg, mustard, salt, Tabasco, and $\frac{1}{3}$ cup of the safflower oil in a blender. With the machine running, slowly pour in the remaining safflower oil and the olive oil in a steady stream. Add the lemon juice and pulse briefly to mix. Add the heavy cream and pulse again. If the mayonnaise seems too thick, add a bit more cream. It should have the consistency of a thick sauce. Adjust the seasonings.

Peel the celery root, then finely julienne using a food processor or a large knife. Put in a large bowl and add half of the mustard mayonnaise, tossing to combine well. Add more mayonnaise as needed to coat the celery root lightly. Chill until ready to serve.

tuscan bread salad

Don't let the bread put you off— this salad is actually quite light. My recipe for summer bread salad is a rendition of the Italian bread salad called panzanella. It's a great way to use stale leftover bread. And it's a perfect accompaniment to grilled meats and fish.

SERVES 6

$2\frac{1}{2}$ cups 1-inch stale bread cubes, crusts removed
6 ripe plum (Roma) tomatoes, cut into large cubes
1 medium red onion, thinly sliced
1 cup slivered fresh basil leaves
$\frac{1}{2}$ cup extra-virgin olive oil
2 tablespoons balsamic vinegar
  Kosher salt and freshly ground pepper

METHOD

Put the bread cubes in a colander and sprinkle with water so the cubes are wet but not mushy; let drain for 1 hour.

In a large bowl, combine the tomatoes, onion, basil, olive oil, vinegar, salt, and pepper. Toss to mix.

Gently squeeze the excess water from the bread cubes and add to the tomatoes. Toss again, then cover with plastic wrap and let stand at room temperature for at least 1 hour before serving.

veal chops with sage butter

Veal chops are very lean and their delicate flavor partners well with the subtle pungency of sage. Butter adds a veil of richness that enhances the meat's tenderness. Veal is one of those meats that many people enjoy only when they're in a restaurant so it's a nice surprise when it's served in a friend's home. The success of this dish depends greatly on the quality of the veal. Look for Plume de Veau or Provimi veal.

SERVES 6

- ¾ cup (1½ sticks) unsalted butter, softened
- 2 teaspoons fresh lemon juice
- 1 tablespoon dry white wine
- 2 tablespoons chopped shallot
- 3 tablespoons chopped fresh sage
- 1 tablespoon chopped fresh parsley
  Kosher salt and freshly ground pepper
- 6 loin veal chops, about 1 inch thick
- 2 tablespoons extra-virgin olive oil
  Fresh sage sprigs

METHOD

In a small bowl, mash together ½ cup of the butter, the lemon juice, wine, shallot, sage, parsley, ¼ teaspoon salt, and ⅛ teaspoon pepper or to taste. Blend until the mixture is smooth. Transfer the mixture to a piece of plastic wrap and form into a log about 6 inches long and 1¼ inches thick. Wrap tightly and refrigerate until firm.

Season the veal chops with salt and pepper. In a large skillet, heat the remaining 4 tablespoons butter and the oil over high heat. When very hot, add the chops (you will probably have to do this in batches) and cook until golden brown, about 2 to 3 minutes on each side. Transfer to a warm platter, cover with aluminum foil, and keep warm as you cook the remaining chops, if working in batches.

To serve, cut the sage butter into ½-inch slices and top each veal chop with a slice. Decorate with fresh sage sprigs and serve immediately.

For a more composed presentation, I molded the salad that accompanies the veal chops in a ramekin and inverted it onto the plate.

hearts of romaine with blue cheese vinaigrette

Invite me to a steakhouse and I will order the hearts of romaine every time. The combination of crunchy lettuce and creamy blue cheese sends me swooning. Here, I have lightened the traditional blue cheese dressing by turning it into a vinaigrette. The swooning effect, however, remains.

SERVES 6

3 tablespoons red wine vinegar
   Kosher salt and freshly ground pepper
$\frac{1}{3}$ to $\frac{1}{2}$ cup extra-virgin olive oil
$\frac{1}{4}$ cup crumbled blue cheese
3 small heads romaine lettuce or 3 large hearts of romaine
$\frac{1}{2}$ cup toasted pine nuts (page 188)

METHOD

In a small bowl, combine the vinegar, salt, and pepper. Stir to dissolve the salt. Slowly add $\frac{1}{3}$ cup of the olive oil in a steady stream, whisking constantly. Taste the vinaigrette and if it is too tart, whisk in a bit more olive oil. Gently stir in the blue cheese.

If using romaine lettuce heads, trim the outer leaves until you reach the smaller, lighter green center leaves—this is the heart. (Reserve the outer leaves for another use.) Trim the stem of the lettuce, but leave it intact. Cut the heart in half. Place a heart half on 6 individual plates. Drizzle with the vinaigrette and scatter the pine nuts on top.

caramelized figs with lavender honey

Ripe, voluptuous figs appear at California farmers' markets in early September along with dusky purple, fragrant bouquets of lavender. They're so splendid in their natural states and seem so made for each other that I am compelled to marry them in a dessert. Lavender honey is sold in specialty stores, but you can make your own by placing unsprayed lavender blossoms in a mild honey and letting it infuse for at least 1 week. The lavender subtly perfumes the figs and the honey imparts a shiny glaze.

SERVES 6

12 fresh figs
$\frac{2}{3}$ cup lavender honey
1 pint best-quality vanilla ice cream

METHOD

Preheat the broiler.

Cut the figs in half and arrange on a baking sheet, cut side up. Drizzle with the honey. Place under the broiler $1\frac{1}{2}$ inches from the heat and broil until the honey caramelizes and the tops begin to brown, 3 to 5 minutes.

To serve, arrange 4 fig halves on each dessert plate along with a scoop of vanilla ice cream.

PRIMER

After-Dinner Cheese

When you're used to having something sweet after a meal, the notion of cheese may seem a bit strange, but try it! After all, the French usually know what they're doing when it comes to food—and indulge!

You'll find the texture and the complex flavor of cheese, particularly when paired with a ripe fruit, perhaps a few nuts, and a glass of wine or Port, contribute to a satisfying and delicious finale to a delicious meal.

Choose three ripe cheeses: a blue, a triple cream, and a goat cheese. Place them on a platter with one type of fruit, such as pears, figs, or grapes, some walnuts, and very thinly sliced crusty bread.

For ideas on fruit and cheese pairings, see page 233.

WINTER

big-deal menu

Caviar Eggs

Filet Mignon Parcels

Sautéed Cherry Tomatoes

Milk Chocolate Pôts de Crème

caviar eggs

Softly scrambled eggs paired with luxurious caviar make a first course that is pure indulgence. Serving the caviar-laced eggs in the eggshell adds whimsy to the presentation, but you could also serve them in demi-tasse cups. I serve this first course with a small glass of very cold vodka.

SERVES 6

6   extra-large or jumbo eggs
    Kosher salt and freshly ground pepper
1   tablespoon unsalted butter
2   tablespoons heavy cream
2   tablespoons minced chives
6   ounces beluga, osetra, or sevruga caviar
6   slices of thin white bread, toasted, crusts removed

METHOD

To remove the tops of the eggshells, place the egg in an egg cup, pointed side up. Invert an empty spice bottle over the egg. Tap the bottom of the bottle along the circumference of its edge with a spoon. Carefully remove the spice bottle. You should have created a crack around the top of the egg. Pry open the top with a sharp knife. Pour the egg into a medium bowl. Rinse the eggshells and tops with boiling water and set aside.

Just before serving, fill a double boiler or medium saucepan three-quarters full with water and bring to a simmer. In a medium bowl, whisk the eggs with 1 teaspoon of water. Season with salt and pepper. Melt the butter in the top of the double boiler or in a stainless steel bowl that will fit snugly in the saucepan without touching the water. Add the eggs and cook, stirring, until the eggs thicken and are softly scrambled, 3 to 4 minutes. Whisk in the cream and chives and cook, stirring, just until the cream is heated, about 30 seconds more. Remove from the heat. Transfer to a cool bowl. Gently stir in half the caviar.

Place the eggshell bottoms in egg cups and spoon equal amounts of the scrambled eggs into them. Top with the remaining caviar, allowing it to mound above the eggshell.

Cut each slice of toast into 4 triangles and serve with the caviar eggs.

filet mignon parcels

This is a modernized version of the classic Beef Wellington, a dish that defined big deal in the fifties—the type of dish that Samantha would have served to Darrin's Mr. Tate during an episode of *Bewitched.* Here, I have substituted phyllo dough for the more stodgy puff pastry and wild mushrooms for the foie gras. If the boss is coming to dinner, you ought to consider this dish quite seriously. It's got that *je ne sais quoi* that will make him pat himself on the back for hiring you.

SERVES 6

6   filet mignons, each approximately ½ pound and
    about 1½ inches thick
    Kosher salt and freshly ground pepper
1   cup (2 sticks) unsalted butter
4   tablespoons extra-virgin olive oil
1   pound assorted mushrooms (a mix of wild and
    domestic), coarsely chopped
¼   cup Madeira wine
3   tablespoons chopped fresh chives
2   packages frozen phyllo dough, defrosted
4   leeks, green parts only, blanched and cut lengthwise
    into six ½-inch strips

METHOD

Preheat the oven to 400°F. Line a baking sheet with parchment.

Pat the filet mignons dry with paper towels and season them with salt and pepper. Heat a sauté pan over high heat. When it's hot, add 2 tablespoons of the butter and 2 tablespoons of the olive oil; when the butter has melted, add the filet mignons and sear just until brown on each side, about 1½ minutes per side. Cool to room temperature.

Melt 6 tablespoons of the butter and the remaining 2 tablespoons of the olive oil in the same sauté pan over medium heat. Add the mushrooms and sauté, stirring, until they release their liquid. Add the Madeira and chives and cook over medium-low heat until soft. Season with salt and pepper to taste. Cool to room temperature.

Melt the remaining stick of butter. Unwrap the phyllo dough and cut the phyllo sheets into twenty-four 12-inch squares. Keep the unused phyllo covered as you're working so it doesn't dry out. (For tips on working with phyllo, see page 148.)

To make the parcels, place 1 phyllo square on a flat surface, brush lightly with butter, place another square on top of the first with the corners turned 45 degrees. Add 2 more sheets in this way, turning each square before placing on top of the previous one so the corners do not align.

Spoon 2 tablespoons of mushrooms into the center of each packet. Place a filet on top of the mushrooms. Top the filet with another 2 tablespoons of mushrooms.

Gather the edges of the phyllo together and gently twist. Tie with a leek ribbon. Transfer the packets to the parchment-lined baking sheet, brush lightly with melted butter, and bake approximately 20 minutes, or until the beef registers 125°F. (medium-rare) on an instant-read thermometer when inserted through the top of the packet into the center of the filet. Serve the parcels immediately.

sautéed cherry tomatoes

While this side dish is perfect during the peak of tomato season in the summer, the heat of the sauté pan does wonders for bringing out the inherent sweetness of cherry tomatoes. Eating these cherry tomatoes is like having a ray of warm sunshine burst in your mouth.

SERVES 6

 2 tablespoons extra-virgin olive oil
 2 garlic cloves, finely chopped
 2½ pints cherry tomatoes, stemmed
 ¼ cup mixed fresh herbs (parsley, basil, thyme, oregano)
  Kosher salt and freshly ground pepper

METHOD

Heat the oil in a large skillet over medium heat. Add the garlic and cook, stirring constantly, until translucent. Add the tomatoes and cook, shaking the pan occasionally, just until the tomatoes soften, about 5 minutes, depending upon their ripeness. Stir in the herbs and salt and pepper to taste. Serve immediately.

milk chocolate pôts de crème

Rich chocolate flavor and a silky texture make these individual custards a luxurious indulgence. Sometimes I will bake the custards in ovenproof coffee cups, which injects a sense of humor into an otherwise serious dessert.

SERVES 6

 1 cup heavy cream
 1 cup milk
 2 ounces milk chocolate
 2 ounces bittersweet or semisweet chocolate
 5 large egg yolks
 ⅓ cup sugar
 ¼ teaspoon kosher salt
 2 teaspoons vanilla extract

METHOD

Preheat the oven to 325°F.

In a medium saucepan, combine the cream, milk, and chocolates. Bring to a boil over medium heat, stirring frequently.

In a medium bowl, beat the egg yolks, sugar, and salt until well blended. Stir in a bit of the hot cream mixture, then slowly whisk in the remaining cream. Stir in the vanilla extract.

Place 6 pôts de crème cups or custard cups in a baking dish. Divide the chocolate mixture evenly among the cups. Pour enough hot tap water into the baking dish to reach halfway up the cups.

Bake in the center of the oven until the custards are set but still jiggle in the center, 30 to 35 minutes. Remove the custards from the water bath and let cool. Cover and chill until ready to serve.

more
big-deal recipes

fava bean crostini

The lively spring green color of this puree is perfectly balanced with the vibrant flavors of fava beans, mint, and lemon. While fresh fava beans do have the best flavor, they are very time-consuming to shell, parboil, and peel. Take this route if you are in need of a mindless yet calming task. Otherwise, use frozen beans. Make the puree a few hours ahead of time if you can so the flavors can meld.

MAKES ABOUT 16 CROSTINI

3 cups fresh or frozen fava beans or lima beans
  Kosher salt
¼ cup extra-virgin olive oil, plus up to ¼ cup more
  as needed
1 teaspoon fresh lemon juice
3 tablespoons minced fresh mint
  Freshly ground pepper
½ loaf French bread (baguette)
  Lemon zest, for garnish

METHOD

Preheat the broiler.

If using fresh fava beans, bring a large pot of water to a boil. Add the fava beans and blanch for 30 seconds. Rinse under cold water. Slit the seams of the beans along their edges and pop the beans out of their skins. Reserve the beans and discard the skins.

Fill a large saucepan with water and bring to a boil. Add a generous pinch of salt and when the water returns to a boil, add the beans. Reduce the heat to low and simmer until the beans are tender, 15 minutes.

Drain the beans and puree them in a food processor, adding a bit of the liquid in which you cooked the beans. Transfer to a medium bowl, stir in ¼ cup of the olive oil, lemon juice, mint, and salt and pepper to taste. Adjust the consistency to your preference—it should be thick and spreadable, not runny. If you pureed the fava beans in a food processor, you may not need ¼ cup olive oil; start by stirring in 2 tablespoons, then add more as needed.

Slice the bread thinly (¼ inch) on the diagonal and arrange on a baking sheet. Place under the broiler and toast until golden, about 20 seconds per side. Lightly brush the toasts on one side with olive oil. Spread with the fava bean puree and top with lemon zest.

Note: If you're pressed for time, serve the fava bean puree in a bowl surrounded by the toasted bread slices or toasted pita triangles.

crabmeat-stuffed artichokes

This pretty dish actually makes a hefty first course, so I would follow it with something relatively light such as grilled fish. I have also served these artichokes as a main course on a hot summer night and as a brunch dish. They may be made a day beforehand. You can purchase cooked crabmeat in most fish markets, and it's certainly a timesaver. If you're going to prepare your own, you will need about two 1½-pound crabs.

SERVES 6

6 medium artichokes
½ lemon
¼ cup watercress leaves
¼ cup parsley leaves
¼ cup basil leaves
½ shallot, minced
1¼ cups mayonnaise
1 tablespoon fresh lemon juice
2 teaspoons dry mustard
  Kosher salt and freshly ground pepper
2½ to 3 cups cooked crabmeat (about 1 pound)
  Grated lemon zest

METHOD

Fill a stockpot with about 3 inches of water and bring to a boil over high heat. Cut off the stems of the artichokes so they will stand upright. Trim about 1½ inches off the top of the artichokes and remove the tough outer leaves. Rub the cut parts with the lemon half. Put the artichokes in the saucepan along with the lemon. Reduce the heat to medium, cover, and simmer until the stems are tender when pierced with a fork, about 20 to 30 minutes.

Remove the artichokes and invert on a rack to drain. When cool enough to handle, gently spread open the leaves of each artichoke and using a spoon, scoop out the prickly choke from the center.

Combine the watercress, parsley, and basil leaves in a food processor and chop finely. Transfer to a medium bowl. Add the shallot, mayonnaise, lemon juice, and dry mustard. Stir well to combine. Season to taste with salt and pepper. Add the crabmeat and stir gently to combine.

Fill the cavity of each artichoke with an equal amount of the crabmeat and sprinkle the tops with the grated lemon zest. Serve chilled.

spinach herb soufflé

No, no, no! Soufflés are not impossible! Just prepare all the ingredients before beginning the recipe, beat the egg whites until stiff peaks form, combine everything with a gentle hand, and you'll achieve perfection. It's all in the attitude.

SERVES 6

 5 tablespoons unsalted butter, softened
 ⅓ cup plus 1 tablespoon freshly grated Parmesan
      cheese
 2 green onions, green parts only, minced
 1 cup cooked spinach, drained, or 1 10-ounce package
      frozen spinach, thawed
 1 tablespoon finely chopped fresh parsley
 2 tablespoons finely chopped fresh basil
 1 tablespoon fresh thyme leaves
      Kosher salt and freshly ground pepper
 1 cup whole milk
 3 tablespoons unbleached all-purpose flour
      Dash of Tabasco Sauce
 4 large egg yolks
 5 large egg whites, cold

METHOD

Preheat the oven to 375° F. Butter a 1½-quart soufflé dish or six 1-cup ramekins and sprinkle with 1 tablespoon of the Parmesan cheese. Set aside.

In a medium skillet, melt 1 tablespoon of the butter over medium heat. Add the green onions and sauté until wilted. Add the spinach, herbs, and a pinch each of salt and pepper. Cook, stirring frequently, until the moisture evaporates. Remove from the heat and reserve.

In a small saucepan, heat the milk over medium heat until small bubbles form around the edges.

In a medium saucepan, melt the remaining 3 tablespoons of butter over medium-high heat. Stir in the flour and whisk until a smooth paste forms, about 2 minutes. Do not allow the flour to brown. Whisk in the hot milk, a pinch of salt, and a dash of Tabasco. Cook, stirring, until the mixture boils and thickens, about 2 minutes. Remove from the heat and beat in the egg yolks one at a time. Fold in the spinach mixture and stir in all but about 1 tablespoon of the remaining Parmesan cheese.

Put the egg whites and a pinch of salt in the bowl of an electric mixer. Beat until stiff peaks form. Stir a large spoonful of the egg whites into the spinach mixture to lighten it, then fold in the remaining egg whites just until combined. Spoon the mixture into the prepared soufflé mold or ramekins. Sprinkle the top with the remaining cheese. Bake until puffed and golden, about 30 to 35 minutes for the large soufflé or 15 to 20 minutes for the small ones. Serve immediately.

style note

ORANGES AND LEMONS CHIMED THE BELLS OF ST. CLEMENS

I know why the bells were singing. What is more perfect than citrus? Available all year long, useful in all types of cooking, possessing a bright aroma and color, citrus fruits are elegant and beautiful in their simplicity. When it comes to cooking and entertaining, I can't imagine where I'd be without them.

• Adding a squeeze of lemon to food—both savory and sweet—will brighten its flavor before serving.

• Float lemon or orange slices in pitchers of water for serving at the table.

• Peel long strands of peel from lemons or oranges and use to garnish drinks.

• Thinly slice kumquats and add to green salads.

• Make candied citrus peel to serve with after-dinner coffee: Cut peel from fruit with a vegetable peeler, slice into slivers, and simmer in a syrup of half water and half sugar. Cool on parchment-lined wire racks.

• Use a lemon zester to carve patterns on citrus and pile in a silver bowl as an aromatic centerpiece.

• Scoop out oranges, lemons, and lime and insert small votive candles. Trim the bottoms a bit so they don't topple.

• Insert cloves into tangerines and lemons to make scented pomanders and put in a wooden bowl in your foyer or entry hall to greet your guests.

• Serve freshly squeezed pink grapefruit juice as a nonalcoholic choice for nondrinkers. Make a celebration spritzer with sparkling water and a dash of berry syrup.

• Wrap blue satin ribbon around oranges, tie a bow at the top, and secure it with a beautiful hat pin. Hang on doorknobs, armoires, or the backs of dining chairs.

gravlax with potato waffles

Gravlax is salmon that has been cured with salt, sugar, and some kind of alcohol, generally aquavit, a caraway-flavored liquor. Prepared gravlax can be found in many specialty food shops but you can substitute smoked salmon. Assemble this dish just before serving so the waffles don't become soggy.

SERVES 6

  4 tablespoons (½ stick) unsalted butter, melted
  1 tablespoon grated lemon zest
    Potato Waffles (recipe follows)
 12 thin slices of gravlax or smoked salmon
  ½ cup sour cream
  ¼ cup chopped red onion
  ⅓ cup capers, rinsed
    Lemon wedges
    Dill sprigs
    Salmon roe (optional)

METHOD

Combine the melted butter and lemon zest. Place 1 waffle on each of 6 individual plates. Brush lightly with the lemon butter. Top each with 2 slices of the gravlax and a dollop of sour cream. Garnish with the red onion, capers, lemon wedges, dill, and a dollop of roe if desired.

potato waffles

Russet potatoes are a must for this dish because they have less starch than boiling potatoes and will yield fluffier waffles. Likewise, when making the mashed potatoes for these waffles, err on the firmer side and you will have lighter waffles. When I don't serve waffles with gravlax as a first course, I often enlist them in the main course as an accompaniment to roasted meats.

SERVES 6

  5 russet potatoes, peeled and quartered
    Kosher salt
  ⅓ cup extra-virgin olive oil
  ½ to ¾ cup whole milk, warm
    Freshly ground pepper
  1 cup all-purpose flour
  1 teaspoon baking powder

METHOD

Put the potatoes in a large saucepan with cold water to cover. Bring to a boil over medium-high heat, add a generous pinch of salt, and cook until fork-tender. Drain the potatoes, then return them to the warm saucepan and gently shake it to get rid of any excess moisture.

Puree the potatoes by putting them through a ricer, or mash with a handheld masher. Stir in the olive oil and gradually add the milk until the potatoes are soft but hold their shape. Season with salt and pepper to taste.

Lightly grease and preheat a waffle iron.

In a large bowl, combine the mashed potatoes, flour, and baking powder. Spoon about ⅓ cup of the mixture onto the hot waffle iron. Cook until the waffles are golden and crisp. Keep the waffles warm in a 250° F. oven while you cook the remaining batter. Serve immediately.

butternut squash and shrimp soup

The alluring flavors and colors of this soup make it well worth the time you will spend preparing it. Once you make the stock, the rest of the soup comes together quickly. This recipe is a good one to prepare in stages. Make the stock early in the week and refrigerate it, then midweek, prepare the soup up to the point where the prawns are added. Finish the soup on the day you'll serve it.

SERVES 6

Stock

1½ cups dry white wine
3½ cups bottled clam juice
3 cups water
2 leeks, white and tender green parts, trimmed and sliced
4 fresh thyme sprigs
6 fresh parsley sprigs

Soup

6 tablespoons (¾ stick) unsalted butter
2 medium yellow onions, thinly sliced
2 pounds butternut squash, peeled and cut into 2-inch chunks
1 fresh rosemary sprig
2 tablespoons fresh lemon juice
18 large shrimp, peeled and deveined
Kosher salt and freshly ground pepper
Few dashes of hot pepper sauce
Rosemary sprigs, for garnish

METHOD

To make the stock, combine all the stock ingredients in a large saucepan over medium-high heat and bring to a boil. Reduce heat to low and simmer, uncovered, for 20 minutes.

Strain the stock through a fine sieve into a bowl. Reserve the stock and discard the solids. You should have about 6 cups of stock.

Cups in all sizes, shapes, and colors are wonderful containers for soup. I especially like to serve hor d'oeuvres–sized "soup sips" in demitasse cups.

To make the soup, in the same saucepan in which you made the stock, melt the butter over medium-low heat. Add the onions and sauté over medium heat until translucent. Add the squash and rosemary, reduce the heat to low, cover, and cook, stirring occasionally, for 10 minutes. Add 5 cups of the reserved stock and the lemon juice. Bring to a boil, reduce the heat to low, cover, and cook until the squash is very tender, 10 to 15 minutes.

Strain the soup, reserving the liquid. Discard the rosemary. Puree the squash in a food processor or blender in small batches. Return the puree to the pan over medium-low heat along with the reserved liquid. Add the remaining 1 cup stock if the soup is too thick.

Slice the shrimp in half lengthwise and add to the soup. Cook until the shrimp turn pink. Transfer them to a warm platter and cover. Season the soup to taste with salt and pepper and a few dashes of hot pepper sauce.

To serve, ladle the hot soup into shallow soup bowls and arrange 6 prawn halves on top of each serving. Garnish with the rosemary.

PRIMER

OUT DARN SPOT!

If you entertain, chances are you will stain. Here are some remedies for banishing that darn spot:

- Regardless of the nature of the stain, here is the course of action to take: Act quickly and blot (don't scrub) the stain. Apply the stain-removal remedy only to the spot or you'll spread the stain. Test the stain-removal remedy on a hidden area before applying to the stain to be sure it is appropriate for the fabric.

- Remove red wine by saturating it with club soda, then blotting it with a mixture of mild dishwashing liquid and white vinegar.

- Eliminate a grease stain by applying a mix of baking soda and mild detergent plus a teaspoon of glycerin (you can buy it at the drugstore).

- Expel fruit and vegetable stains by stretching the linen over a pot or bowl and pouring boiling water through the stain from a height of at least a foot.

- White vinegar is a magic elixir. Diluted with water, it is an effective stain remover and general cleaner.

- Lift candle wax from linens by placing a cotton tea towel over the stain and pressing lightly with a warm iron.

golden beet soup with caviar pearls

Orange juice and sherry vinegar contribute sweetness and tartness to this bright yellow pureed soup and star anise gives it an exotic quality. The soup's color reminds me of Persian silk and the caviar of black pearls that adorn it. The flavor is equally sumptuous.

SERVES 6

- 4 tablespoons (½ stick) unsalted butter
- 1 medium yellow onion, diced
- 2 garlic cloves, sliced
- 2 pounds golden beets, peeled and sliced
- 1 bay leaf
- 1 star anise
  Kosher salt and freshly ground pepper
- 4 cups chicken broth
- ½ cup fresh orange juice
- 2 tablespoons sherry vinegar
- ⅓ cup sour cream
- 3 tablespoons caviar, such as osetra or sevruga

METHOD

In a Dutch oven or medium saucepan, melt the butter over medium-low heat. Add the onion and garlic, reduce the heat to low, cover, and cook, stirring occasionally, until soft but not brown. Add the beets, bay leaf, star anise, a generous pinch each of salt and pepper, the chicken broth, and orange juice. Bring to a boil, then reduce the heat to low, cover, and simmer until the beets are tender, about 30 minutes. Discard the star anise and bay leaf.

Working in batches, use a slotted spoon to transfer the beets to a food mill or food processor and puree until smooth. Once all the beets have been pureed, return them to the saucepan with the broth. Stir in the sherry vinegar and cook over medium-low heat to warm through. Season to taste with salt and pepper.

Ladle the soup into bowls. Garnish each serving with a dollop of sour cream and spoon ½ tablespoon of caviar onto the sour cream.

lily broth with fava beans

This light, aromatic broth heralds spring. The lily family includes all varieties of onions and garlic including leeks and chives. The soft color and texture of fava beans mirror the delicate characteristics of this broth. If you can't find favas, substitute baby lima beans.

SERVES 6

- 2 pounds fresh or frozen fava beans, shelled
- 1 tablespoon extra-virgin olive oil
- 4 ounces pancetta or slab bacon, diced
- 4 large yellow onions, thinly sliced
- 2 shallots, thinly sliced
- 2 leeks, white part plus 2 inches of green, thinly sliced
- 4 green onions, green and white parts, chopped
- 2 green garlic shoots (available at farmers markets or specialty stores), green and white parts, diced (optional)
- ½ cup dry white wine
- 8 cups chicken stock or low-sodium canned broth
  Kosher salt and freshly ground pepper
  Chopped chives and chive flowers, for garnish
  Freshly grated Parmesan cheese

METHOD

If using fresh fava beans, bring a large pot of water to a boil. Add the fava beans and blanch for 30 seconds. Rinse under cold water. Slit the seams of the beans along their edges and pop the beans out of their skins. Reserve the beans and discard the skins.

In a large pot, warm the olive oil over medium heat. Add the pancetta, onions, shallots, leeks, green onions, and green garlic, if using. Sauté until the onions are soft and translucent, 8 to 10 minutes. Add the wine and cook, stirring, for 30 seconds. Add the chicken stock, cover, reduce the heat to low, and simmer for 25 minutes. Add the fava beans and cook for 5 minutes more. Season to taste with salt and pepper.

To serve, ladle the soup into warmed soup bowls and garnish with the chives and chive flowers. Pass the Parmesan cheese at the table.

When an acute case of spring fever gets me, I cover my table with flats of wheat grass (don't forget to line with plastic first!) to create a virtual garden. I tuck spring blooms, such as chive flowers, in the grass.

frilly greens with kumquats

Kumquats, a diminutive member of the citrus family, appear in the winter market. Their skin is sweet but the flesh is tart, so slice them very thinly. If you have trouble finding kumquats, you can substitute oranges. Blood oranges are unusual and their vivid red color is quite attractive.

SERVES 6

Vinaigrette

- 3 to 4 tablespoons rice wine vinegar
- 1 teaspoon sugar
  Kosher salt and freshly ground pepper
- 6 tablespoons peanut oil
- 2 teaspoons hot sesame oil, or more to taste

- 6 large handfuls of mixed "frilly" greens, such as chicory, escarole, frisee
- 4 kumquats, thinly sliced
- 1 medium red onion, thinly sliced

METHOD

In the bottom of a large salad bowl, combine the vinegar, sugar, salt, and pepper. Stir to dissolve the sugar and salt. Whisk in the oils.

Just before serving, toss together the greens, kumquats, and onion. Add to the salad bowl and toss again to coat with the dressing. Serve immediately.

baked halibut with peperonata

Throughout Italy, one finds various versions of peperonata, a dish that always includes bell peppers and as far as I can tell is always delicious. The peppers are cooked to a sweet softness that is lifted by the vibrant flavors of basil, oregano, and sherry vinegar. When baked with the halibut, the peperonata infuses the mild fish with its bright flavor. I like to serve this with couscous to soak up the excess juices.

SERVES 6

- ¼ cup plus 2 tablespoons extra-virgin olive oil
- 2 medium onions, thinly sliced
- 4 garlic cloves, peeled and finely chopped
- 2 red bell peppers, cored and seeded, cut into ½-inch strips
- 2 green bell peppers, cored and seeded, cut into ½-inch strips
- 4 large tomatoes, peeled and chopped
- ¼ cup chopped fresh basil leaves
- 2 tablespoons chopped fresh oregano
- 1 bay leaf
- 1 teaspoon sherry vinegar
  Kosher salt and freshly ground pepper
- 6 halibut fillets or other firm white fish fillets, each about ⅓ pound
  Juice from ½ lemon

METHOD

Preheat the oven to 350°F.

In a shallow ovenproof casserole, heat ¼ cup of the olive oil over moderate heat. Add the onions and garlic and sauté until soft, about 2 minutes. Add the peppers and sauté for 5 minutes. Stir in the tomatoes, herbs, vinegar, and salt and pepper to taste and simmer for 10 minutes. Remove from the heat.

Pat the halibut fillets dry with paper towels and season on both sides with salt and pepper. Arrange on top of the peperonata, squeeze a bit of lemon juice on each, and drizzle with the remaining 2 tablespoons of olive oil. Bake until the halibut is opaque and flakes easily, 20 to 25 minutes.

To serve, spoon some of the peperonata onto each plate and place the halibut fillet on top of it.

For special occasions, Chuck Williams, the founder of Williams-Sonoma (and, to my eyes, the embodiment of casual elegance), likes to serve vichyssoise (what he calls leek and potato soup), steamed crab, and green salad. If that doesn't say "casual" and "elegant," not to mention "simple" and "delicious," I don't know what does.

SERVES 6

Lemon-Lime Butter

1 cup (2 sticks) unsalted butter
1 tablespoon fresh lemon juice
1 tablespoon fresh lime juice
Grated zest of ½ lemon
Grated zest of ½ lime
Kosher salt

Tartar Sauce

2 cups prepared mayonnaise
¼ cup chopped sweet pickles
1 teaspoon dry mustard
2 tablespoons fresh lemon juice
1 teaspoon finely chopped capers
Kosher salt
Dash of hot pepper sauce

Crabs

2 bottles dry white wine
1 lemon, thinly sliced
1 bay leaf
2 garlic cloves, peeled
Sprinkling of red pepper flakes
6 live Dungeness crabs (1½ to 1¾ pounds each) or 36 live blue crabs

METHOD

To make the lemon-lime butter, melt the butter in a small saucepan over low heat. Add the lemon juice, lime juice, lemon zest, lime zest, and salt to taste. Keep warm.

To make the tartar sauce, in a small bowl, combine the mayonnaise, pickles, dry mustard, lemon juice, and capers. Season to taste with salt and hot pepper sauce. Cover and refrigerate until ready to use.

To cook the crab, in the bottom of a large pot with a steamer insert, combine the wine, lemon, bay leaf,

garlic, and red pepper flakes. Add water until the liquid comes to just below the steamer basket and bring to a boil. Put 3 of the Dungeness crabs or 9 of the blue crabs into the steamer and place the steamer over the boiling liquid. Cover and steam until the crabs have turned red, about 30 minutes for the Dungeness crabs and about 15 minutes for the blue crabs.

With tongs, remove the crabs from the pot and transfer to paper towels to cool slightly. Add the 3 remaining Dungeness crabs or the next batch of blue crabs to the steamer and cook in the same manner.

To serve, place the crabs on a large platter or individual plates and serve with small individual bowls of the dipping sauces.

Note: Dungeness crabs are equally succulent whether you serve them hot or chilled; blue crabs are best served hot. Use 2 steaming pots if you'd like to speed up the cooking process and get yourself to the table with your guests!

style note

SCENTED HAND TOWELS

For a refreshing end to a meal, particularly if you have served fish, shellfish, or finger foods, offer your guests scented hand towels.

Dampen small white cotton or terry cloth hand towels or washcloths with water mixed with a bit of lemon oil, rosewater, or lavender oil. Roll the towels and microwave them for a few seconds so they're warm. Arrange on a tray and offer to your guests between the main course and dessert.

scallops with watercress, red pepper, and corn salad

For this main-course salad, I quickly sear large sea scallops to create a golden crust that highlights their luscious texture. A lusty vinaigrette and the peppery bite of watercress balance the shellfish's richness. The bright colors and diverse textures in this dish make for a rather dramatic presentation.

SERVES 6

- ¼ cup sherry vinegar
- 2 teaspoons Dijon mustard
- 1 shallot, minced
- 2 teaspoons finely grated orange zest
  Kosher salt and freshly ground pepper
- ½ cup extra-virgin olive oil

- 36 sea scallops (1½ pounds)
  Kosher salt and freshly ground pepper
- 2 tablespoons extra-virgin olive oil

- 2 bunches watercress, trimmed
- ⅔ cup cooked corn kernels, fresh or thawed frozen
- 6 tablespoons minced red pepper

METHOD

In a small bowl, combine the vinegar, mustard, shallot, orange zest, salt, and pepper. Stir to dissolve the salt. Whisk in the olive oil. Reserve.

Season the scallops with salt and pepper. Heat the olive oil in a large sauté pan over high heat until very hot. Sear the scallops without moving until golden and just cooked, about 1½ minutes per side.

Toss the watercress and corn with half the vinaigrette. Whisk any scallop juices from the skillet into the remaining dressing. Mound the watercress mixture in the center of 6 plates. Arrange the scallops on the greens, dividing them evenly among the 6 plates, and sprinkle with the red pepper. Drizzle with the remaining vinaigrette.

roasted game hens stuffed under the skin with herbed ricotta

If you can stuff a hen inside, why not under the skin? The delicate flavors of herbs, lemon, and ricotta and the beautiful presentation of whole game hens make this a special dish. You can stuff the game hens early in the day and pop them in the oven in the evening.

SERVES 6

- 12 ounces (¾ of a 15-ounce container) part-skim ricotta
- ⅓ cup freshly grated Parmesan cheese
- 1 egg yolk, lightly beaten
- ¼ cup finely chopped fresh basil
- 3 tablespoons finely chopped fresh parsley
- 1½ tablespoons grated lemon zest
- 2 small garlic cloves
  Kosher salt and freshly ground pepper
- 6 Cornish game hens
- 1½ small lemons, cut into 6 quarters
- 1½ small onions, cut into 6 quarters
- ½ cup dry white wine

METHOD

Preheat the oven to 350°F.

Put the ricotta in a fine sieve and drain for 30 minutes. In a medium bowl, combine the drained ricotta, Parmesan, egg yolk, herbs, and lemon zest. Put the garlic cloves through a garlic press and add to the mixture. Combine well, adding salt and pepper to taste.

Rinse the game hens and pat them dry. Season the cavities with salt and pepper and place a lemon quarter and an onion quarter in each cavity.

Loosen the skin on the breasts by sliding your fingers under the skin, being careful not to pierce it. Spoon the ricotta mixture under the skin (about 4 tablespoons of stuffing per bird). Truss the birds.

Place the birds, breast side up, in a shallow roasting pan. Pour the white wine into the pan. Bake for 1 hour, or until the juices run clear when the hen is pierced in the thickest part of the thigh. Remove from the oven, tent lightly with aluminum foil, and let rest 10 minutes. Discard the trussing string and serve with the pan juices spooned over the hens.

chicken breasts with asparagus, fontina, and prosciutto

Years ago, as a student, when I was traveling from Vienna to Rome on my Eurail pass, I had a version of this dish in a small trattoria near the train station in Parma. It may have been my deep yearning for something other than the Cadbury chocolate bars that I had been eating for the past two days (this was before energy bars came on the scene, when chocolate bars with raisins and hazelnuts were hailed as "sportif" bars for their "healthful" ingredients), but the combination of the woodsy asparagus, the creamy fontina, and the salty prosciutto was nothing short of heaven and to this day, the memory evokes hunger pangs. It's a winner!

SERVES 6

- 12 thin asparagus spears, trimmed to 6 inches
   Kosher salt
- 6 skinless, boneless chicken breasts
   Freshly ground pepper
- 6 thin slices of prosciutto (about 4 ounces)
- 6 thin slices of fontina cheese (about 6 ounces)
- ½ cup Marsala wine

METHOD

Preheat the oven to 350°F. Lightly butter a 9×13-inch baking dish.

Halve the asparagus lengthwise. Bring a sauté pan of water to a boil. Add a pinch of salt along with the asparagus and simmer until tender but firm, about 1½ minutes. Remove the asparagus with tongs to a paper towel–lined plate and set aside.

Place the chicken breasts between 2 sheets of plastic wrap and pound gently with a meat pounder or the side of a soup can until about ⅓ inch thick. Season with salt and pepper. Lay the chicken breasts on a work surface. Cover each with 1 piece of prosciutto, then with 1 piece of cheese. Bunch 4 pieces of asparagus at one end of the chicken breast and roll the breast lengthwise to form a bundle. Insert a toothpick through each bundle to ensure they keep their shape during cooking.

Arrange the chicken bundles seam side down in the baking dish. Pour the Marsala around the chicken. Bake until cooked through, 25 to 30 minutes.

To serve, remove the toothpicks and slice each bundle in half on the diagonal to reveal the stuffing.

style note

THE COVER-UP: LINENS

To cover or not to cover? That is the dilemma, particularly when there are so many options available to us for embellishing the table with linens.

• Beautiful table surfaces, ranging from highly polished wood to distressed painted pine to ceramic tile, deserve to be showcased. Rather than covering up its beauty, arrange a runner across the center of the table, with place mats at each setting to protect the table's surface and finish the look.

• Tablecloths can be much more than standard white damask (though it's beautiful in its own special way). Consider a length of organza or mattress ticking, a sari or a large kimono, gauze or mosquito netting, a quilt or a Navajo rug. Each embraces the table with its own personality.

• Coordinate the tablecloth with the chairs; use the same fabric to wrap the chair backs or cushions and tie with a matching ribbon.

• Beyond fabric, natural fibers such as sisal and seagrass make dramatic table coverings and place mats.

• Napkins can be as small or as large as you wish. You can find delicate embroidered tea napkins at secondhand stores. I like to fold them into triangles and offer them with beverages. Large dishcloths in breezy colors are fun—and functional—for messy dinners like Saturday Night Spareribs (page 58).

• If you have the time or inclination, you can trim napkins and place mats with ribbon, tassels, or beads. Fabric paint and a rubber stamp will make you into a textile artist in a snap—think white muslin and bright red and blue sailboats.

• If you're going to spend time around the coffee table, either during before-dinner drinks or with dessert, think about covering it, too.

• To prolong the life of your linen treasures, dry-clean them the day after you use them. This is especially true for the more delicate fabrics such as silk, and embroidered pieces. Linen is very durable and laundering is often preferred to dry cleaning because it rejuvenates and softens the fabric's surface.

• Very old and delicate linen will benefit most from hand washing with a delicate soap such as Ivory Snow, or send the linen to a hand launderer.

• To avoid creases and unnecessary touch-up pressing when it's time to set the table (and when, inevitably, I am harried), I hang my linens on padded hangers or over wooden rods. If you want to fold or roll (even better!) your linens, place acid-free tissue (available from a framing supplier) on them and then fold.

• Don't relegate your lovely linens to the closet. Use them! You'll smile.

moroccan chicken tagine

This stew gets its Moroccan designation from the redolent spices that flavor it. While you might not regard stew as a big-deal meal, the exotic nature of the dish and the richness of the spices, especially the saffron, says "special" to me. It will imbue your kitchen with the aromas of faraway places and entice your guests with promises of delicious things to come.

SERVES 6

2   chickens (about 3 pounds each), each cut into 6 pieces
    Kosher salt and freshly ground pepper
2   tablespoons (¼ stick) unsalted butter
2   tablespoons extra-virgin olive oil
1   large pinch of saffron threads dissolved in ¼ cup warm chicken broth
2   cinnamon sticks
2   teaspoons ground cumin
1   teaspoon curry powder, preferably Madras
4   cilantro sprigs
4   parsley sprigs
2   medium onions, quartered
4   medium tomatoes, seeded and quartered
8   to 10 cups chicken stock or low-sodium canned broth
4   medium carrots, halved lengthwise and cut into 2-inch pieces
4   parsnips, halved lengthwise and cut into 2-inch pieces
6   baby zucchini, trimmed
2   cups cooked chickpeas (garbanzo beans)
¼   teaspoon red pepper flakes
1   cup golden raisins
2   cups quick-cooking couscous
    Long strips of orange zest, for garnish
½   cup unsalted pistachios, for garnish

METHOD

Preheat the oven to 350°F.

Season the chicken pieces with salt and pepper. Combine the butter and olive oil in a large ovenproof casserole or Dutch oven over medium-high heat. When hot, add the chicken in batches and sauté until golden brown on all sides, 5 minutes. Transfer to a platter and reserve.

Add the saffron and the chicken broth it soaked in, cinnamon sticks, cumin, curry powder, cilantro, parsley, onions, and tomatoes to the casserole and sauté over medium-high heat until the onions are soft. Return the chicken to the casserole, add enough chicken stock to cover the ingredients entirely, and bring to a boil, stirring occasionally. Reduce the heat, cover, and simmer for 5 minutes. Transfer to the oven, reduce the temperature to 275°F., and bake 1 hour. Add the carrots and parsnips and bake for 15 more minutes. Add the zucchini, chickpeas, red pepper flakes, and raisins and return to the oven for 15 minutes more.

Remove the chicken from the oven. Transfer the chicken and vegetables to a warm platter and cover with foil. Pour the cooking liquid into a measuring cup and if needed add water to make 2 cups. Put the measured liquid in a medium saucepan and bring to a boil. Add the couscous, cover, and set aside for 10 minutes. Fluff with a fork.

To serve, spoon the couscous onto a serving platter and form a well in the center. Arrange the chicken and vegetables in the well. Garnish with the orange zest and pistachios and serve immediately.

chicken paillards with saffron sauce and tomato confetti

Paillard is the French term for a skinned, boned, and pounded-thin chicken breast. The refreshing tomato "confetti" offers a softly acidic counterpoint to the pungent saffron sauce and the red and yellow color is brilliantly appealing. All told, it's a very special dish.

SERVES 6

- 1 large tomato, peeled, seeded, and finely diced or 1 pint small cherry tomatoes, halved
- 3 tablespoons finely chopped fresh parsley
  Kosher salt and freshly ground pepper
- 6 skinless, boneless chicken breasts
- 1 cup chicken stock or low-sodium canned broth
  Large pinch of saffron threads
- 2 tablespoons (¼ stick) unsalted butter
- 1 tablespoon extra-virgin olive oil
- 1¼ cups sour cream, at room temperature

METHOD

Place the diced tomato in a colander and drain for 30 minutes. Mix with the parsley and salt and pepper to taste.

Place the chicken breasts between 2 sheets of plastic wrap and pound gently until very thin. Season with salt and pepper.

Bring the chicken broth to a boil. Add the saffron; stir to dissolve. Reserve.

In a large sauté pan, heat the butter and olive oil over medium heat. Place 3 chicken breasts in the pan and sauté, turning once, until golden brown and cooked through, about 3 minutes per side. Transfer to a warm platter and keep warm while you sauté the remaining 3 chicken breasts.

Add the chicken stock to the sauté pan and bring to a boil, stirring to scrape up any browned bits from the bottom. Cook until reduced to ½ cup, 3 to 5 minutes. Gently stir about half of the reduced broth into the sour cream. Stir the diluted sour cream into the remaining reduced broth. Heat gently just until warmed through. Do not boil. Stir in about ⅓ cup of the diced tomato. Taste for seasoning, adding more salt and pepper if necessary.

To serve, spoon the sauce over the chicken breasts and sprinkle with the remaining tomato confetti.

style note

CANDLELIGHT

Nothing creates atmosphere more effectively than candles. As an added bonus candlelight makes everybody look beautiful and feel good.

I like to place candles all around the house starting with the foyer so my guests can see them when they first arrive. I group candles of different sizes on tables, the mantel, and windowsills. Sometimes I arrange candles on mirrors because I like the reflection of the light flickering. I put candles in flowerpots, glasses, or bowls, anchored in pebbles, dried beans, or sand. Or I bring out the crystal candlesticks for their simple elegance.

Beeswax is the best candle material because it's smokeless, dripless, and odorless. The beautiful ivory or honey color of beeswax, whether it's in a honeycomb pattern or smooth, complements any table and every decor. I like scented candles in the bathrooms but never around food.

When placing tapers or tall candles on dining tables, be sure that the candle is not directly in front of a guest. The flame can be distracting if it's within one's direct line of vision.

Never put a "naked" wick on the table. This is an old superstition but I am prisoner to it. Light the wick, then blow it out if you won't be using the candle until later.

And finally, use candles only when it's dark outside.

grilled quail with orange and honey mustard marinade

Quail is an elegant yet whimsical choice for a dinner party. Here, I marinated the quail to preserve its moistness while it cooks, as well as to infuse the quail with sprightly flavors that play off its inherent sweetness. You can find quail at specialty butchers and in many supermarkets, albeit oftentimes frozen.

SERVES 6

½ cup honey mustard
¼ cup orange juice
¼ cup dry sherry
⅓ cup extra-virgin olive oil
½ teaspoon dried red pepper flakes
Kosher salt and freshly ground pepper
12 quail, well rinsed and patted dry

METHOD

In a small bowl, whisk together all ingredients except the quail. Put the quail in a large baking dish and pour the marinade over the birds, turning to coat completely. Marinate at room temperature for 1 to 3 hours, turning occasionally.

Prepare a fire in the grill. Remove the quail from the marinade, place breast side down on the grill, and cook 4 to 6 inches from the heat, turning them frequently, for 10 minutes. Brush some marinade on the quail and cook for 3 to 5 minutes more, turning them once or twice and brushing them again with the marinade. The quail should be brown and crispy on the outside and slightly pink and juicy in the center.

Serve 2 quail per person and insist that your guests use their fingers so they will savor every luscious bit.

duck breasts with cherry-cabernet sauce

Duck breasts are an elegant but easy choice for a special occasion. They require nothing more than a quick sauté, which makes the basis of a simple pan sauce, a fruity and slightly acidic cherry-cabernet sauce that is a delicious foil for the duck's robust richness. Assemble the sauce ingredients while the duck is cooking.

SERVES 6

  3 duck magrets (large boned duck breasts), about 10 to 12 ounces each
     Kosher salt and freshly ground pepper
     Ground allspice
  2 tablespoons (¼ stick) unsalted butter
  1 tablespoon extra-virgin olive oil
  1 large shallot, finely chopped
 1½ cups cabernet sauvignon wine
  1 cup beef stock
 1½ cups canned unsweetened cherries with their juice
  ¾ cup heavy cream

METHOD

Score a crisscross pattern on the skin side of each duck breast. Season both sides with salt, pepper, and a bit of allspice.

Heat a large skillet over high heat. When it's hot, add the butter and olive oil. When the butter has melted, add the duck breasts, skin side down (you may have to do this in batches), and sauté for 10 minutes without turning. Reduce the heat to medium, turn the duck breasts over, and cook 5 minutes more. Be advised—they will splatter. Transfer to a warm platter and keep warm.

Pour off most of the fat from the skillet, leaving the brown bits and about 1 tablespoon of fat. Reduce the heat to medium-low. Add the shallot and cook until soft and beginning to brown, about 2 minutes. Increase the heat to high, add the wine, beef stock, and cherry juice, and reduce by two-thirds, about 10 minutes. You should have about 1 cup of liquid. Reduce the heat to medium-low. Add the cream and cherries and cook until you have about 1½ cups of sauce, 3 to 5 minutes more. Season to taste with more salt.

To serve, cut the duck breasts into ¼-inch slices and arrange them in a fan pattern on each plate. Spoon some of the sauce over each serving.

roasted turkey breast with herbes de provence

You don't need a holiday to serve turkey! A whole turkey breast is a wonderful choice for entertaining because it's simple to prepare, its neutral flavor marries well with seasonal ingredients, and its presentation is appealing. Here, I've paired it with herbes de Provence, a blend of thyme, savory, fennel, and often lavender. Sometimes rosemary, sage, or bay leaf is included, too. Herbes de Provence is available at most specialty food shops or you can blend your own.

SERVES 6

  1 whole turkey breast (4 to 5 pounds)
  ½ lemon, thinly sliced
  2 tablespoons extra-virgin olive oil
  ½ teaspoon lemon zest
 1½ tablespoons herbes de Provence
     Kosher salt and freshly ground pepper
  ¾ cup dry white wine

METHOD

Preheat the oven to 350°F.

Using your fingers, gently separate the skin from the breast meat and arrange the lemon slices on top of the meat. Place the turkey breast on a rack in a shallow roasting pan.

In a small bowl, whisk together the olive oil, lemon zest, herbes de Provence, and salt and pepper to taste. Brush the mixture on the turkey breast. (If you have time, let the turkey rest for about 30 minutes, which will allow the meat to absorb the flavors nicely.) Add the wine to the roasting pan.

Roast the turkey until an instant-read thermometer registers 170°F. when inserted in the thickest part of the breast, about 1½ hours. Let sit at least 15 minutes before carving.

style note

CENTERPIECES AND ORBITS

When symmetry ruled the day, the key decorative element on a table was in the center. Today, when anything goes—even in big-deal situations—decorative elements have been liberated from the center of the table and can appear anywhere on the table. I call these "orbits" because rather than being anchored in the center, they are arranged around the table, sort of like planets orbiting around the galaxy. They may sit beside each setting or here and there on the table, in a line from end to end, between place settings, or in unexpected alignments. Orbits add interest and whimsy and engage your guests. Whether you choose a centerpiece or an orbit, the key is to give your table your personal style whether it be fancy, eclectic, or elegant.

CENTERPIECES

- Fill a deep glass bowl with scallop shells, marbles, or goldfish.
- Tuck pinecones and lady apples in a conical glass vase.
- Stack lemons in a tall glass vase, fill with water, then insert a few stems of gerbera daisies or calla lilies into the vase.
- Set a ship's lantern or hurricane lamp in the center and anchor it with pebbles, beach glass, and shells.
- Fill a large candelabra with honeycomb beeswax candles.
- Display a mercury glass or gazing ball.
- Fill a glass compote with eggs in varying eggshell tones.
- Polish apples or pears with a soft, cotton cloth and pile them in a pewter bowl.
- Arrange deep orange persimmons in a green frosted glass bowl.

ORBITS

- Glass balls or Christmas ornaments
- Pansies in demitasse cups
- A mix of oranges, lemons, limes, grapefruits, tangerines, kumquats
- A garland of boxwood or bay leaves; tuck citrus or flowers into it.
- Votive candles in miniature flowerpots
- Different size candles in different size candlesticks and/or holders. (Keep all the candles one color, preferably white or ivory.)
- Bundles of cinnamon tied with ribbon
- Pomegranates
- Tangerine pomanders studded with cloves
- Miniature ivy topiaries
- Frosted glass tumblers filled with beach pebbles and seagrass
- A starfish at every place setting
- Delicate spring posies in silver mint julep cups.

grilled butterflied leg of lamb with mint aioli

Aioli, one of the hallmarks of Provençal cooking, is a mayonnaise made with garlic. In my version of this assertive sauce, I incorporate fresh mint, which lightens the richness of the aioli and adds a fragrant counterpoint to the grilled lamb. Ask your butcher to bone and butterfly the lamb, specifying that he or she cut it to uniform thickness so it cooks evenly.

SERVES 6

- 1 3- to 3½-pound leg of lamb, boned and butterflied
- 1¼ cups plus 2 tablespoons extra-virgin olive oil
- 2 tablespoons dried mint
   Kosher salt and freshly ground pepper
- 2 garlic cloves, peeled and finely chopped
- ½ cup fresh mint leaves
- 2 egg yolks
- 1 tablespoon fresh lemon juice

METHOD

Prepare a fire in the grill. Rub the lamb with 2 tablespoons of the olive oil, dried mint, and salt and pepper to taste. When the coals become gray and ashy, place the lamb on the grill, cover and cook without turning for about 15 minutes. Turn the lamb and continue to cook until an instant-read thermometer registers 130°F. to 135°F. for medium-rare, about 15 to 20 minutes longer. Let the meat rest for 10 minutes before carving.

In the bowl of a food processor, combine the garlic, mint leaves, egg yolks, lemon juice, and salt to taste. With the machine running, add the remaining 1¼ cups of olive oil in a slow, steady stream. Process until thick.

To serve, cut the lamb into thin slices and pass the mint aioli separately.

five-spice pork tenderloin

A versatile meat, pork gladly takes on the flavors with which it is cooked. In this case, the pork is perfumed with Asian flavors, including the aromatic five-spice mixture, which can include, depending upon the brand you buy, a combination of star anise, cinnamon, Sichuan peppercorns, cloves, fennel, or licorice root.

SERVES 6

- 3 pounds pork tenderloin (approximately 3 whole tenderloins)
   Kosher salt and freshly ground pepper
- ½ cup soy sauce
- 2 tablespoons sugar
- 4 tablespoon fresh orange juice
   Finely grated zest from 1 orange
- 1½ tablespoons five-spice powder
- 2 tablespoons grated fresh ginger
- 2 tablespoons peanut oil
- 2 cups chicken broth

METHOD

Season the pork with the salt and pepper. In a small bowl, combine the soy sauce, sugar, 2 tablespoons of the orange juice, orange zest, five-spice powder, and ginger. Rub the soy sauce mixture all over the tenderloins. Wrap tightly in plastic wrap and marinate at least 1 hour.

Warm the peanut oil in a large sauté pan over high heat. When hot, add the tenderloins and sear until brown on all sides, about 5 minutes total. Reduce the heat to medium-low, cover, and cook slowly, turning the tenderloins occasionally, until the pork registers 150°F. on an instant-read thermometer when inserted in the thickest part of the meat, about 18 to 22 minutes. Remove the pork from the pan and transfer it to a cutting board. Cover loosely with aluminum foil.

Increase the heat to high, add the chicken broth and remaining 2 tablespoons orange juice, and cook, scraping the bottom of the pan with a wooden spoon to remove any caramelized bits, until reduced by half, about 5 minutes.

To serve, cut the meat crosswise into 1-inch slices. Arrange the medallions on individual plates and spoon the sauce over them.

filet mignon with red wine shallot sauce

For this luxuriously simple dish, I pair tender, flavorful filet mignon with its natural partner, red wine. Did you know that it has been shown that red wine actually aids the digestion of beef? A divine discovery, as is this dish. Use a good-quality cabernet in the sauce and pass the same one at the table for a marvelous flavor echo.

SERVES 6

- 6 filet mignons, each approximately ½ pound and 1½ inches thick
  Kosher salt and freshly ground pepper
- 5 tablespoons unsalted butter
- 2 tablespoons extra-virgin olive oil
- 3 shallots, thinly sliced
- 1 cup dry red wine, such as a cabernet sauvignon
- 1 cup beef stock or low-sodium canned beef broth

METHOD

Pat the steaks dry with paper towels and season with salt and pepper.

Combine the butter and oil in a large sauté pan or skillet over high heat. Add the filets, working in batches so they are not crowded in the pan, and cook, turning once, until done to your preference, about 3 minutes per side for rare and 3½ to 4 minutes per side for medium-rare. Transfer to a warm platter; keep warm by covering with aluminum foil.

When all the steaks have been cooked, pour off the excess fat in the pan, leaving about 1½ tablespoons. Add the shallots and cook over medium heat until translucent, about 2 minutes. Pour in the red wine and cook, scraping the bottom of the pan to dislodge any browned bits. Add the stock and cook over high heat until reduced by half. Season with salt and pepper to taste. If desired, whisk in 1 tablespoon of butter before serving, which will enrich the sauce and impart a beautiful sheen to it.

To serve, place a filet on each plate and top with some of the sauce.

For a French take on meat and potatoes, I accompany red wine and shallot-sauced Filet Mignon with Potato and Chèvre Galette (page 142). Incroyable!

beefsteak oriental with cilantro vinaigrette

The Asian ingredients in the marinade infuse this steak with exotic flavors. This is an ideal dish to make ahead of time and serve at room temperature, though it is equally good served hot.

SERVES 6

Marinade
- ½ cup dry sherry
- ⅓ cup soy sauce
- 2 tablespoons grated fresh ginger
- 2 tablespoons rice wine vinegar
- 1 tablespoon honey
- 2 garlic cloves, finely chopped
  Kosher salt and freshly ground pepper

- 2 pounds boneless sirloin steak
- 2 tablespoons extra-virgin olive oil

Cilantro Vinaigrette
- ¼ cup red wine vinegar
- ½ teaspoon sugar
  Kosher salt and freshly ground pepper
- ⅔ cup extra-virgin olive oil
- ⅓ cup chopped fresh cilantro leaves

METHOD

In a medium bowl, combine the marinade ingredients. Place the steak in a baking dish and pour the marinade over it, turning to coat completely. Cover and refrigerate at least 1 hour or up to 8 hours.

Preheat the oven to 400°F. Heat a large ovenproof skillet over high heat. When hot, add the olive oil and heat for 30 seconds. Place the steak in the skillet and sear it for 2 minutes on each side. Transfer the skillet to the oven and roast 15 to 20 minutes for rare (125°F. on an instant-read thermometer), or longer according to your taste.

Transfer the steak to a cutting board and let it rest for 10 minutes before carving.

In a small bowl, whisk together the vinegar, sugar, salt, and pepper. Whisk in the oil in a steady stream, then stir in the cilantro.

To serve, slice the steak and drizzle it with the Cilantro Vinaigrette.

roast leg of lamb with pomegranate glaze

Pomegranate juice lends a sweet-tart flavor and a gorgeous mahogany sheen to the lamb. In the winter, when pomegranates are plentiful, you can make your own juice, or opt for the much easier route and purchase pomegranate nectar at Middle Eastern groceries or in the ethnic foods section of your supermarket.

SERVES 6

1 whole leg of lamb (4 to 5 pounds), trimmed of excess fat
2 garlic cloves, thinly sliced
6 small fresh rosemary sprigs
Kosher salt and freshly ground pepper
½ cup fresh orange juice
¾ cup fresh pomegranate juice from 3 small pomegranates (see Note), or bottled pomegranate juice or nectar
2 tablespoons fresh lemon juice
1½ cups dry red wine or water

METHOD

Preheat the oven to 450°F.

Make small slits in the lamb and insert the garlic and rosemary into the slits. Season with salt and pepper. In a small bowl, combine the orange juice, pomegranate juice, and lemon juice.

Place the lamb on a rack in a roasting pan and brush it generously with the juice mixture. Roast the lamb, brushing it frequently with the juice mixture, for 30 minutes, then remove the lamb and turn it over. Return the lamb to the oven, reduce the heat to 325°F., and roast until an instant-read thermometer registers 130°F. to 135°F. for medium-rare when inserted in the thickest portion, about 45 minutes longer. Remove the lamb to a platter and cover loosely with aluminum foil. Let the lamb rest for 10 minutes before carving.

Pour off excess fat from the roasting pan, leaving about 2 tablespoons. Put the pan on top of the stove over medium-high heat. Add the red wine or water along with any remaining juice mixture and bring to a boil, scraping the bottom of the pan with a wooden spoon to loosen any caramelized bits. Cook until the liquid reduces by half, 2 to 3 minutes. Add any juices that have collected around the lamb, season to taste with salt and pepper, and serve in a sauceboat or small pitcher.

To carve the lamb, grasp the shank bone with a clean kitchen towel and, holding the knife parallel to the bone, cut thin slices of meat.

Note: To juice pomegranates, cut them in half horizontally and use a citrus juicer to juice them as you would oranges.

roast loin of pork with cinnamon-roasted pears

On an autumn Saturday, after a day of watching the kids' soccer game or walking Labrador retrievers in the woods, I like to serve roast pork. It's a wonderfully comforting yet refined dinner around which to gather friends. Here, I've paired the pork with cinnamon-dusted pears that roast right along with the meat and make an unexpected and seasonal accompaniment for it.

SERVES 6

2   garlic cloves, peeled and finely chopped
     Kosher salt
     Freshly ground pepper
1   tablespoon chopped dried rosemary
1   bay leaf, crumbled
1   boneless pork loin, about 3 pounds
1   tablespoon extra-virgin olive oil
¼   cup sugar
1   cup dry red wine
2   cinnamon sticks
6   black peppercorns
6   firm but ripe pears, such as Bosc, peeled, cored, and halved

METHOD

Preheat the oven to 450°F.

In a small bowl, combine the garlic, 1½ teaspoons kosher salt, ½ teaspoon ground black pepper, the rosemary, and the crumbled bay leaf. Rub the pork with the olive oil, then rub the seasoning mixture evenly over the pork. Place the loin in a shallow, nonreactive roasting pan and roast 15 minutes.

Meanwhile, in a small saucepan over medium-high heat, combine the sugar, wine, cinnamon, and peppercorns. Bring to a boil, stirring to dissolve the sugar, then reduce the heat to low, add the pears, and simmer for 10 minutes.

After 15 minutes, reduce the oven temperature to 350°F. and continue to roast the pork for 10 minutes. Remove the pork from the oven. Transfer the pears to the roasting pan and spoon the wine syrup over the pears and the pork. Cover the roasting pan with aluminum foil, return to the oven, and roast the pork until an instant-read thermometer registers 150°F. when inserted in the thickest part, and the pears are tender when pierced with the tip of a sharp knife,

20 to 25 minutes longer. Remove the pork and pears from the oven. Transfer the pork to a cutting board and the pears to a warm platter. Cover both loosely with aluminum foil. Let the pork rest 10 minutes before carving.

To serve, slice the pork and arrange on individual plates with the pear halves. Serve immediately.

style note

COMMEMORATIVE TABLECLOTHS

A personalized tablecloth makes an unusual—and reusable—memento for a truly special occasion, whether you keep it for yourself or present it to a guest. Use a plain white tablecloth as your canvas and let the creativity and whimsy flow. To ensure preservation of this keepsake, dry-clean or hand-wash the tablecloth. It's nice to include care instructions when you bestow a commemorative tablecloth as a gift.

• Put permanent markers at each place setting and ask guests to write greetings and draw pictures in commemoration of the guest of honor. Give the tablecloth to the special guest (laundered, of course).

• In commemoration of a life milestone, such as a wedding or anniversary, monogram a tablecloth with the initials of the special couple and their special date, along with memory words such as

"Hawaii 1955" (where they honeymooned) or "St. Lawrence and UVM" (where they attended college).

• Start a keepsake tablecloth. When friends and family are around your table, have them sign their names. Later, embroider the names onto the tablecloth. The keepsake can be used on special occasions or passed on as a treasured gift.

• For a guest of honor with a keen interest, such as gardening or fishing, theme the tablecloth with appropriate motifs, either embroidered, drawn, or painted.

• Stitch fabric square "pockets" onto a tablecloth and ask guests to bring commemorative photographs that can be inserted into the pockets and enjoyed during dinner (the guest of honor gets to take the whole thing home).

crown roast of pork with "triple a" stuffing

The dramatic crown roast is formed by tying together the two trimmed rib ends of a pork loin, a tricky job that is best left to the butcher. After the crown construction, preparing the roast is a snap. It is truly a special-occasion dish, as the succulent loin pork chops are cut to reveal a savory stuffing in the center that has been enriched by the pork juices with which it was cooked. The three "A's" in the stuffing are apricots, almonds, and chicken-apple sausage, a fruity combination that makes this crown roast an elegant centerpiece for an autumn or winter dinner. Pass the flavorful pan juices at the table.

SERVES 6

- 1 crown roast of pork with 12 to 14 chops, about 5 pounds
  Kosher salt and freshly ground pepper
- 2 tablespoons extra-virgin olive oil
- 1 cup dry white wine
- ¼ cup (½ stick) unsalted butter
- 1 small onion, chopped
- 2 garlic cloves, finely chopped
- 1 celery stalk with leaves, chopped
- 1 pound chicken-apple sausage, casing removed
- 3 cups cooked medium-grain rice
- ½ cup chopped dried apricots
- ½ cup chopped dried prunes
- 2 tablespoons chopped toasted almonds
  Grated zest of 1 orange
- 2 teaspoons ground dried sage
- 1 teaspoon ground dried thyme

METHOD

Preheat the oven to 400°F.

Season the pork with salt and pepper and rub with the olive oil. Place the roast on a rack in a roasting pan. Pour the wine into the roasting pan. Roast for 30 minutes, then reduce the heat to 325°F. and continue to roast, basting frequently with the pan juices, for 35 minutes.

Meanwhile, in a large skillet, melt the butter over medium heat. Add the onion, garlic, and celery and sauté until very soft, about 5 minutes. Add the sausage and cook, breaking it up with a spoon, until browned. Pour off any accumulated fat and transfer the mixture to a large bowl. Stir in the rice, apricots, prunes, almonds, orange zest, sage, and thyme. Season to taste with salt and pepper.

Remove the pork from the oven, spoon the stuffing into the center of the crown, and return the pork to the oven. Roast, basting frequently with the pan juices, until the pork registers 150°F. when an instant-read thermometer is inserted in the thickest part and the stuffing is heated through, about 30 minutes longer. Remove the pork from the oven and transfer it to a cutting board. Cover loosely with aluminum foil and let rest 10 minutes before carving.

To serve, transfer the pork roast to a platter and carve at the table. Cut the pork between the bones and arrange 2 chops on each place, along with a spoonful of stuffing.

style note

TASSELS

On a trip to Venice, I came across a shop that sold nothing but handmade tassels. In their various sizes and colors (and prices), they were the embodiment of luxury. I instantly purchased a dozen (what do I know from lire?), recognizing that these tassels exude old-world glamour and even whimsy. I later found many uses for them. You can:

•Wrap napkins with velvet ribbon and tie small satin tassels on them.

•Hang a large cotton-chenille tassel from a chandelier or the light over the table.

•Wrap a candy apple red mop-cotton tassel around the knob of your front door.

•Wrap black tassel curtain tiebacks around your dining room chairs.

•Tie opalesque beaded tassels around wine decanters or bottles, or hang one from the handle of your teapot.

•Pin or sew chenille tassels to the corners of the tablecloth or napkins.

farfalle with asparagus tops and herbs

This is a delicate pasta dish in which the farfalle, or butterflies, float in a simple chicken broth. It's nice to serve in the early spring when asparagus is at its peak and we're ready for lighter fare. It's particularly nice as a first course.

SERVES 6

1½ pounds thin asparagus
  Kosher salt
1½ pounds farfalle (butterfly-shaped) pasta
  3 tablespoons extra-virgin olive oil
  ¾ cup finely chopped shallots
  ½ cup dry white wine
  4 cups chicken broth
  ¼ cup chopped fresh parsley
  2 tablespoons chopped fresh basil
  2 teaspoons fresh thyme leaves
  Freshly ground pepper
  Freshly grated Parmesan cheese

METHOD

Trim off the tough ends of the asparagus and discard. Cut the spears on the diagonal into 1-inch pieces; reserve.

Bring a large pot of water to a boil. Add 2 generous pinches of salt and when the water returns to a boil, add the pasta. Cook until the pasta is al dente. Drain the pasta and transfer to a warm serving bowl.

Meanwhile, heat the oil in a large skillet over medium heat. Add the shallots and cook until translucent, about 3 to 4 minutes. Add the asparagus and cook, stirring, for 1 minute. Add the wine and the chicken broth, bring to a boil, and cook for 5 minutes to reduce it a bit. Add the herbs and stir to mix. Season to taste with salt and pepper.

Add the asparagus mixture to the hot·pasta and toss the mixture well. Serve with freshly grated Parmesan cheese.

linguine with pistachio pesto

Pistachios take the place of pine nuts in this vibrant pesto. It's an exuberant pesto that makes a delightful sauce for pasta. Incidentally, this pesto is also great as a dip for vegetables, thinned a bit, if you wish, with olive oil. I created this recipe for a spring issue of the Williams-Sonoma catalog when we had a windfall of pistachios and a hankering for pasta.

SERVES 6

  2   cups loosely packed basil leaves
 $\frac{1}{3}$ cup shelled unsalted pistachios, plus more for
         garnish
  2   garlic cloves, peeled and crushed
  2   teaspoons grated lemon zest, plus more for garnish
 $\frac{1}{2}$ cup extra-virgin olive oil
 $\frac{1}{4}$ cup freshly grated Parmesan cheese
       Kosher salt
 $1\frac{1}{2}$ pounds linguine

METHOD

Put the basil, pistachios, garlic, and lemon zest in the bowl of a food processor and pulse briefly to combine. With the machine running, add the olive oil through the feed tube in a steady stream. Process until smooth. Transfer to a medium bowl and stir in the Parmesan cheese.

Bring a large pot of water to a boil. Add 2 generous pinches of salt and when the water returns to a boil, add the linguine and cook until al dente. Drain, reserving a few tablespoons of the water.

Put the pasta in a large warm bowl. Thin 1 cup of the pesto with some of the pasta water. Spoon over the pasta and toss gently to mix, adding more pesto if desired. Serve immediately, garnished with chopped pistachios and lemon zest.

If you have extra pesto, transfer it to a small bowl and top it with a thin layer of olive oil. Wrapped tightly and refrigerated, it will last 2 to 3 weeks.

For a spring dinner, I sprinkled pink clover buds around the table and perched them in unexpected places.

long fusilli with pancetta and cream

I like to serve this quick and elegant pasta dish for a late supper, preceded by caviar and toast points if it's an extra-special night, and always followed by a crisp green salad. You're probably familiar with short fusilli, the small corkscrews that are often used in pasta salads. Less common (and far from the deli pasta salad connotations of the short fusilli) is the long fusilli, spaghetti-width curly noodles that hold sauces like this luxurious pancetta and cream sauce beautifully. I've used long fusilli here for that reason and also because they're so much fun to eat. If you can't find long fusilli, substitute spaghetti or vermicelli.

SERVES 6

       Kosher salt
 $1\frac{1}{2}$ pounds long fusilli or other thin noodles
  3   ounces pancetta, diced
 $1\frac{1}{4}$ cups heavy cream
  2   tablespoons ($\frac{1}{4}$ stick) unsalted butter
 $\frac{3}{4}$ cup freshly grated Parmesan cheese
       Freshly ground pepper
       Chopped chives and chive flower petals, for garnish

METHOD

Bring a large pot of water to a boil. Add 2 tablespoons salt. When the water returns to a boil, add the pasta and cook until al dente, 8 to 10 minutes. Drain the pasta, reserving $\frac{3}{4}$ cup of the cooking liquid, then return it to the pot in which it was cooked.

While the pasta is cooking, make the sauce. In a large nonstick skillet, cook the pancetta over medium-high heat until the edges begin to brown. Add 1 cup of the cream and the butter. Cook over medium heat until the butter is melted and the cream thickens a bit, about 3 minutes. Remove from the heat.

Add the cream sauce, reserved cooking liquid, and the remaining cream to the pasta and and cook over low heat, stirring and tossing, until the pasta is coated with the sauce. Add the Parmesan and mix well. Season with salt and pepper to taste. Garnish with chopped chives and chive flower petals.

beet and champagne risotto

Roasted beets, with their sweet, more mellow flavor, are the basis of this unusual risotto. The lush pink of the beets and the sparkle of Champagne make it a spirited dish in both flavor and presentation. This is a great use for leftover Champagne (if such a rarity occurs in your house). The beets can be roasted up to 4 days in advance. Serve this jewel-like risotto with a glass of Champagne and a wedge of Parmesan cheese.

SERVES 6

- 6 small red beets, unpeeled, an inch of green stems attached
- 2 large garlic cloves, unpeeled
   Peel from ½ navel orange, cut into 2 pieces
- 1 bay leaf
- ¾ cup plus 2 tablespoons rosé Champagne or sparkling wine
   Kosher salt and freshly ground pepper

- 2 tablespoons (¼ stick) unsalted butter
- 2 tablespoons extra-virgin olive oil
- ½ large onion, finely chopped
- 1½ cups Arborio rice
- 5 to 6 cups chicken or vegetable broth, heated
- 2 tablespoons grated orange zest
- 2 tablespoons freshly grated Parmesan cheese
- ¼ cup finely chopped parsley
- 6 tablespoons caviar, such as osetra or sevruga (optional)

METHOD

Preheat the oven to 400°F.

Wrap the beets, garlic, orange peels, and bay leaf on a large piece of heavy-duty aluminum foil. Roast until the beets are tender when pierced with the tip of a small sharp knife, approximately 1 hour.

Discard the garlic, orange peels, and bay leaf. When cool enough to handle, remove the stems from the beets and slip off the skins with your fingers. Put the beets in the bowl of a food processor fitted with the metal blade and process until smooth. Stir in 2 tablespoons of the Champagne and salt and pepper to taste. Reserve.

To prepare the risotto, in a large saucepan or Dutch oven, heat the butter and olive oil over medium heat and sauté the onion, stirring frequently, until translu-

cent, 3 to 4 minutes. Add the rice, stir to coat with the oil, and cook, stirring, about 1 minute. Add the remaining ¾ cup Champagne and stir until it is absorbed, about 2 minutes.

Add ¾ cup of the broth and cook, stirring, until the liquid is almost completely absorbed. Continue cooking in this way, adding broth ¾ cup at a time, until the rice begins to plump and soften, about 15 minutes. Stir in the beet puree and orange zest. Continue cooking, adding the broth ½ cup at a time, stirring all the while, until the rice is al dente (tender but still slightly firm in the center) and the mixture is creamy, about 10 minutes more.

Stir in the Parmesan, parsley, and salt and pepper to taste. Spoon into shallow bowls and sprinkle with more parsley, orange zest, and the caviar, if desired. Serve immediately.

lobster risotto

Rich? Yes. Indulgent? Positively. Do you deserve it? Most definitely.

SERVES 6

1	3-pound lobster or 2 1½-pound lobsters
6	tablespoons (¾ stick) unsalted butter
2	tablespoons extra-virgin olive oil
6	shallots, finely chopped
2	cups Arborio rice
½	cup brut Champagne or sparkling wine
¾	cup chopped fresh parsley
2	tablespoons chopped fresh tarragon
	Finely grated zest from 1 lemon
1½	tablespoons fresh lemon juice

METHOD

Fill a pot large enough to hold the lobsters with about 8 cups water and bring to a boil. Add the lobsters and when the water returns to a boil, cook 15 minutes for the 3-pound lobster or 12 minutes for the 1½-pound lobsters. Using tongs, remove the lobsters from the water and rinse under cold water. When cool enough to handle, split it down the center of its back. Remove the tail and claw meat and cut it into generous bite-size pieces. Return the shells and any juices to the cooking water, bring to a boil, and reduce the liquid to 6 cups, about 10 minutes. Strain the cooking liquid into a medium saucepan. Cover and keep warm over low heat.

Heat 2 tablespoons of butter and the olive oil in a large saucepan or Dutch oven over medium heat. Add the shallots and cook until soft, about 3 minutes. Add the rice and cook, stirring to coat it with the oil, for 3 minutes. Add the Champagne or sparkling wine and stir until absorbed, about 1 minute.

Slowly add 1 cup of the hot lobster stock. Stir and let simmer, reducing the heat if necessary, until the rice absorbs the stock. Continue in this way, adding stock ½ cup at a time and stirring continuously, until the rice is creamy and al dente, about 20 minutes. Add the lobster meat, parsley, tarragon, lemon zest, lemon juice, and remaining butter. Combine well and serve immediately.

chestnut risotto

Imagine walking through a grove of chestnut trees somewhere in the French countryside in late autumn. These earthy aromas are captured in this chestnut risotto. I usually present it as a first course followed by roasted meat or game. Serve it with a hearty red wine, such as a Burgundy or Côte-du-Rhône.

SERVES 6

¼	cup extra-virgin olive oil
1	large onion, chopped
2	garlic cloves, finely chopped
3	ounces pancetta, coarsely chopped
2	cups Arborio rice
½	cup dry red wine
6	to 7 cups beef broth, preferably low-sodium, heated
24	whole peeled chestnuts, coarsely chopped (see Note)
	Kosher salt and freshly ground pepper
⅓	cup Parmesan cheese, plus more to pass at table
2	tablespoons chopped fresh parsley

METHOD

Heat the oil in a Dutch oven or flameproof casserole over medium heat. Add the onion, garlic, and pancetta and sauté until the onion is soft, about 5 minutes. Add the rice and cook, stirring to coat it with the oil, for another 5 minutes. Add the wine and cook, stirring, 1 minute.

Increase the heat to medium-high. Slowly add 1 cup of the warm broth to the rice. Stir and allow the rice to absorb the broth. When it has absorbed almost all of the broth, add ½ cup more. Continue in this way, stirring frequently, until almost all the stock has been added, about 20 minutes.

Stir in the chopped chestnuts and another ½ cup broth. Cook 3 to 5 minutes, until the risotto is creamy and the rice is cooked but firm to the bite. Season to taste with salt and pepper. Serve immediately, sprinkled with Parmesan cheese and chopped parsley.

Note: You can find canned or vacuum-packed chestnuts at specialty food shops and some supermarkets. If you're using fresh chestnuts, cut an X on their flat side with a sharp knife and roast them in a 425°F. oven for 20 to 25 minutes. Let cool, then peel.

potato and chèvre galette

I have never met a person who does not like potatoes prepared in some fashion. Their versatility and ability to accompany so many different types of foods make potatoes an ideal choice for entertaining. Here, I've assembled them with goat cheese and rosemary in a flat, round cake called a galette. It is a wonderful accompaniment to roasted meats, or you can serve it on its own with a crisp green salad for a luncheon or light supper.

SERVES 6

- ½ cup extra-virgin olive oil
- 1 medium red onion, sliced thinly
- 1 tablespoon fresh rosemary leaves
- 2 garlic cloves, finely chopped
- 6 medium red potatoes, peeled and very thinly sliced (⅛ inch)
- ½ cup heavy cream
- 4 ounces mild goat cheese, such as chèvre
    Kosher salt and freshly ground pepper

METHOD

Preheat the oven to 400°F.

In a medium skillet, heat the olive oil over medium heat. Add the onion, rosemary, and garlic and sauté for 2 minutes. Place the potatoes in a large bowl and add the oil mixture and the heavy cream, tossing gently to mix. Add the goat cheese and toss again. Generously season with salt and pepper. Transfer the potato mixture to a shallow 1½-quart, 9- or 10-inch baking dish. Bake until the potatoes are tender and the top is golden brown, 40 to 45 minutes. Let the galette rest for 10 minutes before serving.

wilted swiss chard with garlic and balsamic vinegar

My Italian aunts sautéed greens all year long, ranging from Swiss chard in the winter to dandelion greens in the spring to spinach in the summer and autumn. Aside from my aunt Zia's belief that the greens would make us wise and alluring (a belief I take as absolute fact), they're just plain delicious.

SERVES 6

- 2 bunches red or green Swiss chard
    Kosher salt
- 2 tablespoons extra-virgin olive oil
- 1 garlic clove, finely chopped
- 1 tablespoon balsamic vinegar
- 1 teaspoon red pepper flakes

METHOD

Trim the Swiss chard and remove the stems. Bring a large pot of water to a boil; add a large pinch of salt. Add the chard to the water and blanch 1 minute. Drain well.

Heat the oil in a large skillet over medium heat. Add the garlic and cook for 1 minute. Add the chard and cook, tossing and stirring, for 3 minutes, until wilted but still green. Stir in the vinegar and red pepper. Season with salt and more red pepper to taste and serve immediately.

green and yellow beans with tarragon

When I was a kid, yellow beans were called wax beans, a name that prevented me from enjoying them until much later in life. (Listening to my mom do her own waxing about the starving children in Bangladesh as the beans sat untouched in front of me didn't help much either.) Having discovered the fresh flavor and beautiful color of these beans as an adult, I am making up for lost time.

SERVES 6

    Kosher salt
 ¾ pound green beans, trimmed
 ¾ pound yellow wax beans, trimmed
 ¼ cup (½ stick) unsalted butter, melted
 1 tablespoon chopped fresh tarragon
    Freshly ground pepper

METHOD

Bring a large saucepan of water to a boil. Add a large pinch of salt along with the beans. Cook until tender but firm, about 5 minutes. Drain. Combine the melted butter and tarragon and pour over the beans, tossing gently to mix. Season with salt and pepper and serve.

sautéed baby artichokes

It may be because I grew up in Connecticut where we rarely, if ever, ate artichokes but to this day, they have a special appeal for me. They have a meaty but clean taste, particularly when they're young, that I can't get enough of. In this dish, the artichokes are cooked in a warm bath of olive oil, which brings out their fresh, green flavor. If you can't find fresh baby artichokes and you positively must have this dish, opt for frozen artichoke hearts.

SERVES 6

 ½ lemon
 18 fresh baby artichokes
 4 tablespoons (½ stick) unsalted butter
 2 tablespoons extra-virgin olive oil
    Juice and zest of 1 lemon
    Kosher salt and freshly ground pepper
 ¼ cup chopped fresh parsley

METHOD

Fill a large bowl with water and squeeze the ½ lemon into the bowl. Trim the artichokes to their pale green leaves by snapping back the darker outer leaves, cut ½ inch off the tops to remove any thorns, and cut off all but ½ inch of the stems. Cut the artichokes lengthwise into thin slices and transfer them to the acidulated water to prevent them from discoloring.

In a large sauté pan, heat the butter and olive oil over medium-high heat. Drain the artichokes and add them to the pan, along with the lemon juice and zest and salt and pepper, and sauté until the artichokes are tender, about 5 minutes. Add the parsley, toss to mix, and serve immediately.

coconut macaroons

Coconut macaroons are the bonbons of the cookie world and I adore them. These macaroons have soft centers and they're nicely sweet. I like to serve them with fresh fruit or sorbets, which they complement to a T. I wrap the extras in cellophane with pink ribbons (bonbons call for pink) to send home with my guests.

MAKES ABOUT 24

- 1 tablespoon melted butter
- 3 large egg whites
  Pinch of salt
- 1½ teaspoons vanilla extract
- 1 cup sugar
- 1⅔ cups sweetened shredded coconut

METHOD

Preheat the oven to 325°F. Line 2 baking sheets with parchment paper and lightly brush the parchment with melted butter.

Put the egg whites and salt in the bowl of an electric mixer. Beginning on low speed, beat the egg whites until foamy. Add the vanilla, then increase the speed to medium and continue to beat until soft peaks form. Sprinkle 4 tablespoons of the sugar over the egg whites. Increase the speed to high and beat until stiff peaks form.

In a small bowl, combine the remaining ¾ cup of sugar and the coconut. With a rubber spatula, fold the coconut mixture into the egg whites. Using a tablespoon, drop the batter onto the prepared baking sheets. Bake until golden, 15 to 18 minutes. Cool on wire racks for at least 1 hour. Store in airtight tins until ready to serve.

ice cream snowballs with peppermint chocolate sauce

My sister-in-law, Stacy, introduced me to this concept a few years ago, when it was her assignment to bring a dessert to our Christmas Eve dinner. Ever the child in adult's clothing, Stacy—and her dessert—charmed everybody (and you will, too).

SERVES 6

- 2 pints best-quality vanilla ice cream
- 3 cups shredded sweetened coconut
- 1 cup finely crushed peppermint candies
- 4 ounces semisweet chocolate
- ¼ cup (½ stick) unsalted butter
- 1 teaspoon peppermint extract
- ¾ cup half-and-half

METHOD

Scoop the ice cream into 6 snowballs about 3 inches in diameter and freeze for at least 20 minutes. On a large plate or in a large shallow bowl, combine the coconut and crushed peppermint candies. Roll the snowballs in the mixture, pressing it firmly onto the surface, and return to the freezer until ready to serve.

In a double boiler set over simmering water, melt the chocolate with the butter. Add the peppermint extract and half-and-half and stir to combine.

To serve, spoon some of the peppermint chocolate sauce onto each of 6 plates or serve it in a cup alongside. Arrange the snowballs on or around the sauce.

Since the ice cream snowballs are so pretty on their own, I like to serve the peppermint chocolate sauce separately and let guests drizzle—or pour—as they see fit.

melon mélange with blackberry sauce

The candylike sweetness, soft hues, and musky scent of melon lead me to serve it frequently during the warmer months. Set off by the tart zing and deep purple of blackberries, this simple mélange will reawaken the taste buds at the end of a satisfying meal. I like to serve this in large glass compotes so my guests can enjoy the pure beauty of the fruit as much as its taste.

SERVES 6

$\frac{1}{3}$ cup crème de cassis
$\frac{1}{4}$ cup sugar, or more to taste
2 cups fresh blackberries
$\frac{1}{4}$ teaspoon finely grated lime zest
An assortment of fresh melon, such as:
1 small cantaloupe, halved and seeded
1 small honeydew, halved and seeded
$\frac{1}{4}$ casaba or crenshaw melon, seeded
Fresh mint sprigs or lime zests

METHOD

In a small bowl, combine the crème de cassis and sugar, stirring to dissolve the sugar. Add the blackberries and lime zest and stir gently to combine.

Using a melon baller, cut the flesh of all 3 melons into balls and combine.

Spoon the fruit into goblets or compotes. Spoon some of the blackberry sauce over each serving and decorate with the mint sprigs or zests.

I used ice cream scoops in various sizes to create an assortment of melon balls and juxtaposed them with triangular "shards" for drama.

secret ingredient chocolate cake

This dense, flourless chocolate cake is doubly rich in flavor due to the addition of a secret ingredient—framboise (raspberry liqueur). Serve the cake with fresh raspberries and small glasses of framboise for a hint of what's inside.

SERVES 8

$\frac{3}{4}$ cup ($1\frac{1}{2}$ sticks) unsalted butter, cut into pieces
$\frac{3}{4}$ cup granulated sugar
10 ounces bittersweet chocolate, chopped
1 tablespoon framboise (raspberry liqueur)
1 teaspoon vanilla extract
4 large eggs plus 1 egg yolk
$\frac{1}{4}$ cup confectioners' sugar
Fresh whole raspberries, for garnish

METHOD

Preheat the oven to 375°F. Butter a 9-inch springform pan.

In a medium saucepan, melt the butter with $\frac{1}{4}$ cup of the granulated sugar over low heat, stirring to dissolve. Add the chocolate and stir until melted. Remove from the heat and stir in the framboise and vanilla.

In a large bowl, beat the eggs and egg yolk with the remaining $\frac{1}{2}$ cup of granulated sugar until pale yellow, fluffy, and tripled in volume, 5 to 6 minutes. Using a rubber spatula, gently fold about $\frac{1}{2}$ cup of the chocolate mixture into the eggs. Pour the remaining chocolate mixture over the eggs and fold in gently with a rubber spatula. Pour the batter into the prepared pan.

Bake until a crust forms on the top and the cake puffs slightly yet is not completely cooked in the center (a skewer inserted in the center will come out coated with some chunks of batter), about 30 to 35 minutes. Transfer to a rack. Run a small knife around the edges of the cake to loosen them. The center of the cake will fall; you can even it out by pressing down lightly around the edges. Cool. The cake may remain in the pan overnight, if you wish.

Release the pan from the sides and remove them. Sift confectioners' sugar over the cake. Serve garnished with raspberries.

fruit in phyllo nests

The recipe upon which this dessert is based was given to me by a friend who had the pleasure of visiting the Golden Door spa, where this lovely and light dessert is a part of the pampering regimen. I will admit that when I made it the first time, it lacked a certain something and the adage "Fat is the channel of flavor" came to mind. Not surprisingly, a bit of butter did the trick.

SERVES 6

- ¼ cup golden brown sugar
- 2 tablespoons kirsch
- 2 Granny Smith apples, peeled, cored, and diced in ½-inch pieces
- 1 Bosc or d'Anjou pear, peeled, cored, and diced in ½-inch pieces
- ⅓ cup dried cherries
- 1 teaspoon lemon juice
  Pinch each of cinnamon, allspice, and nutmeg
- 4 sheets of phyllo dough
- ½ cup (1 stick) unsalted butter, melted
- ¼ cup hazelnuts
- 1 tablespoon confectioners' sugar
  Best-quality vanilla ice cream, for serving with baskets

METHOD

Preheat the oven to 400° F.

In a small nonreactive saucepan, combine 2 table-spoons of the brown sugar with 1 tablespoon kirsch; cook over medium heat until the sugar melts. Add the apples and bring to a boil, then reduce the heat, cover, and simmer, stirring occasionally, until tender, 8 to 10 minutes. Using a slotted spoon, transfer the apples to a bowl.

Add the remaining 2 tablespoons of brown sugar and 1 tablespoon kirsch to the saucepan and melt over medium heat. Add the pear, bring to a boil, then lower the heat, cover, and simmer, stirring occasionally, until tender, 3 to 5 minutes. Using a slotted spoon, transfer the pear to the bowl with the apples, reserving the cooking liquid. Add the dried cherries and toss to mix.

Increase the heat under the cooking liquid to high, bring to a boil, and reduce until the mixture thickens and becomes syrupy, 3 to 5 minutes. Remove from the heat and stir in the lemon juice and spices. Add to the fruit, toss gently to mix, and set aside.

Spread 1 sheet of phyllo out on a flat surface and brush lightly with the melted butter. (Keep the remaining phyllo sheets covered with a damp towel as you work.) Top with a second sheet of phyllo.

Using a sharp knife, cut the phyllo into four 5-inch squares. Gently fit the squares into four 2½-inch muffin cups, leaving a 1-inch pastry border. Repeat with the remaining 2 sheets of phyllo, cutting two 5-inch squares. Wrap the remaining phyllo dough in plastic and reserve for another use.

Bake the phyllo nests until crisp and golden brown, 5 to 7 minutes. Cool the nests in the pan for 10 minutes, then remove to a rack to finish cooling.

Reduce the oven temperature to 350° F. Spread the hazelnuts on a baking sheet and toast in the oven until lightly browned, 3 to 5 minutes. Let cool, then chop coarsely. (If the hazelnuts have skins, immediately upon removing them from the oven, place them in a tea towel and rub them vigorously to remove the skins.)

To serve, arrange the phyllo nests on individual plates. Divide the fruit mixture among the nests and sprinkle with the hazelnuts. Dust with confectioners' sugar and top with a small scoop of vanilla ice cream.

style note

AFTER DINNER

We're so programmed to regard dessert as a wedge or a slice or a scoop of something sweet. Why not usurp the usual and serve something unexpected? Why not switch the venue and serve dessert away from the table? Once you've been sitting in hard-backed dining chairs, enjoying dessert while sitting in an upholstered club chair is heaven.

Along with coffee and tea, offer cordials and digestifs. Port, brandy, and Madeira are classic offerings, grappa and eau-de-vie provide a continental touch, or try an unfamiliar offering such as Cynar, an Italian liqueur known as a digestivo made from artichokes, or vin Santo, an Italian sweet wine.

Round out the after-dinner menu with candied citrus peel, a bowl of hazelnuts, and gourmet chocolates. A perfectly ripe cheese such as a Stilton would be a nice touch, too.

PART!ES

parties

are the pinnacle of entertaining. Planned and executed with aplomb and style, parties result in fun, festivity, and fond memories for both the host and the guests.

Fear not! You *can* give a spectacular party without losing your sanity. The number one guideline is to plan ahead. If you organize the event, breaking it down into manageable categories such as guest list, invitations, food and beverages, and decorations, and make "to do" lists for each category, you will be golden.

If I begin planning far enough out, I truly enjoy the process and I'm more creative since I'm not feeling stressed by time or obligation. I usually begin planning a party a few months ahead of time. I think about the type of occasion it will be (a holiday, a birthday party, a commemoration of a milestone such as an anniversary). Next I come up with a theme that links all the elements, from the invitations to the food to the decorations.

In this chapter, you will find ideas and guidelines for different types of parties, ranging from Cocktails and Hors d'Oeuvres and an In the Pink ladies luncheon to Thanksgiving at Home and a Holiday Open House.

A TOAST

As the host of the party, you're producer, director, and star all in one. With a bit of planning, you can give a party that will be talked about for years to come. Just don't forget to let yourself enjoy it, too. A host's laughter and goodwill are contagious.

Each of the party sections includes information that is relevant to that specific type of party, along with recipes for food and beverages and decoration ideas.

Regardless of the type of party you're giving, be sure to give attention to *how* you invite your guests and how you accommodate them (and yourself) once they're in your home. Here are my suggestions on both these topics.

THE PLEASURE OF YOUR COMPANY: INVITATIONS

I love the happy surprise of finding a heavy envelope among my bills and supermarket circulars. I hang party invitations on my refrigerator door or my office bulletin board so I can enjoy the rush of anticipation when the invitation catches my eye during the course of a regular day.

Invitations should carry a sense of occasion. To ensure that your invitees will be able to attend, give them time to reserve the party date on their calendars. Send invitations three to four weeks in advance of the party and include an RSVP so you can calculate food and beverage quantities and plan seating.

Let the invitation reflect the personality of the event. Ready-made cards run the gamut from whimsical to elegant and are readily available in stationery stores. All you have to do is fill in the blanks (use an evocative ink color).

If you have the time and inclination, work with a stationer or printer to design your own invitation. Choose the paper, typeface, and graphic images that please you. Stationers have a selection of images or you can bring your own. (If you go this route, begin at least twelve weeks before the party.)

If you have a creative bent, make your own invitations. I often splurge on great paper and use rubber stamps to create invitations. Find old postcards or glue heavy paper to the back of photographs. Fill small boxes with excelsior and insert the invitation along with an icon of the party (sunglasses for a pool party; a disposable camera for a once-in-a-lifetime occasion such as a graduation; a clock or watch for a birthday party).

HELP!

Giving a party is a lot of work, but there are numerous routes you can take to share the burden. Caterers can be lifesavers. They lighten the workload, contribute creativity and professionalism, and enable you to relax and enjoy your own party. If you're going this route, select a caterer based on your firsthand experience with her as a guest at a party or by word-of-mouth recommendation from someone you trust. Along with the requisite budget parameters, have a clear picture in your mind about the type of party you want to give. Even though you're hiring someone to cook and serve, you are still the host of the party and it should reflect your taste and personality. The best caterers ask a lot of questions (as should you), offer ideas, and blend their style with yours.

When I entertain, I love the planning and cooking; it's the cleanup I abhor. For a larger dinner party (8 to 12 people), it's nice to have someone who can help plate the food, serve and clear, and clean the kitchen. For cocktail parties, one or two people to help serve, along with a bartender to mix and serve drinks, saves time and angst.

I have often found inexpensive, enthusiastic help by calling cooking schools in my area or the employment offices at local high schools or colleges. Over the phone, I review with the students their specific duties, length of the party, what they ought to wear, and what I'll pay (by the hour is best). I ask them to come to my home the day before the party so they can familiarize themselves with my kitchen and I walk them through what will be expected of them. This saves a lot of time and confusion during the party and lets everybody relax.

Here's the party-giving mantra: Have fun!

cocktails

cocktails and hors d'oeuvres

No party is more quintessentially American than the cocktail party. There is something inherently elegant about these events, and something reckless, too. Each time I plan a cocktail party, I am swept back to the 1920s, to the north shore of Long Island, to the dock with the green light, to . . . you know where I'm going with this.

I was once invited to a cocktail party where the menu featured nothing but Champagne, caviar, and sugared fruit. The dress was black tie (men and women). Talk about reckless. But talk about elegance, too.

Therein lies the beauty of the cocktail party. It can be as lavish or as spare as you wish it to be. Simply be sure you have enough drinks and hors d'oeuvres, a witty guest or two to keep things interesting, and the rest will work itself out.

The cocktail party traditionally lasts two to three hours. It usually begins at 6:00 P.M., though 4:00 P.M. or 5:00 P.M. on weekends is not unheard of. On your invitation,

you may specify an ending time for the party, which signals that your guests should make their own arrangements for dinner. If you exist in a world of capriciousness and abandon, simply list the time of the party and see what develops. In such a case, you'll want to plan for extra hors d'oeuvres.

In this chapter, I have given you a selection of hors d'oeuvres that you can mix at will. They're wonderful when served en masse, but they'll perform equally well if you select one or two and combine them with some of your own favorite hors d'oeuvre recipes.

The trick is to compose an hors d'oeuvre selection that offers a variety of flavors, colors, and textures. It's nice to offer hot and cold hors d'oeuvres, to combine crunchy items like Cheese Straws with creamy items like Green Olivada, and to juxtapose the elegant (caviar) with the earthy (Roasted Olives).

Along with passed hors d'oeuvres, it's nice to arrange stationary offerings around the party such as bowls of macadamia nuts, Spiced Pumpkin Seeds (page 199), and Baked Potato Crisps, or small arrangements of crudités and dips (plan the crudité by color for a dramatic effect: red and white vegetables and a bright green herb dip, for example).

For a two-hour cocktail party, figure 6 to 8 different hors d'oeuvres, 3 of each hors d'oeuvre per guest.

Consider hors d'oeuvres jewels that need the proper showcase. They're as much about aesthetic impression as they are about taste. I like to present them in unexpected ways, some on trays lined with interesting coverings, some skewered and set in a bowl of black and white beans or emerging from a head of red cabbage, a few presented on crystal pedestal cake stands. Prepare duplicates of each tray so you can quickly substitute a full tray when the first one is empty.

Depending upon the number of guests you are hosting and particularly if you are passing hors d'oeuvres, you may want to consider hiring serving help. This will maintain the flow and energy of the party.

As for the bar, it can be simply stocked with wine and beer or elaborately stocked with hard liquors, mixers, and aperitifs. If the occasion warrants, you may consider offering a standard bar along with a specialty bar that offers martinis, margaritas, or classic cocktails such as Manhattans, old-fashioneds, and highballs.

Smaller cocktail parties can function well with a self-service bar but for larger gatherings (more than twenty guests), you may want to consider help with bar service. You can staff a liquor bar with a bartender who mixes drinks for guests and establish a self-service wine and beer bar in another area of the party. Or guests can help themselves to mixed drinks and you can pass wine, beer, and/or Champagne on trays.

Giving a great cocktail party is a balance between organization and instinct. Assemble a few great hors d'oeuvres, make sure everybody has a drink in hand, introduce guests to one another, and before you know it, the party will take on a rhythm of its own.

In a large bowl, combine the peanut oil, ginger, and lemon zest. Add the shrimp, cover with plastic wrap, and marinate in the refrigerator for 2 hours.

Prepare a fire in the grill or preheat the broiler. Meanwhile, trim the lemongrass by peeling off any dried, brownish leaves and soak the stalks in cold water for 15 minutes. Thread each shrimp on a lemongrass stalk and grill until pink, 2 to 3 minutes, depending upon their thickness.

Note: Lemongrass is available at Asian groceries and many supermarkets.

cheese straws

Not one but three kinds of cheese give these cocktail tidbits more varied flavors and add an element of surprise. If I had room in my freezer, I would make millions of these and serve them every time I had guests in my home. These are definite crowd pleasers.

MAKES 60

- ½ pound prepared puff pastry, thawed
- 2 tablespoons grated Gruyère cheese
  Cayenne
- 2 tablespoons grated Cheddar cheese
- 1 tablespoon grated Parmesan cheese
- 1 tablespoon very finely chopped prosciutto (optional)

METHOD

Line 2 baking sheets with parchment.

Divide the pastry into 3 equal portions. Roll out one portion to a rectangle ⅛ inch thick and 10 inches in length. Sprinkle the Gruyère evenly over the surface and dust very lightly with the cayenne. Use the palms of your hand or a rolling pin to firmly press the cheese into the dough. Cut the dough into ½-inch-wide strips, twist them, and arrange them on the baking sheet. Continue with the remaining pastry, sprinkling Cheddar cheese on one batch and Parmesan and prosciutto, if using, on the other. Chill for at least 30 minutes before baking.

Preheat the oven to 400°F. Bake the straws until puffed and golden brown, 8 to 10 minutes. Cool and serve.

ginger shrimp on lemongrass skewers

Shrimp is always a popular hors d'oeuvre and these shrimp, with their aromatic Asian flavors, will undoubtedly have many takers. I like the notion of lemongrass, a lemony herb that has a tall woody stalk, with these shrimp, but I didn't want to use it in the recipe so I hit upon the idea of using the woody lemongrass stalks as skewers. They reinforce the Asian theme and make a dramatic presentation.

MAKES 24 SKEWERS

- ½ cup peanut oil
- 3 tablespoons chopped fresh ginger
- 1 teaspoon grated lemon zest
- 24 jumbo shrimp, peeled and deveined
- 12 tall lemongrass stalks, halved lengthwise (see Note)

baked potato crisps

I sometimes vary these by adding spices such as cayenne or cumin or by using sweet potatoes or parsnips. You'll need to make these in batches, but once you slice the potatoes, it's a snap. Beware—these will disappear very fast! If you have a bit more time, do consider the herb-filled variation that follows.

SERVES 12

6 tablespoons peanut oil
8 baking potatoes, unpeeled
    Kosher salt and freshly ground pepper
    Cayenne (optional)

METHOD

Preheat the oven to 400°F. Lightly brush 2 nonstick baking sheets with some of the oil.

Using a mandoline or food processor, cut the potatoes into $\frac{1}{16}$-inch slices. Pour the oil into a large bowl, add the potatoes, and toss to coat with the oil. Season with salt and pepper.

Arrange the potato slices on the baking sheets in a single layer and bake, turning once, until crisp and golden brown, about 15 minutes.

Remove from the oven and transfer to paper towels to drain. Adjust the seasoning, adding a dusting of cayenne if desired. Serve immediately or store in airtight tins. Repeat the process with any remaining potatoes.

A LOVELY VARIATION

After tossing the potato slices in the peanut oil, pair together slices of similar shape and size. Press a fresh parsley or sage leaf onto one of the slices and top with the other, pressing together the edges. Transfer to the baking sheet, placing a baking stone or an ovenproof dish on the slices to flatten them. Bake 7 minutes, remove the baking sheet, turn the chips over, and return to the oven until crisp and golden, 7 to 8 minutes more.

Vodka is a perfect foil for caviar's assertive flavor—serve it very cold. Horn or mother-of-pearl spoons showcase caviar's flavor best but stainless or silver will do in a pinch.

PRIMER

Caviar

Ca-vi-ar. Three syllables that are synonymous with three other syllables, lux-u-ry. Caviar is extravagant—and expensive—but fortunately, a little bit goes a long way (though I have always wanted to have a party where I served gobs of the stuff).

Genuine caviar is made from the roe of the sturgeon. Other fish roe is sometimes marketed as caviar and some is quite good, but it's not truly caviar.

If you're taking a no-holds-barred attitude and going for the real thing, you'll find that caviar is available in three grades:

Beluga. The rarest and the most expensive, these are the crown jewels of the caviar family. The roe are large and the mildest-flavored. Beluga is a beautiful pearl-gray color.

Osetra. Also large-grained with a more intense flavor; its color ranges from ocher to gray-white.

Sevruga. This grade is small-pearled with an intense flavor. Its color ranges from a dark gray to dark black.

Caviar is *extremely* perishable. Purchase it from a purveyor whom you know has rapid turnover and if possible, serve it the same day you purchase it. In the unlikely event that you have leftovers, use them within a day or two, stirred into scrambled eggs (see page 106) or sprinkled on top of a vegetable puree.

When serving caviar, less is most definitely more. Skip the chopped egg, onion, and capers and serve it with nothing more than toast points with sweet butter and a glass of iced vodka or cold Champagne. *C'est magnifique*!

roasted olives

The heat of the oven awakens the briny richness of olives. I like to combine different varieties of olives, both green and black, because their distinct characteristics come forth when they're sampled together.

MAKES 4 CUPS

4 cups black and green olives of your choice
   Zest from 1 large orange
   Zest from ½ lemon
   Chopped leaves from 1 large rosemary sprig
2 tablespoons extra-virgin olive oil
   Rosemary sprigs for garnish

METHOD

Preheat the oven to 250°F.

Place the olives in an ovenproof bowl. Add the orange and lemon zest, rosemary, and oil; stir gently to combine.

Place in the oven until warmed through, stirring occasionally, about 15 minutes. Serve warm, garnished with the rosemary sprigs.

PRIMER

How to Assemble a Cocktail-Hour Olive Tasting

Bowls of black, green, and purple olives from Italy, France, Morocco, and California assembled together on a tray or placed on tables singly or in groups are a simple and earthy way to complement drinks. The diverse varieties of olives do differ in flavor and make for interesting conversation—not to mention eating. For fun, write the names of the olive varieties on plastic garden markers and stick them in the bowls.

Olives are readily available at gourmet shops as well as shops specializing in Italian, Middle Eastern, Spanish, and French foods. Many supermarkets carry an array of bottled and "fresh" olives. Let your whim guide you when choosing olives (taste lots!) and strive for a diversity of color, texture, and flavors. Toss in herbs or garlic or citrus zest for zing.

Here are a few of my favorite pairings:

• Niçoise, Kalamata, picholine, Calabrese, and California dry-cured

• Lugano, Gaeta, cracked Provençal, Moroccan oil-cured, spicy Sicilian

• Italian Bella de Cerignola—all by themselves

Don't forget to place small plates or bowls near the olives for pits and before your guests arrive, eat an olive or two and place pits on the plates as an example for your guests to follow. It's no fun to find those pesky pits strewn about the morning after.

If you want to expand the olive tasting to include other bites, think Mediterranean and add bowls of almonds, cherry tomatoes, dried figs, and raisins, especially the big plump Malaga variety, if you can find them.

green olivada on potato rounds

This green olive paste is a departure from the usual black tapenade. Its flavor is greener, too, and by that I mean it's a bit more bitter and briny, and so good when served on sweet Yukon Gold potatoes or even winter squash. It's fun to vary the potato varieties, too. Try purple potatoes or the yellow fingerlings. If you don't want to spend the time creating these hors d'oeuvres, use the olivada as a dip, thinned a bit with olive oil, and serve it with cherry tomatoes or grilled bread. Hors d'oeuvres aside, the olivada is also a great relish for grilled swordfish or tuna. The recipe makes 2 cups of olivada.

MAKES 36 CANAPÉS

3 pounds small yellow Finn or Yukon Gold potatoes, peeled
2 cups pitted green olives, such as Sicilian or picholine
3 tablespoons capers, rinsed and drained
2 garlic cloves
  Freshly ground pepper
6 tablespoons extra-virgin olive oil
2 teaspoons grated lemon zest
  Strips of lemon zest, for garnish

METHOD

Put the potatoes in a large saucepan with salted water to cover. Bring to a boil and cook, uncovered, until just tender when pierced with a fork, 12 to 15 minutes. Drain well and set aside to cool.

Put the olives and capers in a food processor. Pass the garlic cloves through a garlic press onto the olives and capers. Add a generous pinch of pepper. With the motor running, slowly pour the oil through the feed tube and process until smooth. Transfer to a bowl, stir in the grated lemon zest, and adjust the seasoning.

To serve, slice the potatoes into $\frac{1}{8}$-inch slices and spread each slice with some of the olivada. Top with the strips of lemon zest.

wild mushrooms in phyllo bundles

Delicate phyllo dough is transformed into a richly crisp envelope for the warm and savory wild mushroom filling. You can assemble these ahead of time, as long as you keep them covered with a damp cloth or even freeze them. Bake them just before serving.

MAKES 24 BUNDLES

2 pounds fresh wild mushrooms such as shiitakes, chanterelles, or morels
6 tablespoons ($\frac{3}{4}$ stick) unsalted butter
2 tablespoons extra-virgin olive oil
3 shallots, finely chopped
$\frac{1}{2}$ cup Madeira wine
$\frac{1}{2}$ cup heavy cream
6 tablespoons minced fresh parsley
2 tablespoons fresh thyme leaves
  Kosher salt and freshly ground pepper
12 sheets of phyllo dough
6 tablespoons ($\frac{3}{4}$ stick) unsalted butter, melted

METHOD

Cut the mushrooms into $\frac{1}{4}$-inch slices. In a large skillet, melt the butter with the olive oil over medium-high heat. When the butter's foam subsides, add the shallots and sauté for 2 minutes. Add the mushrooms and sauté for 5 minutes. Add the Madeira and cook, stirring, for 30 seconds. Add the cream and cook until the liquid reduces and thickens. Stir in the herbs and season to taste with salt and pepper. Set aside to cool.

Preheat the oven to 400°F. Line 2 baking sheets with parchment.

Spread out 1 sheet of phyllo dough on a work surface and keep the remaining sheets covered with a damp tea towel. Brush the phyllo sheet lightly with the melted butter. Lay another sheet on top of the first and brush with more butter. Repeat with a third sheet. Using a sharp knife, cut the phyllo into six 5-inch squares. Place about 2 to 3 tablespoons of the mushroom mixture into the center of each phyllo square. Draw up the corners of the phyllo and pinch together to make a bundle, leaving the top open a bit. Repeat with the remaining phyllo and mushrooms to make a total of 24 bundles.

Place the bundles on the baking sheets and bake until golden brown, about 12 minutes. Serve immediately.

blue cheese and cider spread

This simple and hearty spread is served in small tapas bars in northern Spain, accompanied by red wine or hard cider. It's a smooth take on the classic blue cheese and green apples pairing. In fact, I serve it on green apple slices as an hors d'oeuvre.

MAKES 20 TO 30 HORS D'OEUVRES

1 pound Spanish blue cheese (cabrales) or other good-quality crumbly blue cheese, such as Maytag blue
1½ to 2 tablespoons apple cider (preferably hard cider, which has a deeper flavor)
Juice from ½ lemon
2 to 3 tart green apples, such as Granny Smith

METHOD

Crumble the blue cheese into a medium bowl. Using a fork to mix and mash, add the cider and stir until a spreadable paste forms.

Just before serving, fill a large bowl with water and add the lemon juice. Halve and core the unpeeled apples, then cut each half into 8 to 10 thin slices, dropping the slices into the acidulated water as you do so to prevent them from discoloring.

To assemble the hors d'oeuvres, drain the apple slices and pat them dry with paper towels. Spread some of the cheese mixture on each apple slice and serve immediately.

the oyster bar

The rule of eating oysters only in months ending with *r* has fallen by the wayside as most oysters are now farm-raised. Named for the bays from which they come (Fanny Bay, Hog Island, Malpeque, and Wellfleet, to name a few), oysters make a fun and fancy addition to a cocktail party. Count on serving 3 per person. You can intersperse cooked shrimp with the oysters for color and variety.

METHOD

To assemble an oyster raw bar:

Find large trays (at least 2 inches deep), galvanized tubs, or wicker baskets (line these with plastic) and fill to the brim with chopped ice.

Cover the ice with seaweed (get it from your fishmonger) or herbs, such as rosemary, chives, parsley, and dill.

Shuck the oysters to the half shell. You can do this yourself (see sidebar at right) but it's a ton of work, so in the spirit of real-life entertaining, I would ask the fishmonger to shuck them just before you arrive to pick them up. Keep the oysters on ice, covered with seaweed or moist paper towels, while you transport them home.

Arrange the oysters in the half shell on the ice and garnish with lime and lemon wedges. Leave room to tuck in a few bottles of Champagne, white wine, or stout, too.

Around the oyster bar arrange bowls of black pepper, bottles of Tabasco sauce, Champagne Mignonette Sauce, Cocktail Sauce, and Tomatillo Sauce (recipes follow).

PRIMER

How to Serve Fresh Oysters

The number one rule about storing oysters (and shellfish in general) is never, never store them directly on ice or in water. Plastic wrap and plastic bags are not a good idea either because live oysters require oxygen.

Instead, put oysters in a dish and cover them with moist paper towels or tea towels (or seaweed, if you can get it). Refrigerate.

Oysters naturally open and close their shells, so store them deep shell down so they don't lose their liquor. Stored this way, oysters will last 3 to 5 days.

Do not attempt to open oysters with a sharp paring knife. A shucking knife, available at cookware stores and some fishmongers, makes the task of freeing oysters from their shells much easier.

According to some oyster farmers I know, a good ol' pair of pliers (a real-life tool if ever there was one) ups the easy quotient yet another notch. Hold the oyster in the palm of your hand on a tea towel with the deep shell on the bottom. With the pliers, snap off a piece of the front edge. Insert the tip of the shucking knife or a table knife into the opening and cut around both sides to release the oyster from the top shell. Cut underneath the oyster to free it from the bottom shell, being careful to keep as much of the liquid as possible.

For traditionalists, insert the tip of the blade near the hinge, twisting gently until you can work the knife under and around the shell as above.

champagne mignonette sauce

Mignonette is a classic French vinegar-based sauce that is traditionally served with oysters. I have gussied it up a bit with the addition of Champagne vinegar and lemon zest.

MAKES 1 CUP

- 3/4 cup Champagne vinegar
- 6 tablespoons finely chopped shallots
- 2 teaspoons finely grated lemon zest
- 2 teaspoons freshly ground white pepper
- 3/4 teaspoon salt

METHOD

In a small bowl, stir together all ingredients. Cover and chill until ready to serve.

cocktail sauce

When I was a kid, I'd spy on my parents' cocktail parties, then scoop the leftover cocktail sauce it into my mouth with Ritz crackers. Now I do this after cocktail parties in my own home, often with a girlfriend (and a bit of party gossip) as my partner in crime.

MAKES 1 CUP

- 1 cup ketchup
- 2 tablespoons prepared horseradish
- 1/2 teaspoon minced jalapeño pepper, or more to taste
- 2 teaspoons Worcestershire sauce
- 1 tablespoon fresh lime juice
  Kosher salt and freshly ground pepper

METHOD

In a small bowl, stir together all the ingredients, seasoning with salt and pepper to taste. Cover and chill until ready to serve.

tomatillo sauce

MAKES 1 CUP

- 1/2 pound tomatillos, papery husks removed
- 3 garlic cloves, unpeeled
- 1 tablespoon extra-virgin olive oil
- 2 medium green chilies, seeds removed
- 2 tablespoons finely chopped cilantro
- 1 tablespoon lime juice
  Kosher salt

METHOD

Preheat the oven to 400°F. Place the tomatillos and 2 of the garlic cloves in a baking dish and roast, uncovered, for 20 minutes. Peel the remaining garlic clove; reserve. In a medium skillet, warm the olive oil over medium heat. Add the chilies and cook until soft; do not brown.

  Remove the skin from the roasted garlic cloves and put in the bowl of a food processor with the raw garlic and tomatillos and puree until smooth, then stir in the cilantro and lime juice. Add salt to taste and the sautéed chilies and process again, adding water if needed to form a very thick sauce. Transfer to a bowl, cover and chill until ready to serve.

champagne cocktail

A Champagne cocktail is a fancy-dress version of the plain bubbly.

SERVES 1

1 sugar cube
1 splash of brandy
1 splash of Angostura bitters
Champagne or sparkling wine, brut

METHOD

Put the sugar cube in a Champagne flute. Add the brandy and bitters, then fill with Champagne.

vodka gimlet

At every party there is always one guest who commands attention simply by striking a cool, I-don't-give-a-damn pose. Surely, she'd be drinking a gimlet.

SERVES 1

1½ ounces vodka
½ ounce Rose's lime juice

METHOD

Combine the vodka and lime juice in a shaker with ice. Shake to mix, then strain into a chilled cocktail glass.

red paisley

Wearing this pattern is not mandatory when sipping this drink—but just think of the effect.

SERVES 1

3 ounces Campari or San Pellegrino non-alcoholic bitters
2 ounces pink grapefruit juice
½ ounce lime juice
Twist of lime

METHOD

Combine the Campari, grapefruit juice, and lime juice in a shaker or jar and shake with ice. Strain over ice into a squat 8-ounce glass and garnish with the lime twist.

kir

Substitute Champagne for the white wine and this becomes a Kir Royale. It's a festive drink that I like to serve at birthday parties and during the holidays, though it lends a nice touch to any cocktail party. When your guests ask for white wine, tell them you want to give them something special and hand them a Kir.

SERVES 1

1½ teaspoons (¼ ounce) cassis liqueur
¼ to ⅓ cup (4 to 6 ounces) chilled white wine (depending upon the size of the glass)
Twist of lemon

METHOD

Pour the cassis into a wineglass, then fill with white wine. Garnish with the lemon twist.

PRIMER

Cheers!

One bottle of wine = six 4-ounce glasses or four 6-ounce glasses

One bottle of Champagne = 6 flutes

One liter of hard liquor = twenty-two 1½-ounce drinks

One case of wine = 12 bottles

One case of beer = 24 bottles

Calculation:

For a 2-hour cocktail party:

Hard liquor: 1 liter bottle for every 10 drinkers

Wine: 1 bottle for every 2 guests who drink wine

Champagne: 1 bottle for every 2 guests who drink Champagne

Beer: 2 to 3 bottles for every guest who drinks beer

But you know your crowd best. Some regions of the country drink more wine than others; some regions drink more hard liquor. It's better to err on the generous side. Most liquor stores will accept unopened bottles of liquor for return, but ask before you purchase.

style note

TRAY CHIC

The trays on which you serve hors d'oeuvres are as much a part of the presentation as the hors d'oeuvres themselves.

- As much as you think about the presentation of the full tray, consider the half-empty tray. Freshness is the mantra here. Don't serve foods with high fat contents such as pastry or cheeses on absorbent surfaces like paper doilies. When the hors d'oeuvre is lifted off, a grease stain will remain. Opt for lemon leaves (get them from your florist) or cabbage or kale leaves.

- Oddly shaped foods such as cherry tomatoes or new potatoes need nests to keep them from toppling. Nestle them in curly parsley or long shreds of daikon radish or carrot (use a manual spiral shredder for this; it's available at kitchenware stores) gathered into "nests."

- Blanch leek greens and weave them into a covering for a tray.

- Wicker, rattan, and seagrass are naturally beautiful. Arrange hors d'oeuvres on these materials in a way that lets their texture show through; i.e., don't crowd them.

- Natural fibers such as raw linen provide softness and richness as a base for toast or pastry hors d'oeuvres.

- Place one glossy green banana leaf on a white platter.

- Pedestal cake stands make interesting serving trays, as do copper plant trays.

- Transform an antique gameboard into a whimsical tray.

- Line trays with rice, dried beans, or a mix of whole spices such as pink peppercorns, allspice, and star anise.

- Scatter rose petals on silver trays.

- Stud skewers in a bowl of Arborio rice or dried black beans, in the top of a pineapple, or around a beautiful head of whole cabbage.

- Set one exotic flower such as a ginger bloom on a tray for dramatic effect.

- Serve dips in natural containers: pineapple, squash, or radicchio cups.

saturday

saturday breakfast with friends

I like to get up early in the morning because the day lasts longer that way. Usually, I am rushing to get out but when it comes to weekend entertaining, a home-made breakfast shared with a few friends is the best reason to stay in (and I can skip the gym).

I prefer breakfast to brunch. The menu is simpler and the atmosphere is more casual. Breakfast is about home-made doughnuts—the ultimate indulgence—and a mug, not a china cup, of steaming coffee. It's about sharing the newspaper with friends as you share the gossip.

I serve this menu as a whole or in parts. If you opt to serve the entire menu, begin with the grapefruit as a first course. It's best served at room temperature and can be made the night before. Everything on this menu can be prepared ahead of time except the shirred eggs, though you could prepare all its components beforehand and then assemble it in the morning. If it's the season, a big bowl of strawberries would round out this menu nicely.

breakfast with friends

PRIMER

A Great Cup o' Joe

Whether you use an electric coffeemaker or a fancy French press, there are four things you can do to guarantee yourself and your guests a great cup of coffee every time:

• Always use fresh beans and fresh cold water (store the beans in the freezer until you're ready to grind them). If you prefer ground coffee, be sure it's fresh (store it in a tightly sealed container in the refrigerator);

• Measure coffee and water precisely (I like 1 tablespoon of coffee to 6 ounces of water);

• Clean the coffeepot after each use.

• If you like flavored coffees, try flavoring them yourself. Add cardamom, orange zest, or cinnamon. Rather than flavoring an entire pot, I offer zests, syrups, and liqueurs, along with milk, sugar, and powdered cinnamon, cardamom, and cocoa for sprinkling on top, to my guests at the table.

old-fashioned buttermilk doughnuts

Sometimes when I'm coming home from an early morning jaunt to the farmers' market, I will make a detour to Early Time Donuts where I am embraced by the heady scent of everything that's "bad" for me and reminded that there do exist places (thank my lucky stars!) where fat is not a dirty word and sugar is not a sin. In fact, they taste positively righteous. Herewith is my culinary ode to all things bad that are good.

MAKES ABOUT 12 DOUGHNUTS

- 2 tablespoons ($\frac{1}{4}$ stick) unsalted butter, melted
- $\frac{1}{2}$ cup buttermilk
- 1 large egg, beaten
- $\frac{1}{3}$ cup sugar, plus extra for dusting
- Pinch of grated nutmeg
- 1 teaspoon ground cinnamon
- 2 teaspoons baking powder
- $\frac{1}{2}$ teaspoon baking soda
- 1 teaspoon salt
- About 2 cups cake flour (not self-rising)
- Vegetable oil or shortening, for frying

METHOD

In a large bowl, mix the melted butter, buttermilk, egg, sugar, nutmeg, cinnamon, baking powder, baking soda, and salt.

Add 1 cup of the flour, stir to combine, then add the rest of the flour a few tablespoons at a time until you have a dough that resembles a soft cookie dough in texture. It should be soft but you should be able to handle it. Turn the dough onto a lightly floured surface and knead it a few times until it is smooth. Cover and chill for 30 minutes.

Roll the dough out to a $\frac{1}{2}$-inch thickness. With a floured doughnut cutter, cut out rounds, transferring them to a sheet of parchment paper as you do so. You can reroll the dough scraps to make more doughnuts.

Heat 3 inches of oil in a deep, heavy saucepan. When it registers 375°F. on a candy thermometer, carefully drop 3 or 4 doughnuts into the oil. As they rise to the surface, turn them and continue to turn them as they cook, 2 to 3 minutes total, or until they are golden on all sides. Transfer the doughnuts to paper towels to drain. Dust with lots of sugar. Continue frying the remaining doughnuts and serve warm.

shirred eggs with asparagus and country ham

A bit more genteel than scrambled or poached eggs (and as easy to prepare), shirred eggs are light yet substantial enough for a breakfast or luncheon entrée. The eggs are baked in the oven in individual baking dishes, enabling you to spend time with your guests instead of with a frying pan.

SERVES 6

6 tablespoons (¾ stick) unsalted butter, melted
   Kosher salt
8 asparagus spears, cut into 1-inch pieces
⅓ pound country ham, diced
12 eggs
   Freshly ground pepper
½ cup freshly grated Parmesan cheese

METHOD

Preheat the oven to 400°F. Divide the melted butter among 6 individual baking dishes or ramekins (the size should be just large enough to hold 2 eggs). Use a pastry brush to coat the sides with the butter.

Bring a medium saucepan of water to a boil. Add a generous pinch of salt and when the water returns to a boil, add the asparagus and cook 1 minute. Drain well.

Divide the asparagus pieces among the gratin dishes and top with the diced ham. Crack 2 eggs into each dish. Season with salt and pepper and sprinkle with the Parmesan cheese. Cover the dishes with aluminum foil and bake for 6 to 8 minutes, until the eggs are set and the cheese has melted.

broiled grapefruit with crystallized ginger

Very fifties, I know, but very tasty, too.

SERVES 6

¾ cup granulated sugar
⅓ cup finely chopped crystallized ginger
3 large pink grapefruits, halved

METHOD

Preheat the broiler.

In a small bowl, combine the sugar and ginger. Arrange the grapefruit halves, cut side up, in a large baking pan. Sprinkle with the sugar-ginger mixture. Broil the grapefruits about 1½ inches from the heat until the sugar caramelizes and the tops begin to brown, 10 to 12 minutes.

Serve at room temperature.

PRIMER

Fresh Juices and Smoothies

In addition to the customary mimosas and Bloody Marys that I serve for weekend breakfast, I like to offer freshly squeezed juices and smoothies, too. When faced with a juicer or blender and an array of fruits and other ingredients, it is amazing the combinations that people come up with. Arrange a big bowl of fruits and vegetables alongside a juicer/extractor, citrus juicer/reamer, or blender, along with juice bar add-ins like protein powder, bee pollen, and spirulina, and let everybody get revved for the day.

Here are some great combinations for your guests to try. (You might even post the choices on a blackboard, à la the local juice counter.)

In the juicer/extractor:

Carrot and apple

Pear and pomegranate nectar (bottled)

Wheatgrass

Spinach and grape

Pineapple and cream of coconut (canned)

In the citrus juicer:

Pink grapefruit juice and grated ginger

Tangerine juice with a squeeze of lime

Orange and cranberry-raspberry juice

In the blender:

Dates, bananas, and vanilla yogurt

Cantaloupe, blueberries, and plain yogurt

Strawberries, mangoes, and lemon sorbet

Nectarines, raspberries, crystallized ginger, and plain yogurt

Cherries, raspberries, and chocolate frozen yogurt

polenta with maple syrup

In Northern Italian households, leftover polenta is fried in olive oil and served for breakfast with sugar or honey. Here, I have substituted butter for the heavier olive oil and given it a good ol' American finishing touch, maple syrup.

SERVES 6

- 3 cups milk
- 6 tablespoons (¾ stick) unsalted butter
- 1 tablespoon sugar
  Pinch of grated nutmeg
  Pinch of salt
- 1 cup coarsely ground yellow cornmeal (polenta)
  Maple syrup

METHOD

In a medium heavy saucepan, combine the milk, 2 tablespoons of the butter, the sugar, nutmeg, and salt. Bring to a simmer over medium heat.

Add the cornmeal by letting it fall through the fingers of one hand while you whisk with the other. Reduce the heat to low and cook, stirring constantly, until the cornmeal has absorbed the liquid and begins to pull away from the sides of the pan, about 10 to 15 minutes.

Grease a jelly roll pan or a shallow baking dish with 2 tablespoons of the butter. Scrape the polenta into the pan, smoothing the surface with the back of a spoon. Cover with plastic wrap and refrigerate until firm, 1½ to 2 hours or overnight.

Using large decorative cutters or a knife, cut the polenta into serving portions. Melt the remaining 2 tablespoons of butter in a large skillet or heat a griddle. Fry the polenta portions until golden on both sides. Alternatively, you can brush the polenta with melted butter and broil until golden.

Serve drizzled with maple syrup.

kumquat marmalade

Tart-sweet kumquats make a bracing marmalade and a rather exotic departure from the usual orange version. This marmalade is delicious served on toasted challah or brioche, or spread on toasted pound cake for dessert.

MAKES APPROXIMATELY 4 CUPS

- 1 pound kumquats, sliced very thinly
- 1 pound sugar
- 1 tablespoon fresh lime juice
- 2 tablespoons Grand Marnier or other orange-flavored liqueur

METHOD

Put the kumquats in a large bowl and cover with cold water. Soak overnight.

Drain the kumquats and put them in a large saucepan with the sugar, lime juice, and liqueur. Bring to a boil, then reduce the heat and simmer for 1 hour. Put a spoonful of the marmalade on a plate and let cool. Gently push the surface of the marmalade with your finger. If it wrinkles, the marmalade is ready. Ladle into warm sterilized jars. Alternatively, the marmalade can be refrigerated in a tightly sealed container for 3 to 4 weeks.

PRIMER

Sweet Toppings for Breakfast Breads

Along with the fruit jams I serve to spread on toast, scones, and muffins, I like to offer sweet butters, too. To softened unsalted butter, stir in grated orange zest, poppy seeds and lemon zest, fruit purees, sugar and cinnamon, rose petals (nonsprayed), honey and ground nuts, or finely chopped crystallized ginger. Pack the butter into decorative molds and unmold before serving, or tamp into ramekins or other small, pretty containers.

Fruit cheeses, pictured at right, aren't cheeses at all but intensely flavored fruit spreads with the consistency of a paste. They make interesting and delectable toppings for breakfast breads. Look for them at specialty food stores.

in the

in the pink

There comes a time in every woman's life when she just wants to be a girl: to gossip, to giggle, to talk about love, lipstick, and luxury items. Baby showers and bridal showers provide the ideal opportunity for such frivolity.

I've found that in entertaining, just as in fashion or decorating, colors can create a mood and evoke an emotional response. I chose the pink theme for this luncheon not only because it's girly but also because it's fresh and fun. It reminds me of an early spring garden, of a sunrise on Cape Cod, of a confectionery in Paris, of a satin sash on a bridesmaid's dress at a summer wedding—all things that make me happy.

A single color can have many values or tones and in this party, the depth of pink is represented in various applications. The food ranges from the rosy pink of salmon caviar to the blush pink of the meringues. Chef's license allowed me to deepen the pink theme further with the addition of cherry tomatoes and radishes. Begin the party with Pink Lady cocktails to get everybody in the mood and if you're so inclined, hand out rose-colored glasses.

172

pink

For invitations, I hand-lettered white correspondence cards with fuchsia ink and tucked them into vellum envelopes with pink rose petals. I haunted secondhand stores to find pink-embellished linens and a few pieces of pink china to complement my white dinnerware. Party favors were pink inspired, too. I filled white tulle beggar's purses with pink jelly beans and tied them with a polka-dot ribbon. Other options might have included pink lipstick, pink rose potpourri, or pots of pink geraniums.

If you're hosting a party to which guests will be bringing gifts, ask them to follow the pink motif in their gift wrapping. Think beyond paper when it comes to wrapping. How about fuchsia pink raw silk, or cotton candy pink-and-white satin? Don't forget the ribbon!

pink lady

If pink had a flavor, this would be it.

SERVES 4

- ¼ cup (4 ounces) black currant–flavored vodka
- 2 tablespoons (2 ounces) Calvados
- 4 egg whites (see Note)
  Juice of 2 limes
  About 10 to 12 dashes of Grenadine
- 4 lime slices, for decoration
- 4 small edible pink flowers, for decoration

METHOD

Put all the ingredients in a large cocktail shaker or a sealable jar with chopped ice and shake energetically. Pour into short glasses and decorate with lime slices and flowers.

Note: Due to the health concerns surrounding raw eggs, you may consider powdered egg whites, found in the baking section of supermarkets. If you use raw egg whites, be sure that the eggs have been refrigerated and there are no cracks in the shells.

ollalieberry lemonade

In northern California, ollalieberries make their summertime debut with the other cane berries, raspberries and blackberries. They're quite similar to blackberries, with a touch softer flavor. If you can't find ollalieberries, raspberries or blackberries work just fine.

MAKES 1½ QUARTS

- 8 large ripe lemons
- 5 cups water
- 1 cup superfine sugar, plus more to taste
- 1 pint (2 cups) ollalieberries
  Lemon slices or edible flowers, for decoration

METHOD

Squeeze the lemons and measure 1½ cups of juice; reserve.

In a large saucepan, combine 3 cups of the water and the sugar. Bring to a boil, stirring to dissolve the sugar. Add the lemon juice and the remaining water and cool.

Put the berries in a food processor or blender and puree until smooth. Add the puree to the lemonade by pressing it through a sieve with the back of a spoon to eliminate the seeds. Stir.

Serve the lemonade over lots of ice, garnished with a lemon slice or an edible flower.

cucumber sandwiches with salmon caviar

Salmon caviar is usually called salmon roe, so look for it labeled this way in your store. To save time, rather than cutting the bread with a cookie cutter, slice in half and in half again for 4 perfectly acceptable triangles.

SERVES 8; MAKES 32 OPEN-FACE SANDWICHES

- ½ cup best-quality prepared mayonnaise
- 2 tablespoons best-quality prepared black olive spread (olivada or tapenade) (see Note)
- ½ teaspoon fresh lemon juice
- 2 large English cucumbers
  Kosher salt
- 8 thin slices of firm-textured white bread
- ¼ cup salmon caviar

METHOD

In a small bowl, stir together the mayonnaise, black olive spread, and lemon juice. Peel and seed the cucumbers, thinly slice, and sprinkle with salt. Drain in a colander for 15 minutes; pat dry.

Trim the crusts from the bread. Using small cookie cutters, cut each slice of bread into 4 pieces, or slice each in half diagonally and in half again for 4 small triangles.

Spread some of the mayonnaise mixture on the bread cutouts and top with the cucumber slices and salmon roe. Serve open-face.

Note: Black olive spread is available at gourmet groceries or specialty kitchenware stores.

wonton ravioli with edible flowers

Transparent wonton wrappers allow the flower petals to show through these delicate and fanciful dumplings as they float in chicken broth. The darker the hue of the petal, the more visible it will be.

SERVES 8

- 1   16-ounce package wonton skins (about 48)
      Petals from 24 fresh edible flowers, preferably pink and red
- 1   egg white, beaten
- 12 cups chicken broth
- $\frac{1}{2}$ cup freshly grated Parmesan cheese
      Rose petals, for decoration.

METHOD

On a work surface, lay out 24 wonton skins. Sprinkle flower petals on each of the skins, leaving a border around the edge. Brush the edges with the beaten egg white and top with wonton skins, pressing along the edges to seal. Trim to make the edges even.

In a large sauté pan over medium-high heat, bring the chicken broth to a boil. Cook the wontons in batches of 8 in a single layer, boiling gently until cooked through, about 5 minutes. As the wontons are cooked, transfer them to warm serving bowls.

To serve, ladle the chicken broth over the wontons. Sprinkle with Parmesan cheese and pink rose petals.

cherry tomato sandwiches with arugula mayonnaise

Sweet cherry tomatoes and peppery arugula play off each other wonderfully, particularly when they're linked with creamy mayonnaise.

SERVES 8

- 8   to 12 cherry tomatoes
- $\frac{1}{2}$ cup best-quality prepared mayonnaise
- $\frac{1}{4}$ pound fresh arugula, stems trimmed
- 1   tablespoon chopped fresh parsley
- $\frac{1}{4}$ teaspoon grated lemon zest
      Kosher salt and freshly ground pepper
- 8   thin slices of firm-textured white bread
      Small arugula leaves, for decoration

METHOD

Thinly slice the tomatoes through the "equator," not the stem.

In a small bowl, combine the mayonnaise, arugula, parsley, lemon zest, and salt and pepper to taste.

Trim the crusts from the bread. Using small cookie or pastry cutters, cut each slice of bread into 4 pieces, or slice each in half and in half again for 4 small triangles.

Spread some of the mayonnaise on the bread cutouts and top with the tomato slices. Serve open face, garnished with an arugula leaf.

radishes with sweet butter

Commonly served on French *pique-niques*, radishes with sweet butter are refreshing, delicious, and oh-so-continental.

SERVES 8

- 1   bunch radishes, trimmed, with a bit of the green stem left on
- 1   cup whipped sweet (unsalted) butter, softened
- $\frac{1}{2}$ cup finely chopped fresh parsley
- 1   teaspoon kosher salt

METHOD

Fill a medium bowl halfway with chopped ice. Arrange the radishes on the ice. Put the butter in a small bowl. In another small bowl, combine the parsley and salt.

To eat, dip a radish in the butter, then in the parsley and pop it in your mouth. Alternatively, guests may serve themselves a bit of butter and parsley and spread the butter on the radish with a small knife. The former method is much more fun.

style note

THE POWDER ROOM

Contrary to its ladylike associations, the powder room was in fact the place where men powdered their wigs during colonial times. Today, it serves as a refuge for both sexes and provides you with an yet another opportunity for thoughtful hospitality.

• Roll small linen hand towels and arrange them in a basket or tuck them into an antique toast rack by the sink. Don't forget to provide a place for discarding used towels.

• Use a butter curler to create curls from a big bar of soap and put them in an antique dish by the sink (there is nothing worse than a wet, used bar of soap!).

• Fill a small antique bottle with liquid soap and insert a pour spout in the top. Ditto with hand lotion.

• Hang a scented ball of roses or lavender on the back doorknob of the bathroom door.

• Hang a small aromatic wreath with wide satin ribbon on your mirror or the back of the bathroom door.

• Infuse the air with heady fragrance with scented candles, rubrum lilies, or tuberose.

• Arrange dental floss, a few toothbrushes, toothpaste, mouthwash, contact lens solution, and aspirin in a basket on the counter for guests' use.

• Arrange bottles of perfume and cologne on a small antique mirror.

• Be sure you have extra toilet tissue, tampons, and tissues in an accessible place.

shrimp and cannellini bean salad

This Italian-inspired salad is as beautiful as it is tasty. The creaminess of the beans highlights the subtle crunchiness of the shrimp, both of which are accented by the fruity green flavor of extra-virgin olive oil and the refreshing lift of lemon juice.

SERVES 8

3 cups dried cannellini beans
1 pound medium shrimp
3 garlic cloves, crushed
4 fresh parsley sprigs
1 bay leaf
  Kosher salt and freshly ground black pepper
¼ cup fresh lemon juice
9 tablespoons extra-virgin olive oil

METHOD

Rinse and pick through the beans. Put them in a large pot over medium-high heat and fill the pot with hot water to cover the beans generously. Bring to a boil, then remove from the heat, cover, and let stand 1 hour.

Rinse the shrimp and place in a steamer basket. Cook over boiling water until just pink and firm, about 3 to 5 minutes. When cool enough to handle, peel, devein, and chill until ready to serve.

Drain the beans and put them in a large pot with 6 cups of hot water. Add the garlic, parsley, and bay leaf and bring to a boil over medium-high heat. Reduce the heat to low, cover, and simmer until tender, about 1 hour. Remove from the heat and let the beans cool in their liquid. Discard the garlic, parsley, and bay leaf. Drain the beans and season to taste with salt and pepper.

While the beans are still warm, sprinkle with 2 tablespoons of the lemon juice. Add 6 tablespoons of olive oil and toss gently to coat. Season to taste with salt and pepper.

In a medium bowl, combine the shrimp with the remaining lemon juice and olive oil. Season to taste with salt and pepper.

To assemble, mound the beans on a platter and arrange the shrimp on top.

peaches with fresh chèvre and pink peppercorns

I was introduced to this seemingly unlikely trio when I was enticed into a farmyard in the south of France by a periwinkle blue hand-lettered sign proclaiming the availability of fresh goat cheese, ripe peaches, and eggs. The patronesse (Madame Farmer?), obviously amused by my ardor for these everyday items (hey! everything is larger than life in France!), sat me down under a tree on her terrace and produced this dish. It was perfect. If you can't find fresh chèvre, use fresh ricotta.

SERVES 8

4 large ripe peaches
8 tablespoons fresh goat cheese (chèvre)
2 teaspoons crushed pink peppercorns (see Note)

METHOD

Slice the peaches in half and remove the pits. Dollop a tablespoon of fresh goat cheese in the center of each peach slice and sprinkle with crushed pink peppercorns.

Note: Pink peppercorns are available at gourmet groceries and specialty kitchenware stores.

pink and white meringue kisses

I love the magic of airy meringues that melt in your mouth so quickly you forget they were there—so you keep reaching for more. The secret to perfect meringues: Don't make them on a humid or rainy day.

MAKES 25

2 large egg whites
Pinch of salt
$\frac{2}{3}$ cup confectioners' sugar
$\frac{1}{2}$ teaspoon vanilla extract
Pink food coloring
Silver dragees and/or pink sugar confetti, if desired

METHOD

Preheat the oven to 250°F. Line 2 baking sheets with parchment paper.

Combine the egg whites and salt in the bowl of an electric mixer. Beat on low speed until frothy, then increase the speed to medium-high and beat until the peaks begin to stiffen. Gradually add the sugar, continuing to beat as you do so, then add the vanilla. Beat until the egg whites are very stiff and shiny. Divide the meringue batter in half. Tint half the batter with the food coloring to the desired degree of pinkness.

Spoon white meringue batter into a pastry bag fitted with a star tip. Pipe onto the parchment paper to make $1\frac{1}{2}$-inch meringues, leaving at least $1\frac{1}{2}$ inches between meringues. Repeat with the pink meringue batter. Alternatively, spoon about $1\frac{1}{2}$ tablespoons of meringue onto the parchment paper and use the tips of your fingers to pull the center into a peak resembling a chocolate kiss.

Decorate with the dragees and/or pink sugar confetti. Bake for 1 hour, or until the meringues are dry. Cool on wire racks.

strawberry mascarpone gelato

In my book of yums, this ice cream warrants a gold star. I can't resist the rich and luxurious texture that the mascarpone, a soft Italian cream cheese, contributes to the fresh strawberry gelato, not to mention its pale pink hue. Make this ice cream the day before the party or early in the day of the party so it is firm for serving.

SERVES 8; MAKES APPROXIMATELY $4\frac{1}{2}$ CUPS

2 cups heavy cream
3 egg yolks
$\frac{2}{3}$ cup sugar
$3\frac{1}{2}$ cups hulled fresh strawberries or frozen unsweetened strawberries
$1\frac{1}{2}$ cups mascarpone cheese
Sliced strawberries or sliced carambola (star fruit), for garnish

METHOD

In a medium saucepan, heat the cream over medium-high heat until bubbles appear around the edges. In a large bowl, whisk together the egg yolks and sugar until pale yellow and smooth. Whisk in about $\frac{1}{4}$ cup of the hot cream, then slowly whisk in the remaining cream. Return the mixture to the saucepan and place over medium-low heat. Cook, stirring constantly with a wooden spoon, until the mixture coats the back of the spoon, 5 to 7 minutes. Do not boil the custard. Remove from the heat and let cool to room temperature.

Meanwhile, combine the strawberries and mascarpone in a food processor or a blender and puree until smooth. Transfer to a large bowl.

Pour the cooled custard into the strawberry-mascarpone puree and whisk to combine. Refrigerate until cold, 1 hour.

Transfer the chilled mixture to an ice cream maker and freeze according to the manufacturer's directions. Place the gelato in a tightly sealed container and freeze until ready to serve, at least 3 hours or overnight.

Serve with sliced strawberries and/or carambola.

july 4th

July Fourth Bring-a-Dish Party

Every year my husband and I host a July Fourth party. This is our annual "invite everybody we know and love and like" party, complete with kids, visiting relatives, and dogs. We choose a different theme each year and our guests are given the charter of bringing foods that relate in some way. It intimidates some people (usually the first timers) because they think they must compete in a culinary contest. But once we've calmed them, they inevitably join in the spirit of fun-filled creativity and whimsy—and they're hooked for years to come.

This is an easy way to entertain because so much of the work is delegated to others. As both host and director of the event, I send invitations that give the usual date-time-place information along with a description of the party theme and—most important—each guest's "to bring" assignment. I divide the assignments into categories (salad, dessert, hors d'oeuvre, etc.) so we don't have a preponderance of any single type of food, but from there, it's up to my guests and their imaginations. I provide the main course, some of the beverages, and fill in the gaps.

bring-a-dish party

Depending upon how large your group is, you may want to make "creature comforts" a category and ask your friends to bring lawn chairs or folding tables.

Let your imagination be your guide when creating a theme. We've hosted a red, white, and blue party where all the food was red, white, or blue. A Mexico a Go-Go theme yielded all manner of Mexican foods.

One of our best themes over the years was a culinary Olympics—that coincided with the summer games. We asked our guests to bring summertime foods to represent a different country. The result was a colorful and flavorful melting pot. I used our large farmhouse kitchen table as the stage for the foods. Dishes were arranged on the table and alongside each, I placed a paper flag signifying the food's country of origin and wrote the name of the dish on the flag. The dining took place outdoors and I covered long tables with fabrics reminiscent of a variety of international settings—the bright colors and intricate patterns of Provence's Soleado fabric, the red and white gingham of the American South, and the fresh blue and white of South Seas batiks.

When you give a party like this, the emphasis should be on fun and informality. A buffet format lends itself naturally to this. Diverse table locations, some in the sun and a few in the shade, cater to your guests' preferences. Don't forget that a quilt spread out on the grass or big cushions alongside the pool function as tables, too.

Self-serve or staffed bars can be set up indoors and out, or you can fill big galvanized tubs with ice and a selection of beers from around the world. White wines, Provençal rosé wines, and perhaps a dry sherry can be iced, too. Red wines, though they shouldn't be chilled, will taste better if they're kept in a cool, shady spot.

Give the party in the later afternoon. Serve hors d'oeuvres and drinks as the guests arrive, then the main course later on. As it becomes dark, you can toast Independence Day with sparklers and then it's off to the fireworks display!

grilled chicken tostaditas

If you don't have time to make guacamole, don't sweat it—simply visit your friendly take-out food section.

SERVES 12

- 2 whole skinless, boneless chicken breasts
  Kosher salt and freshly ground pepper

Guacamole

- 2 ripe avocados
- 2 tablespoons finely chopped red onion
  Hot pepper sauce
- 2 tablespoons finely chopped cilantro
  Fresh lime juice

- 24 round tortilla chips
- 5 cups shredded lettuce
- 1 large red onion, quartered and thinly sliced
- 4 small plum tomatoes, thinly sliced
- 1 cup Tomatillo Sauce (page 163) or prepared
  tomatillo salsa
- 1½ cups crumbled feta cheese

METHOD

Prepare a fire in the grill. Season the chicken breasts with salt and pepper and grill until just cooked through, turning 2 or 3 times, 15 to 20 minutes. Cool the chicken, then use your fingers to shred the meat. Set aside.

Cut each avocado in half, remove the pits, and scoop the avocado into a medium bowl. Using a fork or the back of a spoon, mash the avocado. Add the onion, hot pepper sauce to taste, and cilantro and mix well. Season to taste with lime juice and salt.

Spread a spoonful of guacamole on each tortilla chip. Top with a layer of lettuce, chicken, onion, tomato, Tomatillo Sauce, and cheese.

summer vegetables with herb-yogurt dip

A riotous combination of color, shape, and texture makes this ideal for inclusion in a festive outdoor party. Plus it's healthful.

SERVES 12

- 4 cups plain yogurt
- 1 cup mixed chopped herbs, such as summer savory, chervil, parsley, basil, and marjoram
- 2 tablespoons Dijon mustard
  Kosher salt and freshly ground pepper
  Dash of hot pepper sauce

  An assemblage of the best-tasting, best-looking summer vegetables you can find, such as:
- 2 bunches radishes, trimmed, with a bit of the green stems left on
- 2 pounds sugar snap peas
- 2 pounds baby carrots, trimmed, with a bit of the green stems left on and blanched for 2 minutes
- 2 pounds cherry tomatoes, stems removed
- 4 fennel bulbs, tops removed, quartered

METHOD

In a medium serving bowl, combine the yogurt, herbs, mustard, and salt, pepper, and hot pepper sauce to taste.

Arrange the vegetables on a large platter or in a basket and serve with the herb-yogurt dip.

grilled littleneck clams with lemon-herb butter

Have the grill fired up and begin grilling the clams when guests arrive. Serve them straight from the grill.

SERVES 12

1½ pounds (6 sticks) unsalted butter
1¼ cups dry white wine
½ cup fresh lemon juice, or more to taste
¼ cup minced fresh parsley
2 tablespoons minced fresh thyme
Dash of cayenne
Kosher salt
6 to 8 dozen littleneck or Manila clams, scrubbed

METHOD

Combine the butter, wine, lemon juice, parsley, thyme, cayenne, and salt to taste in a shallow grillproof pan.

Prepare a fire in the grill, leaving one-quarter of it empty of coals. When the coals are ashy and gray, put the saucepan with the butter mixture on the grill to melt, then move the saucepan to the part of the grill that does not have coals to keep warm.

Place the clams on the rack over the hot coals and grill until they open, 8 to 12 minutes. Serve the clams with the lemon-butter sauce for dipping; either let your guests dip their clams into the communal saucepan of lemon-butter or ladle the lemon-butter into small cups for "private" dipping.

tomato, feta, and cucumber salad

By the time July Fourth rolls around, the tomatoes should just be coming into their own. Their sweetness will be offset nicely by fresh oregano, which is a nice change from the basil that will become the tomato's ubiquitous partner by summer's end.

SERVES 12

- 12 large ripe tomatoes, sliced
- 3 large cucumbers, peeled and sliced
- 1 cup crumbled feta cheese
- ½ cup red wine vinegar
  Kosher salt and freshly ground pepper
- 1 cup extra-virgin olive oil
- 1 tablespoon minced red onion
- 2 tablespoons chopped fresh oregano

METHOD

On a large serving platter, arrange the tomatoes in rows alternating with the cucumber slices. Sprinkle the feta cheese over the tomatoes and cucumbers.

In a medium bowl, whisk together the vinegar and salt and pepper to taste. Whisk in the olive oil, then stir in the onion and oregano. Drizzle some of the dressing on the tomatoes and cucumber. Serve the remaining dressing on the side.

boston baked beans

Where I grew up, July Fourth was not July Fourth without baked beans. Make this dish the day before you serve it.

SERVES 12

- 3 cups dried navy beans
- ⅓ pound piece of salt pork or slab bacon
- ½ medium onion, chopped
- 1 cup beer
- ½ cup maple syrup
- ¼ cup ketchup
- 1 tablespoon dry mustard
- 2 teaspoons kosher salt
- 1 bay leaf

METHOD

Rinse and pick through the beans. Put them in a large pot over medium-high heat and fill the pot with hot water to cover the beans generously. Bring to a boil, then remove from the heat, cover, and let stand 1 hour.

Preheat the oven to 275° F. Place the cooked beans in an ovenproof casserole. Add the remaining ingredients. If the beans are not covered with liquid, add enough boiling water to cover. Cover the beans and bake for 5 to 6 hours, adding more boiling water to just cover the beans. Uncover the beans for the last half hour of cooking. Serve directly from the pot.

style note

THE OUTDOOR ROOM

A big secret of successful entertaining is making your guests feel comfortable. This is not difficult to pull off outdoors either. When the weather's nice, think of your outdoor garden, patio, or yard as an extension of your indoor living space.

Cotton slipcovers made especially for outdoor furniture are now readily available, some in waterproof, nonfade fabrics. Use them to cover those rusty chairs that sat outside all winter long. Or think about bringing indoor dining chairs outdoors. Slipcover them in garden-inspired patterns and colors for a change of pace. Put cushions on picnic benches for greater comfort and more sitting longevity. Create intimate mini-rooms by grouping chairs under trees, near the birdbath, or next to a hydrangea in full bloom. Don't forget small tables upon which drinks and hors d'oeuvres may be rested.

Screens help create environments and a sense of intimacy. They hide messes, too. A white paneled screen is reminiscent of a garden fence. Cut square or rectangular "windows" in the panels and hang birdhouses or small lanterns in them. Wrought iron screens can be hung with baskets of flowers.

For balmy evenings that become cool, keep a supply of stadium blankets on hand to warm chilled guests. An assortment of college sweatshirts (purchased from campus stores via mail order) offer casual warmth while igniting friendly rivalries.

Lastly, don't forget flowers, flowers everywhere! Arrange hydrangeas in tin buckets, full-bloom butter-yellow and salmon and ivory garden roses in urns, big white pots of red geraniums, Queen Anne's lace, and black-eyed Susans in blue teapots, pink camellias floating in the birdbath. And give everybody a pot of pansies to take home.

For a nighttime party, arrange pots of gardenias or night-blooming jasmine around your outdoor room for heavenly wafts of heady, romantic fragrance.

provençal stuffed vegetables

Provence is known for its stuffed vegetables, which are often served as an hors d'oeuvre. I like to include them in a buffet because they're pretty and perfect for grazing, as they work either as a first course, side dish, or a light meal on their own. (I've yet to meet anyone who goes the latter route at a buffet, but how thoughtful of you to have anticipated that.)

SERVES 12

Stuffing

- 2 tablespoons (¼ stick) unsalted butter
- 2 tablespoons extra-virgin olive oil
- 1½ cups finely chopped mushrooms
- ½ small onion, finely chopped
- 1½ cups short grain rice
- 3 cups chicken broth
- 1 cup finely chopped tomatoes
- ¼ cup finely chopped black olives
- 2 tablespoons finely chopped parsley
  Kosher salt and freshly ground pepper

Vegetables

- 2 tablespoons (¼ stick) unsalted butter, melted
- 2 medium zucchini, trimmed
- 2 medium tomatoes, trimmed
- 2 Japanese eggplants, trimmed

METHOD

In a medium saucepan or Dutch oven, melt the butter with the olive oil over medium-high heat. When hot, add the mushrooms and sauté until they are tender and most of their moisture has evaporated. Remove to a bowl with a slotted spoon; reserve.

Add the onion to the pan and sauté, stirring, until soft. Add the rice, reduce the heat to medium, and cook, stirring, for 2 minutes. Add the chicken broth, reduce the heat to low, cover, and simmer for 20 minutes, until the stock is absorbed and the rice is tender. Stir in the mushrooms, tomatoes, olives, parsley, and salt and pepper to taste.

Preheat the oven to 350°F. Lightly brush a baking dish with the melted butter.

Bring a saucepan of water to a boil. Add a generous pinch of salt and when the water returns to a boil, add the whole zucchini and cook for 3 minutes. Drain.

When the zucchini are cool enough to handle, cut them in half lengthwise. Using a melon baller or a spoon, scoop out the pulp, leaving a ¼-inch shell. Cut the tops off the tomatoes and scoop out the pulp, leaving a ¼-inch shell. Cut the eggplants in half lengthwise and scoop out the pulp leaving a ¼-inch shell.

Fill the vegetables with the rice mixture and arrange in the baking dish. Bake until the vegetables are tender and the stuffing is heated through, 30 minutes.

broccoli salad with pine nut vinaigrette

Pine nuts offer a rich and unexpected counterpoint to this broccoli recipe. When you toast the nuts, watch them carefully, as they will go from an appealing golden to an appalling black in the blink of an eye.

SERVES 6

- 2 tablespoons olive oil plus ½ cup
- ¼ cup pine nuts
- 2 pounds broccoli, cut into 1-inch florets
- ⅓ cup water
- 1 teaspoon grated lemon zest
- 1 tablespoon red wine vinegar
- 1 tablespoon balsamic binegar
  Salt and pepper, to taste

METHOD

In a large skillet, warm the 2 tablespoons of olive oil over medium heat. When hot, add the pine nuts and cook, stirring, until lightly browned, about 1 minute. Remove wilth a slotted spoon to paper towels to drain.

Add the broccoli, water, and the lemon zest. Decrease the heat to low, cover, and simmer until the broccoli is tender but crisp, about 5 to 6 minutes.

In a small bowl, combine the vinegars with salt to taste and stir until dissolved. Add the remaining ½ cup of olive oil in a steady stream, whisking constantly. Add pepper to taste. Stir in the pine nuts.

Drain the broccoli and transfer to a large bowl. While still warm, pour the dressing over it and toss to coat the broccoli with the dressing. Cover and refrigerate until ready to serve.

PRIMER

Ice, Ice Baby

Summertime parties rely on ice. Why not give it a festive guise? A tip: Use distilled water to prevent cloudy ice.

- To prevent dilution of drinks, fill ice cube trays with the same beverage or a complementary one (lemonade for iced tea or limeade for vodka tonics) and freeze.

- Filled ice cubes are unusual and beautiful. Fill ice cube trays with water and freeze for 1 hour. Pour out the unfrozen water and fill the ice shells with edible flowers, berries, lemon or lime peel, or herbs (basil, rose geranium, lavender). Fill with water; freeze again.

- To make ice molds for keeping cold dishes cold, choose a container such as a cake tin or bundt mold. Fill one-third full with water and freeze. Scatter flowers, herbs, leaves, or citrus slices on the ice and cover with water. If you want to make an indentation to hold a bowl or bottle, place a container such as an empty wine bottle in the water. Freeze again. To remove the container, fill with warm water.

- To make an ice bucket (literally), put an empty bottle in an ice bucket or half-gallon milk container (cut the top off) and fill with water. Freeze until slushy. Push flowers, branches, or fruit into the slush and around the bottle and return to the freezer until frozen. Remove the "ice bucket" from its container. Fill the bottle with warm water to remove and replace it with a chilled bottle of wine or vodka.

- To chill beverages quicker and keep them cold longer, submerge them in a tub filled with ice, water, and salt (about 1 tablespoon per quart of water).

- A cold drink in a frosty glass is heaven on a hot day. Arrange glasses upside down in a bucket of ice next to the beverages.

style note

OUTDOOR LIGHTING

The options for outdoor lighting now go way beyond tiki torches. Little white Christmas lights, called tivoli lights, strung on trees add warmth and an air of festivity. Wrap them around branches or porch columns for a sculpted effect. Likewise, these lights cast a warm glow when strung up around market umbrella poles and onto the umbrella's "fingers."

Old-fashioned train lanterns, lit with kerosene oil, can be set on tables or hung from trees. Use these lanterns, or luminarias (votive candles set in sand inside open paper bags) to line the walkway or perch them along a fence.

Put votive candles everywhere. Clustered or singly, they lend a happy aura to a party. Place them inside hurricane lamps on a bed of moss, plant them in seashells, fill oversized goblets with black beans and nestle them there, too. Votives placed under cheese graters or in Mexican punched-tin containers not only provide diffused light but also create flickering patterns (built-in party entertainment!).

If you have a pool, float white candles and gardenias in the water. The candles' soft light blends with the flowers' sweet aroma and the balmy night air to create a tropical feeling.

If you're near the shore, search for rocks or coral with natural indentations and use them to hold small tapers.

Like that old standby citronella, lavender oil and basil repel pests. Fill torches with lavender oil and place bouquets of basil around the party. Keep them as well as citronella candles away from food; their scent interferes with the flavors of food.

beef tenderloin with fresh horseradish

Grill the beef the morning of the party and serve it at room temperature thinly sliced with crusty bread, sliced ripe tomatoes, and the fresh horseradish. You will need a grill with a cover for this. A word about fresh horseradish (which you can find in the produce section of your supermarket): If you have never seen a horseradish root, be prepared. It's quite a sight. It's also proof that you can't judge a book by its cover because the zingy flavor it yields is unmatched by prepared horseradish. However, if you can't find the real thing to grate yourself, purchase refrigerated prepared horseradish, which will be fresher than the shelf-stable variety.

SERVES 12

2 whole tenderloins of beef (about 5 pounds each)
Kosher salt and fresh cracked black peppercorns
1½ cups peeled and grated fresh horseradish
3 tablespoons fresh lemon juice
1 tablespoon dry mustard
1 teaspoon sugar

METHOD

Trim the excess fat from the beef and coat it with salt and cracked peppercorns.

Prepare a fire in the center of the grill. When the fire is hot, sear the beef well on both sides, about 10 minutes per side. Transfer the beef from the center of the grill to the sides so it is not directly over the heat. Cover the grill, open the vent a bit, and continue to cook until the meat is cooked through, about 25 minutes for rare and 28 to 30 minutes for medium-rare. Let the beef rest at least 15 minutes before slicing or cool, refrigerate, and slice just before serving.

In a small bowl, combine the horseradish, lemon juice, dry mustard, 1½ teaspoons salt, and the sugar. Stir well. Cover and refrigerate until ready to use.

grilled kielbasa with an assortment of condiments

The smokiness of kielbasa makes it a great companion for mustard and in case you haven't looked lately, there are myriad mustard choices out there. Many boutique, or small production, mustards are quite interesting,

PRIMER

Grilling to a "T"(Bone)

The best way to start a charcoal fire is with a stainless steel "chimney" that enables you to stack the coals and light the fire without the chemicals (and odor) of lighter fluid. Steel chimneys are available where grilling equipment is sold.

Charcoal will take 30 to 45 minutes to burn to a red-hot, ashy readiness; wood, such as mesquite, will take about an hour. Put the rack in place on the grill about 10 minutes before you're ready to cook to preheat.

To prevent sticking, brush the grill with vegetable oil or spray it with vegetable cooking spray, and/or marinate the food before cooking.

A charcoal fire's heat radiates upward and the hottest part of the grill is generally in the center. Begin grilling here and move the food to the sides of the grill as they cook or begin to char. More tender foods, like vegetables, will do better if they're grilled toward the outer edges of the grill over less intense heat.

To prevent smaller foods, such as shrimp and pieces of vegetables, from falling through the grill, thread them on skewers. Use metal skewers or small wooden skewers that have been soaked in water for an hour or so to prevent burning. Heartier, "stalkier" herbs and aromatics such as rosemary and lemongrass make handy skewers that also infuse foods with their flavors.

including those flavored with herbs, honeys, and liqueurs. They're an easy and inexpensive way to jazz up the kielbasa. Fresh horseradish from the beef tenderloin recipe (above) works well, too.

SERVES 12

4 pounds smoked kielbasa
An assortment of condiments, such as boutique mustards, horseradish, and sauerkraut

METHOD

Bring a large skillet of water to a boil. Reduce to a simmer, add the kielbasa, and cook gently for 15 minutes. Drain well.

Prepare a fire in the grill by placing coals on both sides of the grill and leaving the center empty. When the coals are ashy and gray, place the kielbasa on the center of the grill so they are not over direct heat. Grill the kielbasa for 15 minutes, turning often.

Slice the kielbasa into links and serve warm or at room temperature with the condiments.

gingersnaps

If you've ever had the dubious pleasure of working in a cubicle environment (everybody in one room, divided by partitions that form cube offices), you know that it's both sociable and annoying. Let's dwell on the sociable. I wouldn't have this fine recipe if it weren't for a colleague who brought homemade gingersnaps into work every Monday and by virtue of doing so, retained his title, uncontested, as most popular co-worker.

MAKES ABOUT 36

¾ cup (1½ sticks) unsalted butter, softened
1 cup sugar, plus additional sugar for rolling the
   cookies
1 large egg
¼ cup dark molasses
2 teaspoons vanilla extract
2½ cups unbleached all-purpose flour
2 teaspoons baking soda
¼ teaspoon salt
1 teaspoon ground cinnamon
½ teaspoon ground cloves
1 teaspoon ground ginger
¼ teaspoon ground white pepper

METHOD

Combine the butter and 1 cup sugar in a large bowl and beat until pale yellow and fluffy. Beat in the egg, molasses, and vanilla.

In a second medium bowl, sift together the flour, baking soda, salt, cinnamon, cloves, ginger, and white pepper. Add to the batter in 3 batches, mixing well. Cover and refrigerate for 30 minutes.

Preheat the oven to 375°F. Line baking sheets with parchment.

Using a teaspoon as a measure, form the cookie dough into balls. Roll the balls in sugar and place on the prepared baking sheets about 1 inch apart. Bake until crinkled on top and brown around the edges, 8 to 10 minutes. Transfer to wire racks to cool completely, then store in an airtight container.

amanda's summer trifle

My friend Amanda has attended every July Fourth party I've hosted. With kids, dog, and husband in tow, she always brings enough food to host the party herself, including this beautiful summer trifle, a delicious concoction of berries, cream, and angel food cake.

SERVES 10 TO 12

2 cups half-and-half
1 vanilla bean, split
   Grated zest from 1 orange
⅔ pound angel food cake, brown crust cut off, cut into
   1½-inch cubes
6 tablespoons vin santo or other sweet wine
1 quart strawberries, hulled and quartered
1 pint raspberries
1 pint blueberries

6 egg yolks
¼ cup granulated sugar
1 cup heavy cream
2 tablespoons confectioners' sugar
2 tablespoons orange liqueur, such as Grand Marnier
   Additional berries, candied orange peel, and/or edible
   flowers

METHOD

Heat the half-and-half with the vanilla bean and orange zest until bubbles form around the edges. Turn off the heat, cover, and let it steep for 15 minutes.

Put the angel food cake cubes in a glass bowl or individual glasses. Sprinkle with the sweet wine and leave to soak for a few minutes. Add the berries to the bowl. Set aside.

In a small bowl, beat the egg yolks and granulated sugar until pale yellow. Reheat the half-and-half until bubbles form around the edges. Reduce the heat to low, whisk in the egg yolks, and cook, stirring, until the custard thickens, 10 to 15 minutes. Remove the vanilla bean and let the custard cool slightly, then pour it over the fruit and cake cubes. Cover and refrigerate.

Before serving, whip the cream with the confectioners' sugar and orange liqueur until stiff peaks form. Pile the whipped cream on top of the trifle and decorate with more berries and/or edible flowers.

style

blackberry ice cream

Fresh blackberries, homemade ice cream—need I say more?

MAKES ABOUT 1 QUART; SERVES 6

- ½ cup whole milk
- 1½ cups heavy cream
- 1 cup sugar
- 2 cups fresh or frozen blackberries
- 1 tablespoon fresh lemon juice
  Pinch of salt

METHOD

Combine the milk and cream in a saucepan and heat until it just reaches the boiling point. Remove from the heat, add ½ cup of the sugar, and stir until completely dissolved. Cool.

Put the blackberries and remaining ½ cup sugar in the bowl of a food processor and pulse to puree coarsely. Stir the lemon juice into the blackberry puree. Add the blackberry puree to the cooled milk/cream mixture along with the pinch of salt. Stir gently to combine.

Pour the mixture into an ice cream machine and freeze according to the manufacturer's directions.

When firm, transfer the ice cream into a sealable container and store in the freezer.

island fruit pops

What could be simpler? No machines, pureeing, or molds are needed for these refreshing and pretty pops that will be as popular with kids as with adults. Cut the fruit into large pieces in graphic shapes such as rectangles, triangles, and semicircles.

SERVES 12

- 12 large pieces of ripe island fruits, such as papaya, mango, melon, pineapple, and star fruit
- 12 popsicle sticks or 12 lemongrass stalks or 12 cinnamon sticks

METHOD

Peel and core the fruit as needed. Cut into large pieces. Insert popsicle sticks or lemongrass stalks or cinnamon sticks. Lay the fruit pops on a baking sheet lined with plastic wrap and freeze for at least 3 hours.

note

Picking Posies

As with food, let the seasons be your guide when selecting flowers for entertaining. Bulb flowers like daffodils, tulips, and hyacinths will add an air of freshness and newness to the table in the springtime. These are the flowers that look beautiful planted in terra-cotta or porcelain pots, topped with soft green moss—reminiscent of the emerging garden. Sweet little violets make delicate arrangements in egg cups or demitasse cups. Long-stemmed white tulips hang their blossoms, like delicate dancers bending, from a crystal vase. Single blossoms of gardenias or peonies look regal floating in silver or glass bowls.

In summer, I like flowers that come from cutting gardens—or look like they do. Favorites include ruffly ranunculus, tall, deep blue delphiniums, straight-forward zinnias, and garden roses in every color. Summer is about profusion and so "arrangement" seems too stiff a word for these displays. It's all about gathering a bunch of blossoms in both hands and setting them in milk pitchers, watering cans, or galvanized buckets. Smaller blooms can rest in china teapots, jelly jars, or in a single-file line of small bottles.

Autumn is for earthy colors and rich textures. Choose flowers and branches with confidence and inner strength like chrysanthe-

mums and sunflowers, maple leaves on branches, twisting grapevines, and sculptural milkweed pods. They need a good foundation in terms of container material and height. Milk cans and French florist buckets work well, as do jewel-toned majolica vases that complement the blooms in both hue and texture. Autumn is also the time to dry blooms for use in winter arrangements.

Winter weather may be gray, but it needn't be drab inside. Now is the time for the dried hydrangeas, roses, and other branches that you dried throughout the garden seasons. I like to display dried hydrangeas in a copper urn or hang small nosegays of dried

roses on the backs of chairs around my dining room table. Evergreen branches become swags to run the length of the table intertwined with lemons and tangerines. I place smaller cuttings around the bases of votive candles or as bobeches or candle collars around tapers.

As winter wanes, it's time to cajole branches into bloom. Collect forsythia, quince, cherry, crab apple, magnolia, or any early blossoming branch that grows near you. Cut the ends on a slant under running water and put in lukewarm water. Change the water periodically and mist the branches occasionally. They will blossom within one to four weeks.

thanksgiving

Thanksgiving at Home

If you like to cook and entertain, only traction would keep you out of the kitchen on Thanksgiving Day. It is the one day of the year that truly centers around the table and all its glorious abundance.

For me, the aroma of turkey roasting in the oven is heaven. My heart swells at the sight of the mixing bowls lined up on the counter full of chopped vegetables for purees, toasted bread crumbs for stuffing, and sliced apples for pie. I don't even mind the annual argument—excuse me, discussion—with my mother-in-law about the proper roasting time for the turkey.

The personal food memories and recipes we bring to our Thanksgivings sustain the traditions that have formed us and our holiday celebrations. I can't imagine a Thanksgiving without an antipasto of fennel, dried Italian sausages, and provolone cheese, the legacy of my father's Italian heritage. Likewise, I could not end a Thanksgiving dinner without my Irish grandmother's plum pudding or, as we called it, suet pudding. She steamed it in coffee cans and served it with a rich, buttery sauce.

at home

Along with the cherished dishes that make annual appearances on my Thanksgiving table, I like to combine familiar Thanksgiving ingredients in innovative ways. These are the recipes that I am sharing with you. I'm sure you have your own "can't live without them" Thanksgiving dishes, and I wouldn't dream of telling you to substitute one of my recipes for those. Consider this collection an enhancement (if you wish) to your favorite standbys. If you're preparing your first Thanksgiving, perhaps these recipes will help you begin your own traditions. However you use these recipes, they are sure to complement your own family dishes.

THANKSGIVING TIMESAVING TIPS

Thanksgiving by its very definition requires a lot of everything—food, cooking, and effort—but real life doesn't stop during the third week of November. Don't panic! If you take an hour in the beginning of November to plot your preparation strategy, you will be more efficient and much more relaxed on Thanksgiving Day.

Two weeks before the big day, determine your menu. Collect the recipes and write down all the ingredients you'll need. Take inventory of your pantry and cupboards, crossing off those ingredients you already have.

Make a turbo shopping list. Establish shopping categories based on the layout of your market (produce, dairy, breadstuffs and grains, beverages, etc.), then note the ingredients you need in each category. You will be amazed at how much time this saves you in the market.

Order your fresh turkey two weeks in advance and pick it up the evening before Thanksgiving so it does not take up valuable refrigerator space. If you're cooking a frozen turkey, remember that it takes 24 hours per 5 pounds of turkey to defrost. Plan for this!

Wash and prepare vegetables for cooking the day before Thanksgiving. You can also set the table the night before. Most important of all, delegate! Put husbands, wives, and children to work. And when guests ask if they can bring something, say, "Yes."

spiced pumpkin seeds

In a nod to the season (and possibly the demise of the Halloween pumpkin), these pumpkin seeds are a nice, salty tidbit for sparking the Thanksgiving palate. Incidentally, they make a lovely match with Champagne.

MAKES ABOUT 6 CUPS

- ¼ cup vegetable oil
- 2 tablespoons chili powder, or more to taste
- 6 cups shelled raw pumpkin seeds (see Note)
  Kosher salt

METHOD

Preheat the oven to 350°F.

In a small saucepan over medium heat, warm the oil with the chili powder until very hot, 2 to 3 minutes.

In a medium bowl, toss the pumpkin seeds with the chili oil. Sprinkle on salt to taste and toss to mix.

Spread the pumpkin seeds on ungreased baking sheets and bake until toasty brown, about 15 minutes. Remove from the heat, return to the mixing bowl, and let cool, tossing occasionally. Adjust for seasoning before serving.

Note: Pumpkin seeds are available at health food stores and whole food markets.

smoked salmon with tarragon crème fraîche

SERVES 10 TO 12

- 1 cup crème fraîche
- 1 tablespoon tarragon mustard
- 1 teaspoon fresh lemon juice
- 2 tablespoons finely chopped fresh tarragon
- ¾ pound sliced smoked salmon
  Thinly sliced dark rye bread

METHOD

In a small bowl, stir together all the ingredients except the salmon and rye bread.

Arrange the salmon on a serving platter, separating the salmon slices to make it easy for your guests to serve themselves. Place the tarragon crème fraîche and rye bread alongside the salmon platter.

wild mushroom broth

This first course carries the earthy, autumn flavors but is not overly rich or heavy. The combination of fresh and dried mushrooms not only adds depth of flavor but is also a pleasing contrast in textures.

SERVES 10 TO 12

- 1 ounce dried porcini mushrooms
- 3 tablespoons unsalted butter
- 3 tablespoons extra-virgin olive oil
- 3 garlic cloves, finely chopped
- ½ pound fresh chanterelle mushrooms, sliced
- ½ pound button mushrooms, sliced
- 1 1-pound can Italian plum tomatoes, with their juice
- 1 tablespoon fresh thyme leaves
- 2½ quarts chicken stock or low-sodium canned broth
  Kosher salt and freshly ground pepper
- 3 button mushrooms, thinly sliced, for garnish
- ¼ cup chopped fresh chives, for garnish

METHOD

Put the porcini mushrooms in a small bowl and add boiling water to cover. Set aside to soak for 20 minutes.

In a large skillet over medium heat, melt the butter with the olive oil. When hot, add the garlic and sauté, stirring, 1 minute. Add the chanterelles and button mushrooms, lower the heat, and cook, stirring often, for 10 minutes.

Meanwhile, put the tomatoes and their juice in a food processor and puree until smooth. Line a strainer with a double layer of paper towels and set it inside a bowl. Pour the porcini mushrooms with their liquid into the strainer, reserving the liquid. Add the porcini mushrooms and the strained liquid to the skillet along with the pureed tomatoes and the thyme. Increase the heat to medium and cook, stirring, for 10 minutes. Add the stock and bring to a boil, then lower the heat and simmer 30 minutes. Season to taste with salt and pepper.

To serve, ladle the soup into individual warmed bowls. Float 2 or 3 mushroom slices and some chopped chives on top of each serving.

maple roast turkey

I grew up in New England where maple syrup is a native ingredient. On this most native of days, it's fitting that maple syrup complement the roast turkey. Figure on roasting the turkey about 12 minutes per pound. If you stuff the turkey (I don't), figure on about 15 minutes per pound. I prefer to bake the stuffing separately because I like the texture it retains when cooked this way.

If you're going to stuff the turkey, omit the onions, celery, lemon, and herb sprigs from the cavity and loosely stuff the turkey instead. Secure the neck flap and continue with the recipe. For health reasons, don't stuff the turkey until you're ready to put it in the oven.

SERVES 10 TO 12

1   15- to 16-pound turkey, preferably fresh, with its giblets
    Kosher salt and freshly ground pepper
2   onions, quartered
4   celery stalks
1   lemon, quartered
4   parsley sprigs, plus 1 tablespoon finely chopped
4   large sage sprigs, plus 1 tablespoon finely chopped
6   tablespoons ($\frac{3}{4}$ stick) unsalted butter, melted
1   cup dry white wine, plus more as needed
2   tablespoons pure maple syrup
2   teaspoons finely grated lemon zest

METHOD

Preheat the oven to 325°F. Remove the giblets from the turkey cavity; reserve for gravy. Rinse the turkey inside and out and pat it dry. Sprinkle the cavity with salt and pepper, then place the onions, celery, lemon, and parsley sprigs in the cavity. With the turkey breast side up, use your fingers to lift the skin from the flesh and place 2 sage sprigs under the breast skin on each side. Fold the skin over the cavity and secure it with a skewer. Place the turkey on a rack in a large roasting pan. Tie the turkey legs together with kitchen string and tuck the wings under the turkey. Brush the turkey with 2 tablespoons of the melted butter and sprinkle with more salt and pepper. Pour the wine into the roasting pan around the turkey.

Roast the turkey, basting with the pan juices every 30 minutes, for 3 hours. Check to make sure the roasting pan does not dry out, adding more wine if needed. In a small bowl, mix together the maple syrup, lemon zest, and remaining 4 tablespoons of butter. Brush the mixture over the turkey and continue roasting until an instant-read thermometer registers 175°F. to 180°F. when inserted into the innermost part of the thigh, away from the bone, about 15 minutes more.

Transfer the turkey to a platter, cover loosely with aluminum foil, and let stand for 30 minutes before carving.

While the turkey is resting, finish making the gravy (recipe follows).

madeira gravy

Simmer the giblets as the turkey is roasting and you'll be ready to finish the gravy when the turkey comes out of the oven.

MAKES ABOUT 3 CUPS

        Turkey giblets (turkey neck, gizzard, heart, liver)
2$\frac{1}{2}$ cups water
1   cup Madeira wine
    Kosher salt and freshly ground pepper
2   medium shallots, finely chopped
2   tablespoons all-purpose flour

METHOD

In a medium saucepan, combine the turkey giblets, water, Madeira, salt, pepper, and shallots. Bring to a boil, then reduce the heat to low and simmer for 2 hours. Remove the giblets with a slotted spoon and chop the neck meat, gizzard, heart, and liver into small pieces. Strain the cooking liquid and set aside.

Pour off all but 2 tablespoons of the fat left in the roasting pan after the turkey has been removed to a platter. Place the pan on the stovetop over medium heat. In a small bowl, stir the flour into $\frac{1}{2}$ cup of the giblet cooking liquid. Add to the roasting pan and cook, stirring and scraping up the brown bits on the bottom of the pan. When the mixture begins to thicken, 1 to 2 minutes, add the remaining giblet cooking liquid. Simmer on low heat for 10 minutes. Season with salt and pepper to taste, stir in the reserved giblet meat, pour into a gravy boat, and serve.

PRIMER

"The Best Ever"

Each Thanksgiving as we sit around the table enjoying our dinner in all its resplendent excess, someone will inevitably say, "This turkey is the best ever." Funny thing is, I never veer from my tried-and-true procedure when it comes to shopping for and preparing the bird.

Here are my steps for ensuring a moist, flavorful bird. May yours be "the best ever."

- Buy a fresh turkey. Fresh *is* better. Organic or free-range birds that are void of chemicals and allowed room to move about and peck have a better flavor.

- Bring the turkey to room temperature before roasting so it cooks more evenly.

- Preheat the oven at least 20 minutes before roasting.

- Brush the turkey with olive oil or melted butter and sprinkle with salt and pepper before roasting. Insert sage leaves or rosemary sprigs under the skin if you wish.

- Don't crowd the oven.

- Baste the turkey every 30 minutes.

- Test the turkey for doneness with an instant-read thermometer (it's the most accurate) inserted into the meatiest part of the thigh away from the bone. Begin testing 30 minutes before you expect it to be done. The turkey is done when the instant-read thermometer registers 175°F. to 180°F.

- Let the turkey rest at least 30 minutes before carving. This will make the turkey easier to carve and juicier to eat. Tent it with foil to keep it warm.

style note

A WARM WELCOME

At Thanksgiving, I like to engage all the senses in an abundant celebration of the harvest. My husband, who fancies himself a woodsman, likes to comb the back roads and trails of our neighborhood for appropriate natural "props." The fact that he is a designer and can create wonderful scenarios with the treasures he collects doesn't hurt either.

Every year, big pumpkins greet our guests from the front step. Often, we set them against a backdrop of tall stalks of Indian corn. After this treat for the eyes, the first thing our guests experience when they enter into the foyer are the wonderful aromas of the day. The fragrance of warm mulled cider envelops them as they walk in and then, as if by some posthypnotic suggestion (issued by the turkey roasting in the oven, I think), everyone is drawn into the kitchen for a peek at what's to come.

Whether I'm serving a buffet or a sit-down dinner, I like to create a sense of the season and the day's sentiment at the table. Our theme changes each year but as much as possible, we keep the setting and decorations natural. Here are some ideas:

- Use big red and yellow leaves as place cards or cut slits in apples and insert cards.

- Mix orange and green squashes with persimmons and pears for a still life centerpiece. If it's evening, tuck tapers in crystal holders into the display.

- Place fresh cranberries in vases and insert flowers, then fill with water.

- Hollow out minipumpkins and use as vases (fill with purple mums) or votive candleholders.

- Use old round breadboards as chargers beneath dinner plates.

- Drape undyed gauze or raw linen over wood dining chairs and tie in place with twine.

- Likewise, cover the table with gauze and tie it at each corner with twine, raffia, or 2-inch tapestry ribbon.

- Hang colored leaves, still on their branches, from the backs of chairs.

- Display whole nuts and tangerines in brown paper lunch bags. The nuts are decorations for your house and snacks for your guests simultaneously.

- Showcase one large, oddly shaped squash or gourd on a sideboard.

202

chestnut and apple dressing

This is the fancy version of my mom's dressing which, to this day, I love but cannot print as the recipe is published each year by the Pepperidge Farm company on the back of its crouton package. If you're going to cook this dressing inside the turkey (at which point it would become stuffing), spoon it loosely into the cavity of the turkey just before putting the turkey in the oven and remember that the turkey will take longer to cook stuffed than unstuffed.

SERVES 12

4 cups stale bread cubes (challah, brioche, or other egg bread), in ¾-inch cubes
¼ cup (½ stick) unsalted butter, melted
¼ cup (½ stick) unsalted butter
2 medium onions, finely chopped
6 celery stalks, including leaves, finely chopped
1 tablespoon dried thyme
1 tablespoon dried sage
1 cup chopped fresh parsley
2 cups chopped cooked chestnuts (see Note)
2 cups chopped unpeeled apples, such as Granny Smith or Pippin
   Kosher salt and freshly ground pepper
¼ cup Calvados
½ cup dry white wine

METHOD

Preheat the oven to 350°F. Lightly butter a large baking dish.

Put the bread cubes in a large bowl. Drizzle in the ¼ cup melted butter while stirring and tossing the bread cubes constantly to distribute the butter evenly. Set aside.

Melt the remaining ¼ cup butter in a large skillet over medium-high heat. Add the onions and celery and sauté until transparent, 3 to 4 minutes. Mix in the herbs, chestnuts, and apples and stir to coat with butter. Season to taste with salt and pepper.

Pour the vegetable mixture over the bread cubes and toss well to mix. Drizzle on the Calvados and toss again. Add the wine and toss again. If the dressing is too dry for your liking, add a bit of water or broth. Taste for seasoning.

Transfer to the prepared baking dish and bake,

uncovered, until heated through and golden brown on top, about 30 minutes.

Note: Cooked chestnuts are available canned or vacuum-packed at gourmet groceries or specialty retailers. If you prefer to use fresh chestnuts, please refer to Note, page 141 for preparation instructions.

vino bianco braised broccoli

Along with the pasta that accompanied the Thanksgiving turkey in our Italian household this was an annual tradition. It's a festive way to prepare this familiar vegetable.

SERVES 10 TO 12

¼ cup extra-virgin olive oil
2 garlic cloves, minced
4 heads broccoli, trimmed into florets
2 cups dry Italian white wine, such as Pinot Grigio
   Kosher salt and red pepper flakes

METHOD

In a large braising pan or Dutch oven, heat the oil over medium heat. Add the garlic and cook, stirring, for 30 seconds. Add the broccoli, stirring to coat it with the oil, and cook for 2 minutes. Add the wine and a pinch of salt. Cover, reduce the heat, and simmer for 10 to 12 minutes, or until tender. Remove the cover, increase the heat, and cook until the liquid is reduced by half. Adjust the seasonings, adding more salt and red pepper flakes to taste. Transfer the broccoli to a serving bowl and drizzle with the wine sauce.

mashed potato and celery root

If you cook the potatoes and celery roots at the same time, you will not have to reheat them and it will be easier to combine them. Celery root and potato are a smashing duo. The celery root lightens the potato and the potato gives girth to the celery root, making it a perfect balancing act.

SERVES 10 TO 12

8 medium red potatoes, peeled and halved
2 medium celery roots, peeled and cut into chunks
   Kosher salt
½ cup heavy cream
1 cup whole milk
6 tablespoons (¾ stick) unsalted butter
   Freshly ground pepper

METHOD

Put the potatoes and celery roots into separate saucepans and cover with cold water. Place both over medium-high heat and bring to a boil. When the water boils, add 2 generous pinches of salt and cook until tender, about 20 minutes for the celery root and 30 minutes for the potatoes; drain. Puree through a potato ricer or a food mill into a large bowl. Cover and set aside.

Combine the heavy cream, milk, and butter in a small saucepan. Cook over medium heat until the butter melts and the milk begins to bubble around the edges.

Add the celery root puree to the potatoes and stir. Pour in the milk bit by bit until the puree reaches the desired consistency. Season to taste with salt and pepper.

PRIMER

Smooth or Lumpy?

What type of potato makes the best mashed potatoes? Depends upon who you ask. If you like your potatoes fluffy, russet baking potatoes are the choice because they contain less starch. If you're a creamy mashed potato fan, opt for boiling potatoes.

Smooth or lumpy? A potato ricer or a food mill makes velvety smooth mashed potatoes; use a good old-fashioned potato masher or a fork and your potatoes will retain some lumps.

Whatever your preferences, there is one ironclad rule: Never ever use a food processor to mash potatoes. You'll wind up with glue.

cipolline onions with balsamic-cranberry glaze

Cipolline onions are small flat Italian onions that are quite sweet. If you can't find them, substitute boiling onions.

SERVES 10 TO 12

4 tablespoons (½ stick) unsalted butter
2 pounds cipolline onions, peeled, roots trimmed, left whole (see Note)
¼ cup balsamic vinegar
¼ cup cranberry juice
¾ cup chicken broth
   Kosher salt and freshly ground pepper

METHOD

In a large sauté pan, melt the butter over medium heat. When hot, add the onions and sauté, turning occasionally, until golden, about 5 minutes. Reduce the heat to low and add the vinegar, cranberry juice, and broth. Cover and cook until the onions are tender, about 30 minutes. Uncover the pan, increase the heat to medium-high, and cook until the liquid reduces to a glaze, about 5 minutes. Stir the onions to coat them with the glaze. Season to taste with salt and pepper.

Note: To make peeling small onions easier, cut a small "x" in the root of each onion. Bring a medium or large saucepan of water to a boil. Add the unpeeled onions, and boil 1 minute; drain. When cool enough to handle, peel. The skins will slide right off.

roasted winter squash rings

I am a huge fan of winter squash, as much for its sweet, nutty flavor as for its brilliant color. Squash slices roast quickly and the presentation is lovely. I especially like to roast acorn squash because the scalloped edges look so pretty.

SERVES 12

- 6 small winter squashes, such as acorn, butternut, or buttercup, peeled
- $\frac{1}{2}$ cup (1 stick) unsalted butter, melted
- $\frac{1}{4}$ cup maple syrup
  freshly grated nutmeg

METHOD

Preheat the oven to 350°F. Slice the squash crosswise into $\frac{1}{2}$-inch slices. Remove the seeds, using a serrated grapefruit spoon, round cookie cutter, or paring knife. Arrange the squash rings on a lightly buttered or parchment-lined baking sheet in a single layer.

In a small bowl, combine the melted butter and the maple syrup. Brush the squash rings with the melted butter mixture and sprinkle with the nutmeg. Bake until tender when pierced with a fork, 12 to 15 minutes.

perfect pie pastry

This produces a buttery, flaky pastry that's not difficult to make. Just be sure you don't overmix the flour and fat and that you don't handle the pastry too much. Make a few batches of pastry and pat into flat rounds large enough to fit a pie tin or small enough for individual tartlets. Wrap in plastic and freeze until ready to use. Defrosting takes about 30 minutes. With pastry at the ready and the addition of seasonal fruits tossed in sugar, you can make pies and tarts anytime. Frozen pastry will keep up to 1 month.

MAKES A DOUBLE-CRUST 9-INCH PIE

- $2\frac{1}{4}$ cups unbleached all-purpose flour
- $\frac{1}{2}$ teaspoon kosher salt
- $\frac{1}{2}$ cup (1 stick) chilled unsalted butter, cut into cubes
- $\frac{1}{4}$ cup chilled vegetable shortening
- 5 to 6 tablespoons ice water

METHOD

In the bowl of a food processor, combine the flour, salt, butter, and shortening. Process with quick on-off pulses until the mixture resembles oatmeal, 12 to 15 pulses. Sprinkle 5 tablespoons of the water over the mixture and process quickly again, 5 to 7 pulses. At this point, check the dough's consistency by pinching some between 2 fingers. If it holds together, it's ready. If not, add a few teaspoonfuls of water and pulse once or twice more.

Turn the dough out onto a very lightly floured surface and pat into 2 flat disks, making one slightly larger than the other (this will be the bottom crust). Knead it once or twice, wrap tightly in plastic, and chill until ready to use.

PRIMER

Flavoring Pastry

Adding flavor to pastry is an interesting and unexpected way to round out the filling inside the pie. When making pastry, sprinkle spices or zests in with the flour or add a dash of liqueur to the ice water. Try cinnamon for an apple pie, cardamom for a pear tart, lemon zest for a blueberry pie, framboise (raspberry liqueur) for a tart of summer fruit.

three-apple pie with calvados whipped cream

The singular characteristics of different apple varieties intermingle to add depth of flavor and texture to this pie. The addition of Calvados, an apple brandy, adds another apple flavor dimension to the dessert.

SERVES 8 GENEROUSLY, 10 AS PART OF A DESSERT MEDLEY

Perfect Pie Pastry (page 205)
3 Granny Smith apples, peeled, cored, and cut into 2-inch chunks
3 Pippin apples, peeled, cored, and cut into 2-inch chunks
2 of your favorite local apples, such as Rome Beauty, Cortland, Gravenstein, or Winesap, peeled, cored, and cut into 2-inch chunks
$\frac{1}{2}$ cup granulated sugar
1 tablespoon fresh lemon juice
1 teaspoon ground cinnamon
$\frac{1}{4}$ teaspoon ground allspice
 Pinch of grated nutmeg
1 tablespoon all-purpose flour
2 tablespoons ($\frac{1}{4}$ stick) cold unsalted butter, cut into small pieces
1 large egg beaten with 2 tablespoons milk, for glaze

Calvados Whipped Cream
1 cup heavy cream
$\frac{1}{2}$ teaspoon vanilla extract
1 tablespoon Calvados (apple brandy)
$\frac{1}{4}$ cup confectioners' sugar

METHOD

Preheat the oven to 425°F.

Remove the larger disk of pie pastry from the refrigerator and place on a lightly floured surface. Let rest about 3 minutes. Roll out to a 12-inch circle that is $\frac{1}{8}$ inch thick. Gently transfer to a 9-inch pie pan. Pat it in on the bottom and around the sides. Set aside.

In a large bowl, toss together the apples, sugar, lemon juice, spices, and flour. Transfer to the pie tin, mounding the apples in the middle. Dot with the butter.

Roll out the remaining pastry and carefully place it over the fruit. Trim off any pastry that is hanging over the rim and crimp the edges to seal. Brush the pastry all over with the egg-milk glaze. Cut a small vent or two in the pastry to allow steam to escape. Bake for 20 minutes, then reduce the heat to 350°F. and bake until the pastry is golden brown and the juices are bubbling, 30 to 40 minutes more.

Remove from the oven and cool on a wire rack.

Prior to serving, whip the cream with the vanilla, Calvados, and confectioners' sugar until soft peaks form. Serve a dollop alongside each wedge of pie.

tante marie's cold pumpkin soufflé

Tante Marie is the name of a cooking school in San Francisco and it is also the nom de cuisine for one of my great friends, Mary Risley, who owns that school. Like Mary herself, this dessert is straightforward, inventive, and a pleasure to have at the table.

SERVES 6

¼ cup dark rum
1½ tablespoons powdered gelatin
1 cup heavy cream
6 eggs
1 cup sugar
1½ cups pureed cooked pumpkin
¾ teaspoon ground cinnamon
¾ teaspoon ground ginger
½ teaspoon ground mace
½ teaspoon ground cloves
1 cup heavy cream
Candied fruit for decoration, optional
Sweetened whipped cream

METHOD

Put the rum in a small heatproof bowl or measuring cup and sprinkle the gelatin over it. Place the bowl in a pan filled with enough simmering water to reach halfway up the sides of the bowl and let the gelatin dissolve, 3 to 5 minutes. Wrap a 6-inch band of wax paper around a 1-quart soufflé dish and secure it with kitchen string to form a standing collar.

In a medium saucepan over moderate heat, warm the cream until bubbles form around the edges. As the cream is heating, put the eggs in a large bowl and beat until pale yellow. Gradually add the sugar and continue to beat until the mixture is smooth and very thick, 3 to 5 minutes. Stir in a bit of the hot cream to temper the eggs, then slowly pour in the remaining cream, beating continuously. Return the mixture to the saucepan and cook over low heat until the mixture coats the back of a wooden spoon, 6 to 8 minutes.

Pour the custard mixture into a large bowl and stir in the pumpkin and spices. Stir in the softened gelatin, mixing well to make sure it is fully incorporated. Fill a large bowl or dishpan (large enough for the mixing bowl to fit into) with ice. Make an indentation in the ice and set the mixing bowl into it. Stir the custard until you feel the gelatin is beginning to set (the custard will feel thick and sluggish). Whip the cream until soft peaks form and fold it into the custard.

Pour the mixture into the prepared soufflé dish, cover loosely with plastic wrap, and refrigerate until it is set, at least 4 hours or overnight.

To serve, carefully remove the collar and decorate the soufflé with candied fruit, if desired. Serve the pumpkin soufflé with lightly sweetened whipped cream.

mother's chip and date cake

My mom's chip and date cake has been present at every significant occasion in my family for as long as I can remember. Its rich autumnal flavors make it particularly appropriate for Thanksgiving.

SERVES 10 TO 12

24 dried dates, chopped
1½ cups boiling water
2¼ teaspoons baking soda
¾ cup vegetable shortening
2¼ cups sugar
2 eggs
1¾ cups all-purpose flour
½ teaspoon kosher salt
2 cups semisweet chocolate chips
¾ cup chopped walnuts

METHOD

Preheat the oven to 350° F. Grease and lightly flour a 9 × 13-inch cake pan.

In a medium bowl, combine the dates, boiling water, and 1½ teaspoons of baking soda. Stir; let cool.

In the bowl of an electric mixer, combine the vegetable shortening, 1 cup of sugar, and the eggs. Beat until fluffy and well mixed. Stir in the cooled date mixture.

In a medium bowl, sift together the flour, the remaining ¾ teaspoon of baking soda, and the salt. Add to the cake batter, beating just until combined.

In a small bowl, mix together the chocolate chips, the remaining 1¼ cups of sugar, and the nuts. Pour the batter into the prepared cake pan and sprinkle evenly with the chocolate chip mixture.

Bake until golden brown and set in the center, 40 to 50 minutes.

holiday

Holiday Open House

An open house is a wonderful way to celebrate any time of the year but it's particularly appropriate for the holidays. By nature, it's informal, festive, and inclusive, as pleasurable for children as it is for adults. Guests can come and go at their leisure and are free to wander in and out of rooms as they please.

Because the action of this type of party tends to flow naturally, I like to organize the food in different areas of the house. In the den, guests are greeted with a bowl of homemade eggnog and a galvanized tub of Champagne, along with bowls of dried fruit and nuts.

The dining room is laid with a main-course buffet of foods that can be served hot or at room temperature. A baked ham glazed with cranberry and mustard and a citrus-infused roast duck are the stars of the feast. Salads, including a toss of red and white greens and herbs in honor of Christmas and black-eyed peas as an edible charm for good luck in the New Year, join vegetables and buttermilk popovers as accompaniments to the roasts.

In the kitchen, cookies, popcorn balls, and hot cocoa await the children (no minimum age required). Spiced wine mulls things over on the stovetop.

The living room holds the holiday desserts: a panettone bread pudding with cognac caramel sauce, lemon-scented sugar cookies, and a tropical fruit platter. Here, by the fire, Christmas wishes are shared.

Throughout the house, small edible surprises, like bowls of gold-wrapped chocolate coins, ribbon candy, and peppermint sticks, await those intrepid souls who happen upon them. A silver punch bowl on the bench in the foyer is chock-full of Christmas crackers and gingerbread cookies wrapped in cellophane.

As guests depart, they're given a sugarplum to put under their pillows to ensure sweet Christmas dreams.

Setting the Buffet

To ensure easy flow, particularly for a large party, pull the buffet table or sideboard away from the wall so guests can walk around its entire perimeter.

Arrange the dishes on the table in the same way you would serve a sit-down dinner. Begin with first course dishes like soup or salad, followed by the main course and accompaniments. Dessert may be served in another room or brought out later. If you have a particularly beautiful dessert, like a croquembouche, by all means display it as a centerpiece—it will entice guests about what's to come.

Place dinner plates at the beginning of the buffet and utensils and napkins at the end of the buffet. This will enable your guests to serve themselves unencumbered.

Carve a portion of the roast before setting it on the buffet.

Make sure appropriate serving utensils are situated nearby their respective dishes.

With its abundance of beautiful food, the buffet is decoration in itself. Showcase these dishes by displaying them at different heights. Use pedestal cake stands and serving dishes with feet. Or invert flowerpots, small corrugated boxes, or bakeware (soufflé dishes or charlotte molds) on the table, then cover with a tablecloth.

The buffet is not a tableau for heavy decoration that will hinder guests from serving themselves with ease. Place one dramatic arrangement of flowers or a candelabra in the center if the buffet is being accessed on both sides or against the wall if the buffet is being accessed on one side only.

Check the buffet periodically to replenish platters as they are depleted and to tidy up. Remove empty dishes immediately.

dried cherry rhubarb relish

This chunky relish, bursting with tart rhubarb, sweet cherries, and pungent spices, is a fitting accompaniment to the baked ham. As it cooks, it will fill the kitchen with its marvelous seasonal aroma. This relish also makes a nice homemade holiday gift—make a big batch and give it to your guests as a party memento. At this time of year, you'll find frozen rhubarb in your market, as fresh rhubarb appears in the spring.

MAKES 2 CUPS

- 4 cups chopped rhubarb
- 1 cup dried cherries
- 1 teaspoon ground cloves
- 1 teaspoon dry mustard
- 2 cinnamon sticks
- 1/2 teaspoon ground allspice
- 2 tablespoons finely chopped fresh ginger
  Grated zest from 1 orange
  Grated zest from 1/2 lemon
- 3/4 cup packed dark brown sugar
- 2 tablespoons orange juice
- 1/4 cup balsamic vinegar

METHOD

In a large nonreactive saucepan, combine the rhubarb with the remaining ingredients. Bring to a boil, then simmer over low heat until the rhubarb is tender but still maintains its shape, 10 to 12 minutes. Do not stir too often or the rhubarb will begin to disintegrate. Taste for sweetness, adding a bit more brown sugar if needed. Spoon into small jars, cover, and refrigerate up to 3 weeks. Serve at room temperature.

holiday salad

The festive hue of red radicchio and the vibrant green colors of Belgian endive, watercress, and arugula, tossed with a tangy mustard vinaigrette, make this salad a perfect addition to the holiday buffet.

SERVES 10 TO 12

- 2 tablespoons red wine vinegar
- 1/2 teaspoon Dijon mustard
  Kosher salt and freshly ground pepper
- 1/3 cup extra-virgin olive oil
- 2 teaspoons minced fresh parsley
- 2 teaspoons minced fresh chives
- 3 bunches arugula, torn into bite-size pieces
- 1 bunch watercress, tough stems removed
- 1 medium radicchio, torn into bite-size pieces
- 4 Belgian endives, cut crosswise into 1-inch pieces
- 1 small head fennel, trimmed and sliced
  Shavings of Parmesan cheese, for garnish

METHOD

In a small bowl, stir together the vinegar, mustard, and salt and pepper to taste. Slowly add the oil in a steady stream, whisking as you do so. Stir in the parsley and chives. Reserve.

In a large bowl, toss together the arugula, watercress, radicchio, endives, and fennel. Drizzle with the vinaigrette, toss, and garnish with the Parmesan shavings.

Glaze

      Juice from 1 orange

      Juice from 1 lemon

1   cup honey

½ cup Grand Marnier or other orange-flavored liqueur

METHOD

Preheat the oven to 450° F.

Pat the ducks dry inside and out. Gently lift the skin on the breasts and insert the lemon and orange slices. Into each cavity insert half an onion, 1 bay leaf, 2 cloves, and 3 rosemary sprigs. Rub the exterior of the ducks with the garlic cloves and salt.

Place the ducks in a roasting pan and pour the white wine around them. Roast for 20 minutes, then lower the heat to 350° F. and continue roasting for 1 hour.

In a small saucepan, heat the citrus juices, honey, and brandy. Brush the duck with the glaze, return to the oven, and roast until tender, about 30 minutes longer.

To serve, slice the duck meat and arrange on a platter. Alternatively, carve each duck into 6 serving pieces.

cranberry-mustard baked ham

Baked ham is a spectacular addition to a buffet because of its versatility—it can be served hot or at room temperature—and its beauty. Presented on a large platter and decorated with herbs, cranberries, and kumquats, it strikes a festive pose.

SERVES 10 TO 12

1   12- to 14-pound shankless, skinless cured ham

      Whole cloves, for studding the ham

½ cup cranberry jelly

2   tablespoons Dijon mustard

METHOD

Preheat the oven to 350° F.

Score the ham in a diamond pattern and stud the center of each diamond with a clove. Place the ham on a rack in a roasting pan and bake for 1½ hours.

In a small saucepan, stir together the jelly and mustard. Cook over medium-low heat until melted. Spoon the glaze over the ham and bake 30 to 40 minutes more, until the top is golden brown and glistening.

Let the ham rest for 15 minutes before carving.

roast duck with citrus and honey

Oranges, lemons, and honey endow this roast duck with a golden glaze and imbue it with luscious tart-fruity flavor. When I serve duck as part of a buffet, I slice it as I would a roast chicken and arrange the slices on a platter. Definitely leave the skin on as it is an incredible treat!

SERVES 10 TO 12

2   whole ducks, 6 pounds each

1   lemon, thinly sliced

1   orange, thinly sliced

1   onion, halved

2   bay leaves

4   whole cloves

6   fresh rosemary sprigs

4   garlic cloves, peeled and crushed

      Kosher salt

½ cup dry white wine

style note

DECKING, TRIMMING, AND ADORNING

- Ask your local Christmas tree lot for leftover cuttings and use them to line the mantel, gild door and window moldings, or arrange along the length of the table.

- Choose a color theme for holiday decorating and use it to link each room. Red is warm and festive. Pile chili peppers in a bowl, queue up pomegranates along a windowsill, fill red juice glasses with beans and nestle votive candles in them, clip red cardinal millinery ornaments on the Christmas tree.

- The combination of white and silver is oh, so sophisticated: white candles in silver candlesticks, white poinsettias in galvanized pails by the fireplace, sugar-frosted green grapes on a crystal compote. For a change, trim the tree with nothing but tinsel and shimmering tivoli lights.

- Music is a must-have holiday adornment. Play old standbys by Frank and Bing all day and all night. For a party, rent a piano and hire music school students to serenade guests.

- Having houseguests for the holidays? Hang an evergreen wreath on both sides of the bedroom door.

- Put rosemary topiaries in burlap bags, tie with wide red ribbon, and arrange throughout the house for holiday cheer and aroma in every room of the house.

- Fill oversized terra-cotta pots with sand (plug up the hole first) and insert tall pillar candles (like the ones in church), then place outside the front door for an illuminated welcome.

- Greet party guests with red ribbon–tied mistletoe boutonnieres—and a peck on the cheek to go with!

- Put pinecones everywhere!

PRIMER

How to Sugar Fruit

For a frosted, fairy-tale decoration, dip fresh fruits into beaten egg white and roll in granulated sugar. Display in a silver or pewter bowl or glass compote and decorate with ivy or holly.

buttermilk popovers

Here's the secret to high, fluffy popovers: Do not over-mix the batter and be sure it's cold before you bake it.

MAKES 12

- 4 large eggs
- 1 cup unbleached all-purpose flour
  Kosher salt and freshly ground pepper
- 1 cup buttermilk
- ½ cup heavy cream
- 2 tablespoons (¼ stick) unsalted butter, melted

METHOD

In the bowl of a food processor, combine the eggs, flour, a pinch of salt, and pepper. Pulse to mix. In a 2-cup measuring cup, combine the buttermilk, cream, and butter. With the machine running, pour the milk mixture through the feed tube in a steady stream and process until the batter is smooth. Chill for 30 minutes.

Preheat the oven to 400° F.

Grease a 12-cup popover tin or large 12-cup muffin tin. Fill two-thirds full with the batter. Bake for 10 minutes, then reduce the heat to 350° F. and bake until puffed and golden brown, 25 to 30 minutes more. Do not open the oven door when baking or the popovers may collapse. Serve the hot popovers immediately.

black-eyed pea salad

Black-eyed peas are eaten in the South on New Year's Eve as an edible charm to bring good fortune in the coming year. I love the notion of my friends and family—and yours, too—eating their way to good luck.

SERVES 10 TO 12

- 1 pound dried black-eyed peas
- 1 onion, studded with 2 whole cloves
- 2 garlic cloves, peeled
- 1 bay leaf
- 1 medium red onion, finely chopped
- 1 shallot, finely chopped
- 2 medium carrots, finely chopped
- ¼ cup finely chopped fresh parsley
- 3 tablespoons sherry vinegar
- ½ to ⅔ cup extra-virgin olive oil
  Kosher salt and freshly ground pepper

METHOD

Put the peas in a large saucepan or bowl, cover with water, and soak overnight. Alternatively, quick-soak the peas by placing them in a large saucepan, covering them with cold water, and boiling them, uncovered, over high heat for 2 minutes. Remove the peas from the heat, cover, and let stand for 1 hour; drain.

Put the peas in a large saucepan with the onion, garlic, and bay leaf. Bring to a boil, lower the heat, and simmer until the peas are tender, 1½ to 2 hours; drain.

Transfer the peas to a large bowl. Add the remaining ingredients, seasoning to taste with salt and pepper; toss to mix. Serve warm or at room temperature.

green beans with lemon and red pepper

I serve green beans all year long, matched with different flavors according to the season and the occasion. This quick, piquant version is one of my favorites.

SERVES 10 TO 12

- Kosher salt
- 3½ pounds green beans, trimmed
- ¼ cup extra-virgin olive oil
- 1 tablespoon grated lemon zest
- ¼ teaspoon red pepper flakes, or more to taste

METHOD

Bring a large pot of water to a boil. Add a generous pinch of salt and when the water returns to a boil, add the beans and cook, uncovered, until crisp-tender, 5 to 7 minutes. Drain the beans, return to the pot, and add the oil, lemon zest, red pepper, and salt to taste. Cook over medium-low heat for 2 minutes to heat through and awaken the flavors.

tropical fruit platter

The vibrant colors and dazzling sweetness of tropical fruits transport us (at least in our dreams) to faraway islands. For their sunny flavors and for their tonic effect against the gray chill of winter, I like to serve a platter of tropical fruits during the holidays. This is the combination I like, but choose what suits you.

SERVES 10 TO 12

- 3 mangoes, peeled, seeded, and sliced
- 2 papayas, peeled, seeded, and sliced
- 2 pineapples, trimmed of skin and eyes, cored, and sliced
- 4 to 6 star fruit, sliced
- 4 to 6 blood oranges, peeled and sliced
- 4 limes, cut into wedges

METHOD

Arrange the prepared fruits on a large platter. Use 1 or 2 of the lime wedges to squeeze lime juice on the papayas (it brings out their flavor). Garnish the platter with the remaining lime wedges.

style

note

Clove-studded citrus fruits called pomanders do triple holiday duty: They cast a fresh, spicy aroma throughout your home; they can be piled high in bowls or in a compote or hung on a Christmas tree or from doorknobs; they make thoughtful party favors and gifts.

Choose firm whole citrus and whole cloves. Use a wooden skewer or hat pin to pierce the citrus (or you'll pierce your finger, guaranteed) and push the cloves into the holes. Experiment with making patterns with the cloves or opt for a single ring of cloves around the fruit's middle.

To ready the pomander for hanging, wrap a ribbon from top to bottom and secure it to the bottom and top with a pin. Make sure you use enough ribbon so you can tie a bow on the top. If you're having trouble with the ribbon sliding off the fruit, dab a few drops of fabric glue on the fruit and press the ribbon onto it.

panettone bread pudding with cognac-caramel sauce

Panettone is a traditional Italian Christmas bread. It's light, rich, and studded with dried fruits. You will find it in specialty food shops during the holidays. It's divine on its own but takes on distinct heavenly characteristics when transformed into this bread pudding and drizzled with a luscious cognac-caramel sauce. You have two options for serving this dessert: Slice it and arrange it on individual plates or unmold the pudding on a platter and let guests serve themselves.

SERVES 6

- 8 1-inch slices of day-old panettone, challah, or brioche, crusts removed
- 6 tablespoons (¾ stick) unsalted butter, melted
- 2 cups whole milk
- 1 cup heavy cream
- 4 large eggs
- 3 egg yolks
- ⅓ cup Cognac
- ⅔ cup sugar
- 1 teaspoon ground ginger
- 1 teaspoon cinnamon
- 1 teaspoon vanilla extract
  Cognac-Caramel Sauce (recipe follows)

METHOD

Preheat the oven to 400°F.

Brush the slices of bread with the melted butter and toast on both sides in the oven until golden brown. Remove the bread and lower the oven temperature to 350°F.

In a large mixing bowl, whisk together the milk, cream, eggs, egg yolks, Cognac, sugar, ginger, cinnamon, and vanilla.

Arrange a layer of the panettone slices on the bottom of a 9×5-inch loaf pan so the entire surface is covered with no gaps between slices. Continue in this way, layering the panettone slices until you reach about 1 inch of space from the top of the pan. Pour the custard over the panettone about ½ cup at a time, pausing to let the panettone absorb the liquid before adding more.

Place the loaf pan in a deep baking dish. Pour boiling water into the baking dish until it reaches halfway up the sides of the loaf pan. Place the baking dish in the oven and bake until the pudding is set, about 45 minutes. Remove the baking dish from the oven and transfer the loaf pan to a wire rack.

To serve, place a slice of panettone bread pudding on a plate and spoon the sauce over it.

cognac-caramel sauce

MAKES 2 CUPS

- 1½ cups sugar
- ½ cup water
- 2 cups heavy cream, warm
- 2 tablespoons Cognac

METHOD

In a medium saucepan over low heat, combine the sugar and water. Cook without stirring until the sugar melts and the mixture turns golden, 5 to 7 minutes. Remove from the heat and add the cream and Cognac. Stir until smooth.

lemon-scented sugar cookies

The confectioners' sugar in this great, all-purpose cookie recipe gives them a shortbreadlike tenderness. If you're pressed for time and don't want to go through the rolling and cutting ritual, simply scoop tablespoonfuls of the chilled dough and place at least 2 inches apart on the cookie sheet. Flatten with the bottom of a glass.

MAKES ABOUT FORTY-EIGHT 3-INCH COOKIES

- 1 cup (2 sticks) unsalted butter
- 1¼ cups confectioners' sugar
- 1 egg yolk
- 1 large egg
- 2 teaspoons vanilla extract
- 2 teaspoons grated lemon zest
- 2½ cups all-purpose flour
- 1 teaspoon baking powder
- ½ teaspoon kosher salt
  Decorating sugar (optional)
  Decorative Icing (recipe follows), optional

METHOD

In the large bowl of an electric mixer, combine the butter and sugar and beat on medium speed until light and fluffy. Beat in the egg yolk, then the whole egg, vanilla, and lemon zest.

In a medium bowl, sift together the flour, baking powder, and salt. Add to the batter and beat on low speed just until combined. Divide the dough in half; flatten each portion into a disk, wrap tightly in plastic, and chill for at least 1 hour. (You can refrigerate the dough up to 2 days or freeze it for up to 1 month.)

Preheat the oven to 350°F. Line baking sheets with parchment paper.

Turn the dough out onto a lightly floured surface and roll out to ⅛-inch thickness. Using cookie cutters, cut out cookies. Transfer the cookies to baking sheets, spacing them at least ½ inch apart. Gather dough scraps, reroll, and cut out more cookies. At this point, sprinkle the cookies with decorating sugars, if desired.

Bake the cookies until golden brown around the edges, about 8 to 10 minutes. Transfer to wire racks to cool. If desired, decorate the thoroughly cooled cookies with icing.

decorative icing

This icing can be spread on the cookies or piped. Adding an egg white to the icing helps it harden when it's on the cookies. Paste food coloring, which can be found at stores that carry cake decorating supplies, will yield deeper, richer colors.

MAKES ABOUT 1 CUP

- 1¼ cups confectioners' sugar
- 1 egg white
  Pinch of kosher salt
- 2 teaspoons water, lemon juice, or orange juice
  Food coloring of choice

METHOD

In a small bowl, combine the sugar, egg white, salt, and water or juice. Add food coloring to the icing, stirring well to blend. Use the icing immediately.

PRIMER

Cookie Variations

One sugar cookie dough has many flavor possibilities. Here are some ideas:

Candied Ginger:
Stir ⅓ cup very finely chopped candied ginger into the finished dough. For a double ginger whammy, add 1 teaspoon ground ginger to the flour mixture.

Chocolate Dots:
Stir ¾ cup finely chopped bittersweet chocolate into the finished dough.

Cinnamon:
Add 1½ teaspoons ground cinnamon to the flour mixture.

Nut:
Add 1 cup finely ground hazelnuts, pecans, or walnuts with the vanilla.

Orange:
Add 1½ teaspoons grated orange zest with the vanilla.

Peppermint Stick:
Stir ½ cup finely crushed candy canes into the finished dough.

WAYS WITH

TAKE-AWAY

the

British call take-out food "take-away" and because I like the more refined connotations of that term more than I do the slam-dunk, gimme-a-dog-with-everything-on-it cadence of "take-out," I am calling this section "Ways with Take-Away."

Let me absolve you of guilt straightaway. Take-away food, the prepared dishes we find in gourmet delis and supermarkets, exists for one reason: People are busy and have little time to cook. It is a fact of real-life that while the spirit may long to entertain, sometimes the body simply can't. We're tired, we're busy, we're up to our ears in stuff. When these times are upon you, take a breath, give yourself a break, and be thankful we live in a time when convenient options are available to us.

Happily, take-away food is becoming more wholesome and more sophisticated every day. The take-away foods that are available to us range from farmhouse cheeses and country olives to roasted meats and smoked fish to vegetable gratins and grain salads. Why shouldn't we enhance our entertaining menus with the best that take-away has to offer?

I have a foolproof method for entertaining with take-away foods. It's called half-scratch. Since half the work is done for me by the wonderful cooks who prepare the take-away dishes, I just need to do the other half. The other half generally consists of refreshing the food's flavor in simple ways by adding fresh herbs or a squeeze of lemon juice, for instance. It includes complementing the take-away food with other appropriate dishes, whether they're homemade or purchased. And it always involves enhancing the food's presentation.

Of course, you can make as little or as much of the meal yourself as you choose. This tends to assuage the guilt that descends upon so many of us doers when we opt for an easier route. In my book, if you make just one hors d'oeuvre there's no reason you can't call the whole spread "homemade."

If you're partial to dessert making, you can concentrate on creating a stellar finale and purchase the main course. If hors d'oeuvres are the last thing you think about, don't think about them and let someone else prepare them for you. Or, if you're seriously harried, liberate yourself! Compose a simple menu entirely of take-away and relax!

Menus based on take-away foods can be as varied as the selections at take-out food counters. And this is the point. Depending upon where you live, your take-out food options will vary according to local tastes and the decisions of the chef. The menus that I have assembled on pages 232–235 are based on what is available in my neck of the woods, yet include foods that I see appearing on take-out menus, at salad bars, and even in well-stocked supermarkets, across America. Use these menus merely as guidelines, and if they call for a food that you cannot obtain (sorry!), consider it an opportunity to substitute and augment with your own local specialties and regional offerings.

Serve it forth.

"LET ME ABSOLVE YOU OF GUILT STRAIGHTAWAY."

roast chicken

roast chicken

Years ago, someone very smart tapped into the idea that roast chicken is universally appealing and began selling it. Now it's widely available. Rotisserie chicken hot off the spit and packaged roast chicken are wonderful foods for entertaining—and so versatile, too. Here are some ideas for gilding the lily:

EASY ACCESS ACCOMPANIMENTS

Roast chicken, served warm or at room temperature, can be complemented with other take-away foods or quickly prepared side dishes, such as:

■ Sliced ripe tomatoes with finely chopped red onions and slivered black olives, dressed with a drizzle of olive oil and a splash of red wine vinegar.

■ Guacamole, tomatillo salsa, and warm flour tortillas sprinkled with chili powder. Serve a bowl of lime wedges alongside.

■ Tomatoes stuffed with creamed corn, topped with chives and Monterey Jack cheese, and baked until heated through.

■ Leftover rice pilaf or risotto formed into patties and cooked in a skillet with a bit of butter until golden brown.

No-work accompaniments (buy already made from the supermarket or deli):

■ Tabbouleh, hummus, and baba ghanouj.

■ Potato salad and coleslaw.

■ Focaccias with assorted toppings—serve warm.

■ Vegetable salads with oil- and vinegar-based dressings that can be served warm, such as green beans with a mustard dressing.

■ Slice it and serve it at room temperature with a variety of chutneys and relishes, a green salad, and crusty bread.

■ If it's cold outside, add a warm vegetable soup such as a mushroom bisque. If you're purchasing the mushroom bisque, add a dash of sherry before serving. If it's a hot summer evening, chilled gazpacho's the thing. Top it with diced cucumbers and green peppers.

■ Slice grilled chicken breasts and serve over greens dressed with a Caesar vinaigrette.

■ Dice cooked chicken and combine with diced red peppers, diced scallions, and chopped fresh cilantro. Toss with a vinaigrette made with soy sauce, rice wine vinegar, lime juice, and grated fresh ginger. Serve on butter lettuce leaves.

■ Top each chicken breast with a slice of mozzarella and a basil leaf. Put in a baking dish and spoon tomato sauce over all. Cover with plastic wrap and microwave until the cheese melts.

■ Spread black olive tapenade on chicken breasts and serve warm.

soups

Most prepared-food shops and many supermarkets offer a selection of "homemade" soups for carry-out. I like soup any time of the year for the way it anchors a meal, gives a homey spin to a dinner, and satisfies hungry guests at a moment's notice. Most prepared soups will benefit from a squeeze of lemon and the addition of a fresh herb to perk up long-cooked flavors. Taste for seasoning and add salt and/or pepper if necessary.

TOPPINGS

Finishing touches, such as those I've listed here, dress up ordinary soups for entertaining. These are the details that make a soup special:

■ Make croutons by slicing bread, cutting off the crust, and cubing it. Or use miniature cookie cutters to create shapes. Melt butter or heat olive oil in a skillet and toss the bread cubes in it until browned. Experiment with bread flavors: rosemary focaccia for vegetable soups; dark rye for a squash or potato soup; sourdough for a fish soup.

■ Sprinkle fresh herbs or place an herb sprig on top of each bowl of soup before serving.

■ Whisk in a bit of cream or pesto into a pureed soup to create a design on the soup's surface.

■ Float a thinly sliced lemon or lime on each serving.

■ Ladle soup into individual ovenproof bowls, top with puff pastry, and bake until golden.

CONTAINERS

■ Look for bowls of various sizes in interesting colors and shapes. The possibilities are only as limited as your imagination (and sense of humor). Bowls don't have to match. I say, the more the merrier—and the more interesting.

■ Fill an oversized cookie jar in the shape of an acorn with an autumnal soup such as squash or mushroom.

■ Use a large, deep glass salad bowl to showcase a vibrantly colored vegetable puree soup.

■ Pull out your grandmother's good china; an old porcelain tureen that says "stodgy" when sitting on a shelf becomes an elegant serving piece for watercress soup.

■ Try earthenware bowls you might normally use to serve nuts and olives to present corn chowder in a homey way.

■ And don't forget to employ the natural containers—squash, peppers, and rustic bread rounds—that add color and whimsy to the soup course.

ACCOMPANIMENTS

■ Fresh country bread with flavored butters made by stirring chopped fresh herbs, olives, or pesto into softened butter.

■ One perfectly ripe cheese.

■ Cheese Straws (page 157).

■ Pita triangles or flour tortillas brushed with olive oil, sprinkled with cumin or sweet paprika, and toasted under the broiler.

■ Dips such as baba ghanouj (eggplant puree) or hummus (chickpea puree), homemade or store-bought, with pita crisps to accompany them.

stews

Satisfying and robust stews have a place on casual or more formal tables as well as on buffets. They can be dressed up or dressed down by varying their presentation according to the occasion. Here are some suggestions:

■ Make edible "bowls" by fitting sheets of phyllo dough into large, greased muffin tins and baking until golden. Place on individual plates and spoon stew into the phyllo bowl.

■ Make or buy polenta and serve stew over it.

■ Pack warm cooked rice or purchased rice pilaf into a greased timbale mold or ramekin and unmold onto the center of the plate. Spoon stew around the rice. Sprinkle with chopped fresh parsley.

■ Cut the tops off large bread rolls, hollow out, and fill with stew. Similarly, cut off the tops of smaller pumpkins or squashes, hollow out, warm in a microwave, and fill with stew.

■ Place stew in a baking dish. Top with mashed potatoes, brush with butter, and bake until golden brown.

cooked shrimp

Shrimp is elegant, fun, and delicious, but it's a pain to peel and devein. I like to leave this time-devouring task to the fishmonger. You can find cooked shrimp in your market's fish department or frozen in the frozen foods section. The former route is the one to take since the shrimp's texture will be crunchier and its flavor more vibrant.

■ Serve with mayonnaise mixed with chopped garlic, sweet paprika, and a squeeze of lemon.

■ Make a shrimp cocktail by whisking together 2 parts ketchup to 1 part each whipped cream, lemon juice, horseradish, and Worcestershire sauce. Serve in a martini glass.

■ Thread on skewers, alternating with pitted green olives and orange slices. Stick skewers in a bowl of sea salt to anchor them and serve as an hors d'oeuvre with cold fino sherry.

■ Melt butter in a nonstick pan and sauté with chopped garlic, chopped fresh ginger, and scallion for a minute or so. Add shrimp and toss until heated through. Serve with steamed jasmine rice.

■ Place in a microwave-safe bowl with chopped tomatoes, minced tarragon, and lemon zest. Cover and microwave until hot. Serve with crusty bread as a first course.

■ Serve do-it-yourself spring rolls for your guests to assemble at the table with chopped shrimp, bean sprouts, mint, and shredded lettuce and wrap in rice paper. Dip in store-bought plum sauce.

■ Pile unpeeled boiled shrimp on a platter. Serve with coleslaw, chips, and cold beer. Line a table with newspaper, place buckets at both ends for the shells, and go for it!

roast meats: beef, lamb, pork

Sliced and served on a platter with herb bouquets, roast meats make an elegant dinner with simple embellishments to round out the presentation. Many stores roast meats daily. If you can't find them in your meat department, try the deli section. While most often these meats are sold sliced, you can request an uncut portion, or the whole roast.

■ Make homemade mayonnaise by whisking together (or pulsing in a food processor) 1 whole egg, 1 tablespoon white wine vinegar or other flavored vinegar, and a pinch of salt and pepper. Add 1 cup canola oil in a steady stream as you whisk or pulse. Slice the roast meat and serve with the mayonnaise, along with chutneys and relishes, crusty bread, and a green salad.

■ Make a lamb salad by slicing roast lamb thinly, placing atop greens, and drizzling with a mint vinaigrette (red wine vinegar, chopped fresh mint, olive oil, salt, and pepper). Sprinkle with goat cheese.

■ Warm beef, tightly wrapped in aluminum foil, in the oven. Puree canned chipotle chili peppers and thin to the desired consistency with lime juice and corn oil. Warm in a microwave or over low heat. Spoon some chipotle sauce onto each plate and place a slice of beef on top. Garnish with cilantro sprigs.

■ Cut pork in thin strips and combine with chopped scallions, chopped cilantro, grated fresh ginger, lime juice, and sesame oil. Wrap in lettuce leaves. Pass soy sauce mixed with lime juice and mint.

■ Cook lentils with chopped onions, chopped carrots, and chopped garlic. Serve alongside lamb or pork for a hearty winter meal. Alternatively, serve with couscous, warm or at room temperature.

■ Store-bought demi-glace, a highly concentrated stock, can be diluted a bit with water or wine and heated for an instant sauce to drizzle over beef, lamb, or veal roasts.

vegetables

Vegetables in various guises abound in take-away departments. Most will taste best served warm or at room temperature since cold dulls flavor. Taste the vegetables for seasoning before serving. Adding fresh herbs (use either the same herbs that have been used to flavor the dish or a sprinkle of chopped fresh parsley) or a squeeze of lemon to prepared vegetables will enliven their flavor.

■ Heat vegetables prepared with oil- and vinegar-based dressings in a microwave or toss them in a large sauté pan just until warmed through.

■ Add marinated vegetables, such as mushrooms in vinaigrette or beets in orange dressing, to green salads or stir them into pasta.

■ Changing the shape of vegetables casts them in a new light. Cut harder prepared vegetables such as carrots or beets into very thin matchstick slices or into a fine dice and scatter over baked, broiled, or grilled fish to enhance its presentation.

■ Multiplicity adds interest. Purchase a variety of prepared vegetable dishes and serve them as several salads on a plate.

■ Stuff bell peppers with prepared couscous, place in a baking dish, pour a bit of water or wine in the bottom, cover, and bake until the peppers are tender.

■ Transform prepared vegetable dishes such as ratatouille into a gratin by placing in a shallow baking dish, sprinkling with cheese or buttered bread crumbs, and broiling until golden.

mashed potatoes and cooked rice

Mashed potatoes have become standard fare at carry-out counters. While sometimes they're flavored with gourmet ingredients and perfectly acceptable as they are, often a sleight of hand at home will enhance them greatly. Ditto for prepared rice as found in rice salads and risotto.

■ Spoon mashed potatoes into a shallow baking dish, top with grated cheese, and bake until golden.

■ Stir truffle oil into mashed potatoes.

■ Sauté wild mushrooms in butter, add Madeira, and serve over mashed potatoes.

■ Mix mashed potatoes or rice with finely chopped vegetables or smoked salmon. Form into pancakes and cook in butter in a skillet until golden brown.

■ Form balls of cooked rice. Insert a small piece of melting cheese such as mozzarella in the center, making sure that the rice encloses it completely. Heat 1 inch of oil in a sauté pan and fry until golden.

■ Make a vinaigrette with red wine vinegar, olive oil, and herbs. Mix with cold cooked rice and cooked shrimp for a salad.

■ Stir coconut milk and cinnamon into cooked white rice and serve warm or chilled for dessert.

pasta

Pasta is a convenience food in itself, particularly if you sauce it with ingredients gleaned from the take-away case, fresh or frozen vegetables, and bottled condiments. Here are a few ideas:

■ Combine canned tuna in oil, chopped parsley, lemon juice, and red pepper flakes to taste.

■ Toss frozen fava or lima beans (defrosted) with chopped fresh mint and melted unsalted butter; top with shavings of ricotta salata.

■ Stir together black olive tapenade, fresh basil, and slivered sun-dried tomatoes (along with some of their oil) and mix with some of the pasta cooking water to make a sauce; sprinkle with grated Parmesan.

■ Toss diced beets from a prepared beet salad in vinaigrette, a bit of its dressing, and crumbled Roquefort.

■ Puree roasted red peppers with a dash of orange juice and stir together with slivered black olives and chunks of feta.

■ Whisk ricotta with imported Italian tomato paste and a bit of olive oil.

■ Embellish purchased pesto with crumbled walnuts and finely sliced basil.

■ Melt unsalted butter and mix with freshly grated Parmesan and freshly ground black pepper.

antipasto

As the center of an Italian buffet, an ample first course, or a meal in itself, you can't go wrong with antipasto. Fortunately, you can buy virtually everything you need for a spectacular antipasto spread at Italian salumerias or the deli department of many grocery stores. Fill out the table with items from your pantry (see page 17) and fresh fruits and vegetables, mixing and matching ingredients based on seasonal availability and your own preference.

Green and black olives

Salami, pepperoni, soppressata

Roasted red peppers

Sliced fresh mozzarella, fontina, and provolone

A wedge of Parmigiano-Reggiano

Canned tuna in olive oil

Prosciutto wrapped around thinly sliced fennel

Dried figs, sliced lengthwise to create a pocket, stuffed with an almond and a piece of prosciutto ham

Marinated artichoke hearts

Marinated mushrooms

Sun-dried tomatoes in olive oil

Chickpeas with olive oil, lemon juice, and parsley

Caper buds

Loaves of focaccia and ciabatta (flat crusty Italian bread)

Assembly:

Group salads and vegetables together on a large platter, clustering complementary colors and shapes such as artichoke hearts, chickpeas, and sun-dried tomatoes. Let the cheeses, meats, and breads stand on their own.

Intersperse small bowls with olives or caper buds between the platters.

Decant wines into interesting bottles and serve Italian beer and sparkling water.

For dessert, serve fresh fruit (melon if it's summer, oranges if it's winter), raisins macerated in grappa, biscotti, and black coffee.

PRIMER

Cheese and Fruit

No other dessert combines the ease of preparation and sophistication of fruit and cheese. Here are a few classic combinations for elegant endings—or beginnings—or anytime:

- Stilton and dried dates
- Parmigiano-Reggiano and pears
- Roquefort and green apples (Granny Smith or Pippin)
- Feta and watermelon
- Chèvre and peaches
- St. André and dried apricots
- Gorgonzola dolce and fresh purple figs
- Havarti and cantaloupe
- Mascarpone and strawberries
- Brillat-Savarin and cherries
- Sharp Cheddar and red apples (Rome Beauties, Red Delicious, or Macs)

sensational sandwiches

I am a huge fan of sandwiches and I eat them for breakfast, lunch, and dinner. Their compact size, ease of preparation, and versatility—not to mention the fact that they are composed primarily of take-away items—rate them A-1 with me. Here are a few ideas for sensational sandwiches:

■ Grilled chicken strips, guacamole, and chopped tomato wrapped in a flour tortilla.

■ Albacore tuna, slivered black olives, scallions, and Dijon mustard packed into a hollowed-out baguette, then cut into serving slices.

■ Egg salad, chopped sweet pickles, and a dash of caviar on pumpernickel.

■ Smoked turkey, cranberry relish, and watercress on challah or brioche.

■ Meat loaf and ketchup on white (really!).

■ Sharp Cheddar and red apple slices on an English muffin—grilled open-face under the broiler.

■ Sliced lamb, baba ghanouj (eggplant puree), and tomato slices on country bread.

■ Ripe tomatoes, fresh mozzarella, and pesto on a hard roll.

■ Scrambled eggs, smoked trout, and sliced red onion on a croissant.

■ Your favorite cheese on a panini or ficelle.

PRIMER

Charcuterie

Every French village has its charcuterie, a term used to describe both the shop that sells cooked meat products and the meats themselves. Today, charcuterie is not limited strictly to meat. In addition to the innumerable versions of sausages, hams, and cured meats and pâtés, it encompasses a wealth of fish and vegetable pâtés, terrines, and prepared salads.

A charcuterie spread lends itself well to real-life entertaining because it is so easy to assemble and serve and makes a lovely presentation. Charcuterie tastes best at room temperature, which makes it even easier for the host to serve.

Serve charcuterie on a large platter or wooden board and enjoy it communally. Alternatively, you can plate a charcuterie selection individually for each of your guests.

When assembling a charcuterie, look for pâtés with unusual flavorings: wild mushrooms with pork, apples with chicken livers, port with duck, game with truffles and sherry. Many pâtés and terrines have colorful layers, particularly those that contain vegetable purees or nuts.

Serve soft pâtés and terrines in pretty crocks and bowls. Unmold firmer pâtés, slice them, and serve on lettuce leaves.

Don't forget that selections give your guests the opportunity to taste, compare, and converse. Try:

A selection of three pâtés: one pork, one vegetable, one game

A selection of sausages: Arles (garlicky), soppressata (lots of peppercorns), salami (you choose)

A selection of hams: prosciutto, coppa (spicy), Westphalian

Traditional complements for charcuterie include cornichon pickles, mustards, olives, pickled onions, lingonberries (for game pâtés), and dry toast, crackers, or thinly sliced French bread. Small bouquets of fresh herbs and edible flowers complement the charcuterie's presentation.

A green salad dressed with a vinaigrette will balance the richness of the charcuterie. You could also add cheeses and miniature quiches to round out the menu. Finish off with seasonal fruits and cookies. Don't forget the wine! Carry on the French theme and opt for a hearty red such as Burgundy.

desserts

Pulling a cake from a bakery box is surely acceptable but taking the extra few minutes—or less—to personalize a prepared dessert makes a world of difference. Here's how:

WAYS WITH CAKE...

■ Flavor melted bittersweet chocolate with framboise (raspberry-flavored liqueur) and drizzle on pound cake or vanilla ice cream.

■ Whip cream with almond extract and use to frost individual angel food cakes. Dust with cocoa powder.

■ Cut bakery cakes and tarts in smaller than serving-size pieces and present on a cake stand or candy trivet with coffee.

■ Toast pound cake under the broiler, spread with orange marmalade and shave bittersweet chocolate over it.

...AND ICE CREAM

■ Mix softened vanilla ice cream with diced mangoes, nutmeg, and a dash of rum or chopped pistachios, shredded coconut, and ground cardamom.

■ Melt premium-quality vanilla ice cream and use as a sauce for fruit or cake.

■ Place scoops of slightly softened ice cream between 2 cookies for a quick ice cream sandwich. Serve on a pool of warm chocolate sauce.

■ Make ginger ice cream sodas by putting a scoop or two of vanilla ice cream in a tall glass with a squeeze of fresh lime juice; fill the glass with ginger ale and top with crystallized ginger.

■ Fill ice cream molds with premium-quality ice cream in assorted flavors. Serve with fruit purees or chocolate sauce—try white chocolate for a change of pace.

■ Hollow out lemons, limes, and oranges and fill with sorbets. Refreeze until ready to serve.

FRUIT-FILLED IDEAS

■ Flavor mascarpone with vin santo, a sweet Italian dessert wine, and serve with berries.

■ Sprinkle sliced strawberries with best-quality balsamic vinegar.

■ Fold grated orange zest and a dash of orange-flavored liqueur into ricotta and serve with store-bought fruit salad, pound cake, or a peach half.

■ Fill a big bowl with the biggest, ripest strawberries and serve with bowls of confectioners' sugar, melted chocolate, and balsamic vinegar for dipping.

■ Cut peaches in half, sprinkle brown sugar on them, and place under a broiler until the sugar melts. Top with a dollop of sour cream.

■ Freeze seedless grapes and serve as a cooling summer dessert.

■ Whisk jam or honey into plain yogurt and serve with fruit.

■ Fill pear poached halves with crushed amaretti cookies, drizzle with amaretto, and place in the oven until hot. Serve with sweetened cream and a dusting of ground cloves.

FOR CHOCOLATE LOVERS

■ Serve a chocolate tray instead of a cheese tray: Place big bars of premium-quality bittersweet chocolate, milk chocolate, and dark chocolate on a wood cutting board with a cheese knife alongside.

ONE MORE IDEA

Spoon store-bought custards and puddings into coffee cups—a different design (and maybe a different flavor) for each guest.

menu ideas

après-ski family dinner

Black bean soup

Warm roasted chicken

Baked sweet potatoes

Corn tortillas

Brownies *and* ice cream

midsummer al fresco dinner

Assorted olives

Cool gazpacho

Sliced flank steak *on* dressed greens

French bread

Honeydew melon *and* blackberry sorbet

company for dinner

Green salad *with* red onions *and* feta

Chicken breasts *with* tapenade

Creamed corn–stuffed tomatoes

Green beans

Pound cake *with* bittersweet chocolate sauce *and* orange slices

an asian sojourn

Chinese chicken salad

Pan-warmed shrimp *with* scallions, ginger, *and* garlic

Jasmine rice

Sliced mangoes *with* coconut ice cream

spring celebration

Smoked trout *with* Dijon mustard *and* toast points

Roasted lamb tenderloin *with* lemon mayonnaise

Truffle oil mashed potatoes

Asparagus

Angel food cake *with* cocoa whipped cream *and* berries

mad for pasta!

Linguine *with* canned tuna *in* oil *and* black olives

Ravioli *with* roasted red pepper puree

Tagliarini *with* melted butter *and* Parmesan

Green salad *with* olive oil *and* lemon juice

Citrus sorbets

summer dinner by the sea

Clam chowder

Shrimp *with* cocktail sauce *and* tartar sauce

Green salad

Corn *on the* cob

Fresh fruit salad *with* lemon sorbet

index

American cooks use standard containers, the 8-ounce cup and a tablespoon that takes exactly 16 level fillings to fill that cup level. Measuring by cup makes it very difficult to give weight equivalents, as a cup of densely packed butter will weigh considerably more than a cup of flour. The easiest way therefore to deal with cup measurements in recipes is to take the amount by volume rather than by weight. Thus the equation reads:

1 cup = 240 ml = 8 fl. oz.   ½ cup = 120 ml = 4 fl. oz.

It is possible to buy a set of American cup measures in major stores around the world.

In the States, butter is often measured in sticks. One stick is the equivalent of 8 tablespoons. One tablespoon of butter is therefore the equivalent to ½ ounce/15 grams.

LIQUID MEASURES

Fluid Ounces	U.S.	Imperial	Milliliters
	1 teaspoon	1 teaspoon	5
¼	2 teaspoons	1 dessertspoon	10
½	1 tablespoon	1 tablespoon	14
1	2 tablespoons	2 tablespoons	28
2	¼ cup	4 tablespoons	56
4	½ cup		110
5		¼ pint or 1 gill	140
6	¾ cup		170
8	1 cup		225
9			250, ¼ liter
10	1¼ cups	½ pint	280
12	1½ cups		340
15		¾ pint	420
16	2 cups		450
18	2¼ cups		500, ½ liter
20	2½ cups	1 pint	560
24	3 cups		675
25		1¼ pints	700
27	3½ cups		750
30	3¾ cups	1½ pints	840
32	4 cups or 1 quart		900
35		1¾ pints	980
36	4½ cups		1000, 1 liter
40	5 cups	2 pints or 1 quart	1120

SOLID MEASURES

U.S. and Imperial Measures		Metric Measures	
Ounces	Pounds	Grams	Kilos
1		28	
2		56	
3½		100	
4	¼	112	
5		140	
6		168	
8	½	225	
9		250	¼
12	¾	340	
16	1	450	
18		500	½
20	1¼	560	
24	1½	675	
27		750	¾
28	1¾	780	
32	2	900	
36	2¼	1000	1
40	2½	1100	
48	3	1350	
54		1500	1½

OVEN TEMPERATURE EQUIVALENTS

Fahrenheit	Celsius	Gas Mark	Description
225	110	¼	Cool
250	130	½	
275	140	1	Very Slow
300	150	2	
325	170	3	Slow
350	180	4	Moderate
375	190	5	
400	200	6	Moderately Hot
425	220	7	Fairly Hot
450	230	8	Hot
475	240	9	Very Hot
500	250	10	Extremely Hot

Any broiling recipes can be used with the grill of the oven, but beware of high-temperature grills.

EQUIVALENTS FOR INGREDIENTS

all-purpose flour—plain flour
coarse salt—kitchen salt
cornstarch—cornflour
eggplant—aubergine

half and half—12% fat milk
heavy cream—double cream
light cream—single cream
lima beans—broad beans

scallion—spring onion
unbleached flour—strong, white flour
zest—rind
zucchini—courgettes or marrow